WOMEN IN SEARCH OF UTOPIA

Mavericks and Mythmakers

Edited and with Introductions by Ruby Rohrlich and Elaine Hoffman Baruch

SCHOCKEN BOOKS · NEW YORK

First published by Schocken Books 1984
10 9 8 7 6 5 4 3 2 1   84 85 86 87
Copyright © 1984 Ruby Rohrlich and Elaine Hoffman Baruch

Library of Congress Cataloging in Publication Data
Main entry under title:
Women in search of utopia, mavericks and mythmakers.
    Bibliography: p.
    Includes index.
    1. Women—History—Addresses, essays, lectures.
2. Utopias—History—Addresses, essays, lectures.
3. Feminism—History—Addresses, essays, lectures.
I. Rohrlich, Ruby.   II. Baruch, Elaine Hoffman.
HQ1122.W65   1984   305.4′09   83-40467

Designed by Nancy Dale Muldoon
Manufactured in the United States of America
ISBN 0–8052–3900–6 hardcover
        0–8052–0762–7 paperback

    Grateful acknowledgment is extended to Mary Anne Shea for the cartoons
throughout the book, copyright © 1984 Mary Anne Shea.
    Elaine Hoffman Baruch would like to thank the National Endowment of the
Humanities and the PSC-BHE Research Award Program of the City University
of New York for enabling her to do some of the research for her introductions
and article in this book.

Dedicated to MARGARET MEAD, who showed us utopias of the past and pointed the way in "Towards More Vivid Utopias."

Contents

Part Four: VISIONS OF UTOPIA

Preface: What Do Women Want?

RUBY ROHRLICH

"SOMETHING very essential is missing in our studies of communes and communities," observed sociologist Jessie Bernard at a Conference on Communes in 1975, "and that is the female structure," which we must discover or uncover. Women's search for this missing essential in intentional communities, is what this book is all about. In the utopias men create, women are peripheral; *our* vision is centered on women. What do *women* want?

First, we think not of utopia, but of utopias. We imagine a world of mavericks creating new myths based on the naturalness of diversity—cultural, social and biological—as indicated by the substance and form of this book. Its theme encompasses several literary genres—essays, poems, reviews, science fiction, journal entries; the art of cartoons; anthropological and historical studies. We envision a world of homosocial and heterosocial communities consisting of every racial mix. A world with a multitude of family forms. A world in which contradictions abound and resolutions are always in process. As Margaret Mead sums it up in "Towards More Vivid Utopias":

> . . . the utopian vision . . . is built upon the great diversity of human propensities and gifts. It must be, in terms of modern information theory, redundant enough to catch the developed imagination of each so-different member of any society.*

We are grateful to Mary Anne Shea for her help with many aspects of our book. We thank Mary Brown Parlee, Director of the Center for the Study of Women and Society, Graduate Center of the City University of New York, for her unfailing support and for the use of the Center's facilities.

Science, No. 126 (November 8, 1957), 959.

Introduction: The Quest and the Questions

I: ELAINE HOFFMAN BARUCH

THE idea of utopia has been with us at least as long as Plato's *Republic*. It has had its name since 1516 when Sir Thomas More's *Utopia* was published. More was punning on two Greek terms, *ou topos* meaning no place and *eu topos* meaning good place. As the idea of utopia developed, the term came to contain within itself antithetical meanings. *Utopia* today means both a longed for ideal and a crackpot scheme. It signifies both change and stasis. It points to both the future and the past. And it is different for women and men.

To the feminist critique of sexist societies it is now important to add the exploration of alternate possibilities. This book presents the social experiments women have engaged in, with men or apart from them, and visions of utopia by women and men. We hope that the utopias described here will give rise to new visions and social structures, for the idea of utopia changes in the search for it.

Is utopia dead? Such has been the predominant view of the (generally male) critics of this century, who point to the great dystopias of earlier decades: Zamyatin's *We,* Huxley's *Brave New World,* and Orwell's *1984.* They point also to the great social experiments that failed, or at least are found wanting, particularly those of Russia and China. But there is one place where the idea of utopia is alive and well: among women writers and thinkers. And it is not just the literary genre of utopia that is thriving, but a great social movement as well.

Why is it that recent books on utopia—for example, Frank and Fritzie Manuel's massive *Utopian Thought in the Western*

World—do not consider feminism a type of utopian thought and action?[1] Perhaps it is because they do not consider feminism at all. But surely its emphasis on new modes of living with regard to the individual, the family, and the state, and its attempt to change "human nature" as men traditionally have defined it, entitle feminism to a place among the grand visionary schemes. If male utopias, whether in literary or social thought, seek to turn the world upside down, then feminism is the arch utopia with its negation not only of a particular social order, but of the entire principle of patriarchy, of what the French call the name and weight of the father.[2]

It should not be surprising that women's utopias differ from men's. Not freedom, but escape from freedom seems to be the message of many male utopias. For men, utopia has often involved imposing control over the individual who is seen as a threat to the group. For women, on the contrary, utopia is a way of arriving at freedom. Perhaps because they have been allowed so little individuation, women do not see the individual as a threat to society. Men seem to want to recover an imaginary perfection through rules and restrictions. Women want to eliminate those restrictions, having been in the prison of gender for so long.

For men, utopia is the ideal state; for most women, utopia is statelessness and the overcoming of hierarchy and the traditional splits between human beings and nature, subject and other, man and woman, parent and child. In Book V of *The Republic,* Plato also tried to break down the traditional divisions and to eliminate the status system based on possession, sex, and parentage, at least in his ruling class. But this was to benefit the state. Perhaps women are better able than men to reconcile the individual and the group because women have traditionally subordinated their needs to those of others.[3] But also revealed in women's utopias is the new attempt to claim their share of inner space, the space of the imagination, as well as outer space, the space of cultural institutions that has for so long been under the domination of men.

Though utopias are often projected onto the future, some

are set in the past. Men generally return to a mythical past of some dreamlike arcadia. In contrast, women's utopian quest is often an attempt to recover a real past. What we now call utopia was once our reality. In many ways, the contemporary dream of equality existed in pre-state egalitarian societies, a few of which are still extant in some form today. (See Part One.)

The genres of utopian fiction and science fiction have long been as different as men and women's utopias. While one of the purposes of men's science fiction is to depict the uses and abuses of science in a technological tour de force, that of their utopian fiction (which interests them hardly at all today) has been to reveal alternate social structures. Now that more women are writing science fiction, the boundaries between the genres are becoming more fluid. Women's science fiction is marked by greater emphasis on characterization than is men's. Conversely, despite the antipathy of some contemporary feminists to science as a tool of male domination, women's utopian as well as science fiction makes much use of technology. But it is always directed toward human needs or used in the interests of art (e.g., Adam's "Therrillium," Part Four), and is never an end in itself.

A major question in both utopian thought and utopian communities has been what to do with the body. As our book shows, attempts to control reproduction and to express or repress sexuality have ranged from the celibacy of the Shakers to the "complex marriage" of the Oneidans to the lesbianism of some separatist groups. Some feminist utopian novelists and theorists today claim that the only route to equality is through biological engineering, by having reproduction *ex utero* (See Lees and Gearhart, Part Four). Others believe that sexual hierarchy can be eliminated by changing social institutions and not the body. While most want to eliminate gender roles, we note that some utopian societies were able to achieve equality of difference (See LeBow, Part One and Rohrlich, Part Two).

What literary utopias reveal as much as future possibilities are the problems in the societies which conceive them. The reason that so many feminist utopias envision modes of reproduction, outside the natural (See Gearhart, Part Four), is the precarious control that women have over their own bodies in reality. The Supreme Court decision of 1973 which granted women a limited right to abortion (further limited by the Hyde Amendment) is increasingly under attack by orthodox religious establishments and the New Right, which recognize, no less than feminists do, that the personal is political and that the right to abortion contributes to autonomy and sexual freedom, which are inextricably linked to economic, social, and political freedom.[4]

We are all subject now to what might be called the dystopian threat—the massive centralized state and the use of technology to control and pervert rather than to liberate—as depicted in Huxley's *Brave New World* and Orwell's *1984*. Yet in some ways, Huxley and Orwell saw contemporary patriarchy as a kind of utopia, notably in its sexual arrangements. For all of his socialist underpinnings, Orwell models his lovers, Winston Smith and Julia on the traditional bourgeois couple.[5] Huxley, as well as Orwell, feared that catastrophe would ensue if gender roles and the traditional family were eliminated.

Perhaps the antidotes for the pessimism of *1984* are the feminist utopian experiments that are taking place now (see Part Three) and feminist utopian novels, with their new arrangements for living (Part Four). "New utopias," Northrop Frye said a while back, "would have to derive their form from the shifting and dissolving movement of society that is gradually replacing the fixed locations of life. They would not be rational cities evolved by a philosopher's dialectic; they would be rooted in the body as well as in the mind, in the unconscious as well as the conscious, in forests and desert as well as highways and buildings, in bed as in the symposium."[6] This sounds much like the location of the feminist utopia, for example, Marge Piercy's *Woman on the Edge of Time*. As I have said elsewhere, "despite its rejection of the nuclear family, viviparous motherhood, monogamy, and sex for procreation, Piercy's utopia is no *Brave New World*. There is considerable joy, color, and warmth in Piercy's future,"[7] which brings together elements of the traditional utopia, with its emphasis on the group, and of arcadia, the land of personal pleasure. In general, women's utopias allow for art and complexity of feeling, along with equality, a fusion lacking in most male utopias. The task before the utopian thinker is to find or create such freedom and richness in the real world.

NOTES

1. Frank E. Manuel and Fritzie P. Manuel, *Utopian Thought in the Western World* (Cambridge, Ma.: Harvard University Press, 1979).

2. For a provocative sampling of French feminist thought, see *New French Feminists*, edited by Elaine Marks and Isabelle de Courtivron (Amherst: The University of Massachusetts Press, 1980; New York: Schocken Books, 1981).

3. See Nancy Chodorow, *The Reproduction of Mothering: Psychoanalysis and the Sociology of Gender* (Berkeley, Calif.: University of California Press, 1978); Judith Kegan Gardiner, "On Female Identity and Writing by Women," *Critical Inquiry* (Winter 1981), pp. 347–61; Carol Gilligan, *In a Different Voice: Psychological Theory and Women's Development* (Cambridge, Mass.: Harvard University Press, 1982).

4. See Rosalind Petchesky, *Abortion and Woman's Choice: The State, Sexuality, and Reproductive Freedom* (New York: Longman, 1984).

5. See my article, " 'The Golden Country': Sex and Love in *1984*," in *1984 Revisited,* Irving Howe, ed. (New York: Harper & Row, Publishers, 1983).

6. Northrop Frye, "Varieties of Literary Utopias," in *Utopias and Utopian Thought,* Frank E. Manuel, ed. (Boston: Houghton-Mifflin, 1966), p. 49.

7. Elaine Hoffman Baruch, "A Natural and Necessary Monster: Women in Utopia," *Alternative Futures: The Journal of Utopian Thought* (Winter 1979), p. 44.

II: RUBY ROHRLICH

SINCE our primary interest in exploring utopian societies is their significance for women, we believe that a heterosocial/homosocial framework provides the most relevant context for the communities discussed in this book. We are concerned with how women fare in communities consisting of both women and men, and in those consisting of women. How do the structures of heterosocial communities differ from homosocial groups? In our culture the words "homosexual" and "heterosexual" are attached to genital sex and sexual preference. By using "social" instead of "sexual" the richness of human connection and interaction is not reduced to a purely sexualized connotation, but is emphasized in its full sociality.

We take the Hopi, the early Celts, and Minoan Crete (Part One) as the utopian prototypes for the societies that preceded the patriarchal, militaristic state. These three cultures demonstrate the variety of gender relationships available in egalitarian communities. Western feminists generally believe that when gender roles are differentiated, hierarchy is inevitable, but what the Hopi in LeBow's essay illustrate is that, in the absence of hierarchical dualisms, such roles do not generate inequality, that is, unequal economic rewards, political power, and social prestige based on gender. In contrast to equality of difference, Minoan Crete offered a high degree of autonomy to both sexes through androgynous roles. [The term "androgyny" itself indicates credence in discrete female and male principles which are merged and reveals a linguistic hierarchy which gives primacy of placement to the male component. Embedded in the language are the very problems we seek to overcome (See Gershuny; and Thorne, Kramarae and Henley, Part Three).]

As the early class-stratified patriarchies emerged, women and men were divided against each other as women in each stratum were subordinated to men by the construction of the inferior class, women (Rohrlich, Part One). But as organic utopias were transformed into dystopias, women and men began their unceasing struggles to re-establish the former ways of life in new contexts—in communities separate from the mainstream, both heterosocial and homosocial, outside and inside the patriarchal system.

It is most likely that the initial separatist societies were created by women who, refusing to submit to an unprecedented subjugation, escaped from the patriarchies and formed homosocial communities which they defended by force of arms.

The historicity of these so-called Amazon societies is accepted by such eminent ancient writers as Herodotus, Pliny, Plutarch, Diodorus Siculus and Arrian (considered authorities on *other* historical matters[1]), and by some contemporary writers, such as the historian Emanuel Kantor. A fictional counterpart to these societies is Monique Wittig's *Les Guérillères*.[2] More recent real-life analogies are the Peruvian Indian women who, in the 17th century, fled from the Spanish *conquistadores* to the *puna*, the high, almost inaccessible Andean tablelands very distant from their native communities. "Vigorously rejecting the colonial ideology which reinforced their oppression,"[3] these women formed their own societies, incorporating pre-Incan and pre-colonial social relations and religion. One of these women, accused of being a sorceress and priestess of heresy, indicates the unprecedented nature of their oppression: "The universe has turned inside out; for we are being persecuted."[4]

In contemporary Andean culture, the *puna* is still considered "women's territory, and is the center of women's society."[5] Male village members are afraid to go to the *puna,* and say, "If the women in the *puna* do not like what we are doing, they will stone us."[6] On the other hand, they acknowledge that "The women in the *puna* are living in the ways our ancestors lived years ago, they are defending our customs, they are defending our culture."[7]

It seems to be the case that women seeking alternatives to patriarchal oppression joined with like-minded men when communities provided equal access to resources and roles, as did some of the early Christian sects. In *The Gnostic Gospels* Pagels points out that in many of the initial Christian communities both women and men were prophets and priests, healers and teachers, their roles changing continually according to lots drawn at each meeting to prevent the formation of hierarchy. Some of their texts held that "the God in whose image we are made must also be both masculine—and feminine—both Father and Mother";[8] they reject that early example of womb envy in which Eve is created from Adam's rib by a biological sleight-of-hand. Prefiguring the feminist commentators in the *Women's Bible* centuries later, they saw Eve as the human spiritual principle who raised Adam from his merely material condition. They

viewed wisdom as a specifically female attribute, with the ser-
pent the symbol of divine wisdom, as in Minoan Crete, and
among the Hopi.

The Christian Golden Age lasted for about two centuries;
"by the late second century, the orthodox community came to
accept the domination of men over women as the divinely ordained order."[9] By this time "every one of the secret texts which
gnostic groups revered was omitted from the canonical collection
and branded heretical by those who called themselves orthodox
Christians"[10]—utopia becoming heresy. As Pagels points out, "It
is the winners who write history—their way."

Gnostic Christians were the model for the many religious
sects that began to emerge with the Protestant Reformation in
the 16th century. Proliferating in the antebellum United States,
and to a lesser degree in the counter-cultural ferment of the
1960s and 1970s, such groups include several of the recent and
current religious societies discussed in this book: the Shakers
and Perfectionists (Part Two), and the Children of God (Part
Three).

Like the early Christians these communities were heterosocial and held their goods in common, but unlike the Gnostics,
male dominance and/or hierarchical structure were the norm,
together with what were considered extreme forms of sexuality.
The contemporary Children of God were headed by a profligate
patriarch who instituted the virtual prostitution of women members as the means of bringing wealthy converts into the fold.

The Shakers and Perfectionists in the 19th century regulated sexuality in totally different ways, but both were viewed as
extreme and dangerous. The Shakers, vowed to celibacy, de-
nounced marriage as the breeding ground for "lusts of the
flesh," the source of every evil on earth, while the Perfectionists
practiced "group" marriage, abolishing exclusiveness in persons
as in property because it offered insufficient pleasure and in-
terfered with the solidarity of the community. Among the
Shakers, founded by a woman, Ann Lee, women shared equally
in all aspects of leadership; among the Perfectionists, founded
by a man, John Humphrey Noyes, men were formally domi-

nant, but the sexual division of labor was less rigid than among the Shakers.

Alone among all the utopians, religious and secular, the Christian Noyes and the theist Fourier, who influenced Noyes, were concerned with the sexuality of older women, Noyes because intercourse with post-menopausal women did not require men to control ejaculation. Both men recommended that older people initiate younger ones into sex. Fourier also suggested that older women, more experienced and sensitive, should serve as sex counsellors, and at Oneida they served as liaison between women and men who sought sexual relations with one another. Fourier formulated the famous proposition: "The extension of privileges to women is the general principle of all social progress."[11]

Comparing the status of women among the religious Shakers and anti-religious Owenite Socialists discussed by Harsin (Part Two), it appears that the Shaker women had "a degree of equality in leadership that even the most militant socialist advocates of women's rights were unable or unwilling to achieve."[12] In the Owenite communities women were responsible for all domestic labor, both communal and private, worked many more hours per day and week than the men, and had minimal say in government and decision-making.

The factors that "freed Shaker women for an active role in Church leadership at all levels," according to Foster,[13] were, first and foremost, the practice of celibacy, by which women achieved total control over their bodies, combined with communal rearing of the children of individuals joining the Shakers and of the orphans they adopted. Celibacy was a more effective form of birth control than the male control of ejaculation practiced at Oneida, where some unwanted children were born. The loosening of traditional sex roles among the Perfectionists did not lead to gender equality, perhaps because the men maintained control of women's sexuality and reproduction (Noyes deciding which men would be fathers) while the maintenance of traditional roles did not subvert gender equality among the Shakers.

Although many of the nineteenth-century intentional communities, especially those based on socialist principles, intended to implement gender equality, few succeeded. Fewer still were committed to racial equality and interracial living, even among the abolitionist communities. And only two, as far as we know, envisioned both goals, the Shakers and Nashoba (Bensman, Part Two), founded by women. Did the comparative success of the Shaker communes that were interracial derive from their celibacy?

With contemporary women in greater control of their reproduction and sexuality, two small-scale heterosocial communities discussed in this book now offer women the prospect of utopia. Both Findhorn in Scotland and Twin Oaks in the United States (Part Three) have eliminated gender roles and created egalitarian structures. As a New Age spiritual community, with nurturing relations to plants and animals, and respect for non-destructive technology, Findhorn forms part of the feminist/ecology movement that seeks to preserve the planet. However, the sexual invisibility of older women indicates, according to Sheer, that Findhorn is not altogether immune to media culture. At Twin Oaks "the objective structure for liberation is profound," writes Weinbaum. All labor from child care to auto repair is given equal credit, and the "recognition that women's previous labor was unpaid and now needs to be counted is subversive and makes room for other possible changes."

A notable heterosocial organization is CARASA, the Committee for Abortion Rights and Against Sterilization Abuse, which consists of women and some men "of different ages, races and religions,"[14] primarily concerned with the vital issue of reproductive freedom. CARASA members, both grass-roots and academic, recognize that, in a democratic society, reproductive freedom is not "just" a woman's issue but at least as basic a freedom as freedom of speech, freedom of religion, freedom of assembly, and freedom of the press.

Turning to the homosocial communities in the early modern period, we begin with the Beguines. In October, 1976, a women's conference in New York City defined itself as "A Celebration of the Beguines." It is ironic that contemporary feminists involved in creating women's communities that are often homosexual and anti-religious have adopted as their fore-mothers the religious Beguines of the late Middle Ages, who were vowed to celibacy. However, religious or not, celibate or not, the Beguines developed a free and independent way of life, transcending class divisions among women in ways that the current women's movement has yet to achieve. In the 13th and 14th centuries, hundreds of thousands of women managed to form homosocial communities that flourished for at least half a dozen generations in the towns of France, Flanders, and Germany. "Women in every part of society drew strength from personal contact with Beguines and the vigorous alternatives they offered to life with men."[15]

What is remarkable about these communities is that they enabled women in all classes to create ties with one another as they shared support and skills. Since the burgeoning cloth industry in the new towns employed mainly women, working-class women predominated in the Beguine movement, older women often being leaders. Controlling their own property to a great extent, many lived together in their own buildings, chose their own activities and companions, and often travelled together to other cities. But the Church became increasingly hostile to their independence and eventually required them to take permanent vows as lay associates of male monasteries. After the 1330s, this led to the decline of Beguine communities into charity homes and sheltered workshops. Nevertheless, at the height of the movement, they "enjoyed more freedom and more power to expand their lives in any direction than any of their contemporaries, male or female."[16]

The decline of the Beguines marks the beginning of a period when European women were increasingly restricted in their public activities. It was no coincidence that the Salic Law of 1328, barring women from inheriting the French crown, was passed at a time when the Beguines were losing their freedom. In this period, when the modern European states and bourgeois society were emerging, the line between private and public life began to be drawn with increasing firmness for middle-class and even noble women. As the economic, political, and cultural power enjoyed by aristocratic women in the Middle Ages began to decline, and middle-class women were being domesticated, the pre-industrial patriarchal household emerged as the basic social unit, together with the "new gender construction of the domestic lady."[17]

The new secular humanist culture of early modern Europe was accompanied by "the hanging or burning alive of some 100,000 or more women as witches,"[18] which, no doubt, deterred women from continuing to resist the status being imposed on them. Except intermittently, during the English Revolution of the seventeenth century and the French Revolution of the late eighteenth, periods when they regained a measure of freedom, women became increasingly segregated from men and the public domain. By the nineteenth century the roles of men and women in Western industrial societies were fully defined as separate and "complementary" in the public and private spheres; that is, the "unwaged and unacknowledged work" of women in the home "kept them dependent on men" and "bound to a subordinate servicing role."[19] However, most women, including many feminists and socialists, came to "defend and prize the so-called female realm" and its values of purity, piety and superior morality[20] and used them as strategies to achieve their own goals, particularly in the formation of homosocial communities and organizations.

In the midst of hundreds of heterosocial intentional communities in the nineteenth century, the Women's Commonwealth of Belton, Texas, was a unique example of a community formed by women for women only including "battered wives and wives of alcoholics."[21] Using the tradition of women's private networks, the economic ideas of intentional communities, the tenets of social reform and particularly of personal revelation (Andreadis, Part Two, and influenced by the women's movement of the period), the Belton Sanctificationists, as they were also known, rejected as "unholy" the sex and money of their husbands. Despite the threats, vilification and abuse heaped upon them, these middle-class women supported themselves by their own labor from 1868 to 1918.

Acting on their "separate unique female identity," women in

the late nineteenth and early twentieth centuries in the United States extended their private networks into the public domain, and formed separate organizations which enabled them to act politically on behalf of women.[22] Examples are the General Federation of Women's Clubs, which campaigned for social reform and suffrage; the Women's Christian Temperance Union, "which became a strong pro-suffrage organization, committed to righting all wrongs against any woman, through any means";[23] the Women's Trade Union League, which provided valuable services in organizing women workers; and the women's colleges.

In the settlement house movement described by Blanche Cook (Part Three), social workers and nurses, the first generation of twentieth-century feminists, both lived and worked together, drawing strength and emotional support from their homosocial lesbian communities as they succored the poor, battled corrupt politicians and United States imperialism, and fought for suffrage. Like the Women's Commonwealth in Texas, they were abused and threatened.

In these same years, women anarchists in Spain found they could carry out both their feminist and anarchist goals far more effectively in their own autonomous association *Mujeres Libres* (Ackelsberg, Part Three) than in the male-dominated anarchist groups. If the Spanish Republic had survived, these "liberated women" might have provided the leadership necessary to establish a truly egalitarian and democratic government.

A separatist women's organization which linked traditional female culture in the United States with the contemporary women's movement is Women Strike for Peace (WSP), consisting of "women of all races, creeds and political persuasions . . . dedicated to the achievement of general and complete disarmament under effective international control."[24] Called up before the House Committee on Un-American Activities on suspicion of Communist infiltration, these women gave a performance that "was so original, so winning and so 'feminine' in the traditional sense that it succeeded in capturing the sympathy and support of large sections of the national media and in strengthening the movement instead of destroying it."[25] WSP was strongly feminist:

By emphasizing the fact that the men in power could no longer be counted on for protection in the nuclear age, WSP implied that the traditional sex-gender contract no longer worked. And by stressing global issues and international sisterhood, rather than domestic responsibilities, WSP challenged the privatization and isolation of women which was a key element of the feminine mystique.

However, "it alienated a new generation of younger women," who admired WSP for its stand on peace but rejected its heavy reliance "on the politics of motherhood" and "its acquiescence to sex role stereotypes."[26] As WSP was outstanding in the struggle against nuclear armament in the 1960s, so the women's peace camps in Europe and the United States constitute the most effective demonstrators for peace in the 1980s, as well as ongoing homosocial communities deserving intensive study.

Women worked with men in reformist and radical movements in both the nineteenth and twentieth centuries until male oppression forced them to form their own organizations. As Kelly points out:

> Women will not forget how this phase of the women's movement was forced to repeat the first wave in its inception. Women's groups developed out of the radical movements of the 1960s much as they did in the 1840s and 50s when women from the abolition and peace movements came to form their own organizations because men, in those very movements against oppression, retained sex-oppressive structures and behavior.[27]

Since the late 1960's, this generation of both younger *and* older women has formed separatist groups of all kinds: political caucuses within and outside the mainstream political parties; coalitions of women trade unionists; welfare mothers' organizations; the wages-for-housewives movement; women's centers in the colleges and universities; self-help health collectives; collectives of women artists, musicians, photographers, film-makers; collectives publishing feminist journals and newspapers; groups learning self-defense against rape and street harassment; shelters for battered women; collectives fighting sexual harassment in the workplace, and perhaps most important of all, the women's peace encampments.

This generation of feminists has gone off to live together in its own communities in the cities and on farms, usually having tried mixed collectives first and found them wanting. The women on the farms in the United States experience economic, political and interpersonal problems, particularly when dyadic relationships compete with the claims of the group, which occurs in most intentional communities, homosocial and heterosocial. But they are a retreat for "burned-out" women (Weinbaum, Part Three), a place where they can learn non-traditional skills and explore various forms of psychic healing.

In Copenhagen, Denmark, the communities I visited in 1975 had both lesbian and heterosexual members. These were students or workers who had chosen to live in women's collectives primarily because, as active members of the women's movement, they found it convenient and pleasurable to live with women who had the same interests and goals. They also felt that in their own communities they could develop new strengths and skills and learn to depend on themselves and other women. In mixed groups, they said, gender roles remain "astonishingly strong"; women often unconsciously slip into physical and mental dependence, men dominate in decision-making and discussion, and are reluctant to share domestic chores.

All-women utopias are a new phenomenon in fiction, and raise the question of "Why there are no utopias which are made up entirely of men" (Gearhart, Part Four). In her analysis of eleven utopian novels by women, Gearhart notes that in the eight lesbian societies women exercise complete control over reproduction, a central feminist concern, in a variety of ways: by using men for insemination, mating with stallions, through parthenogenesis, and by a form of ovular merging.

The main criticism of separatist societies, writes Gearhart, is that they are never really separate; "complete separatism is impossible at present." There's always some connection to the male system. But according to Kelly:

> We need both separatism and full social participation to liberate ourselves from our several forms of sex oppression; and sex oppression will not itself be overcome without liberation from all forms of domination and hierarchy.[28]

NOTES

1. In the first chapter of her book *The War Against the Amazons* (New York: McGraw Hill, 1983) Abby Kleinbaum conscientiously cites all the Greek and Roman writers who accepted the historicity of the Amazons. She then denies their existence, insisting that they are but a figment of the male imagination. If this is so, then all the data presented by these Greek and Roman writers and accepted as historical must also be rejected.

2. Monique Wittig, *Les Guérillères*, trans. Peter Owen (New York: The Viking Press, 1971).

3. Irene Silberblatt, "Andean Women Under Spanish Rule," in *Women and Colonization*, eds. Mona Etienne and Eleanor B. Leacock (New York: Praeger Publishers, 1980), p. 177.

4. Silberblatt, "Andean Women," p. 173.

5. Silberblatt, p. 180.

6. *Ibid.*

7. *Ibid.*

8. Elaine Pagels, *The Gnostic Gospels* (New York: Vintage Books, 1981), p. 59.

9. Pagels, p. 79.

10. Pagels, p. 68.

11. Charles Fourier, *Design for Utopia: Selected Writings of Charles Fourier*, trans. Julia Franklin (New York: Schocken Books, 1971), p. 77.

12. Lawrence Foster, *Religion and Sexuality* (New York: Oxford University Press, 1981), p. 38.

13. *Ibid.*

14. *Women Under Attack* (New York: Committee for Abortion Rights and Against Sterilization Abuse, 1979), p. 60.

15. Gracia Clark, "The Beguines: A Medieval Women's Community," in Charlotte Bunch, *et al.*, eds., *Building Feminist Theory* (New York: Longmans, Inc., 1981), p. 237.

16. Clark, p. 241.

17. Joan Kelly, "Early Feminist Theory and the *Querelle des Femmes*, 1400–1789," *Signs* (Autumn 1982), p. 7.

18. Kelly, "Early Feminist Theory," p. 27.

19. Joan Kelly, "The Doubled Vision of Feminist Theory," *Feminist Studies* (Spring 1979), p. 217.

20. Kelly, "The Doubled Vision," p. 219.

21. Elizabeth Pleck, "Feminist Response to 'Crimes Against Women,' 1868–1896," *Signs* (Spring 1983), p. 45.

22. Estelle Freedman, "Separation as Strategy: Female Institution Building and American Feminism, 1870–1930," *Feminist Studies* (Fall 1979), p. 517.

23. Amy Swerdlow, "Ladies' Day at the Capitol: Women Strike for Peace *versus* HUAC," *Feminist Studies* (Fall 1982), p. 499.

24. Swerdlow, p. 501.

25. Swerdlow, p. 515.

26. Swerdlow, p. 516.

27. Kelly, "The Doubled Vision," p. 219.

28. *Ibid.,* p. 220.

Part One

THE DISTANT PAST

Introduction

RUBY ROHRLICH

T HE word "utopia" translates into both "good place" and "no place." Skeptics combine the two, convinced that no place was there ever a good place. For them, a golden age, like a matriarchy, like the Amazons, is to be found only in fiction and fantasy. Yet students of society, contemporary and ancient, have documented ways of life that, from our perspective, are utopian prototypes. Unlike the lost Atlantis, or a planet in outer space, the societies discussed below actually existed, with flesh-and-blood people, in specific geographical areas, at particular times, on this earth. These peoples, or their descendants, are still with us, though their societies have suffered violent change.

But a crucial *caveat* for all social systems (for that matter, all forms of life) is that they are in process, as Khanna points out (Part Four); thus, our utopias are neither finite nor perfect. Unlike the planned, rigidly controlled, and static utopias, real and fictional, generally devised by men, these societies are subject to transformation as the world within and around them changes. In fact, our "good place" also illustrates the forces that may turn utopia into dystopia.

The societies selected as utopian models—typical of many of the societies that the Europeans colonized beginning in the late 15th century—are the Hopi (Pueblo Indians) in North America, and the Celts and the Cretans in Europe. Their impressive achievements in the arts and crafts, science and technology, were for the most part indigenous, deriving from their respective histories and skilful adaptations to their environment, which produced food surpluses permitting the creative use of surplus energy. Contrary to the widespread Western belief that a managerial class is essential for complex social production, these societies demonstrate that voluntary labor on behalf of an egalitarian community, holding land and basic resources in common, can achieve remarkable feats.

Their architecture, for example, refutes the notion that monumental works are created only in state societies. The Hopi built elaborate four- and five-storied structures of stone masonry, the first apartment houses in North America, and great ceremonial subterranean *kivas,* symbolizing the body of Mother Earth. The megalithic burial chambers of the Celts, "the earliest stone monuments in the world,"[1] and the imposing circular tombs, the *tholos,* of the early Cretans go back more than 5,000 years, long before the Pyramids. The Celtic and Cretan buildings were meeting places for the ceremonials of the living, as well as abodes for the dead, and were associated with "belief in the great Mother Goddess."[2]

While the three societies have roots in the ancient past, only the Hopi still retain, "to a remarkable degree,"[3] the culture of their forbears. Their direct ancestors were the *Hitsan Sinom,* or Basket-makers, who stemmed from the Archaic Desert culture established in the southwestern part of North America more than 10,000 years ago. When the Spaniards arrived, the Pueblo Indians were living in peaceful symbiosis with the Apache.[4] Despite their self-designation as "people of peace," they rose up against the atrocities of their Spanish conquerors in the late seventeenth century and massacred them.

Notwithstanding the enormous pressures of their arid environment and the onslaught first of the Spaniards and then of the Anglo-Americans, "the tenacity of the Pueblos to survive as a people and as tightly knit communities over many centuries"[5] refutes anthropological stereotypes about the fragility of matrilineal societies. Such societies provide women and their children with socioeconomic and emotional security without degrading male status, according to female anthropologists who have studied the Hopi, and whose findings LeBow compares with those of male anthropologists. (Rohrlich *et al.* present similar disparities between male and female anthropological findings about Australian aboriginal women.)[6] Nor does the sexual division of labor lead to gender inequality in matrilineal, matrifocal pre-state societies, unlike the patriarchal state societies in which differentiated roles keep women out of highly rewarded and prestigious occupations. The active social roles of Hopi men and women are reflected in sexual practices[7] that attest to their exuberance and humor—practices so shocking to the Catholic and Protestant missionaries who were, on the whole, unsuccessful in converting them.

Lest we think that contemporary physicists[8] or utopian fiction writers (cf. Pearson's "Of Time and Revolution," Part Four) originated non-linear, multi-dimensional concepts of reality, a glimpse of the Hopi cosmology reveals a much earlier origin for these views, as well as for the "reciprocally balanced" dualism which underlies their differentiated and egalitarian gender roles:

> . . . the conception of change in linear, cause-and-effect terms, common among us, is absent in the thinking of these people, who see life in terms of inter-related and multi-manifested wholes in the process of metamorphosis, each according to its own mode, rhythm and tempo. Moreover, the Hopi concept of the balanced, correlative interdependence of the manifold aspects of reality excludes an arbitrary over-all dual division, such as that which structures our own thinking and forms the basis for our traditional ethical concept of the competing forces of good and evil. Duality in the Hopi world view exists only insofar as it represents two correlates conceived as an indispensable part of the whole, neither one being essentially subordinate to the other.[9]

The Indo-European Celts ranged widely over Europe, from the British Isles to Spain, during the Iron Age. Long ago, their descendants settled down in Brittany, Cornwall, the Isle of Man, Wales, Scotland, and Ireland. Gaelic, a Celtic dialect, is still spoken in Ireland and Scotland, and Celtic mythology and folklore, ancient documents and archaeological artifacts, attest to a rich historical and literary heritage. Celtic women shared with men the roles of farmer, herder, gatherer, fisher, teacher, poet, healer, priest, warrior, and god, in tribes that remained essentially egalitarian through redistribution of wealth, even when headed by chiefs. McNelly reveals the sophisticated world view of Medb, the Irish queen who, in her "pillow talk" with her husband, comprehends the intertwined tragedy and comedy of love in terms of the unstable natural elements. Their dialogue also illustrates the male-female conflicts that germinated with the acquisition and private ownership of large quantities of goods, mainly the spoils of raiding, no longer rare in this society with a hereditary noble lineage on the way to becoming warlike and patriarchal.

The Minoan matriarchy, the first European civilization, was a "pristine and original creation"[10] which owed little to the "arrival of wise men from the east,"[11] i.e., from Sumer and Egypt. Initially, the roughly contemporaneous Cretan and Sumerian cultures had much in common: both were egalitarian Neolithic societies, organized in corporate kinship clans where women, pre-eminent in plant cultivation and its associated inventions, played ascendant roles. At this stage, we regard both as utopian prototypes. The later divergence between Crete and Sumer is illustrated by the differences in their artistic development. Minoan arts and crafts reached heights not attained by any other Bronze Age civilization, in a society that left the artists, and the people as a whole, relatively autonomous. Since Minoan Crete remained at peace with the world for about 1500 years, political power was widely diffused, with clan structures comparatively intact. Female deities were served by a priesthood of women and men, headed by the women rulers.[12] In Sumer, art reached its zenith at the threshold of state formation; thereafter, it became increasingly stereotyped and static, compelled to glorify the exploits of the warring kings. As warfare became chronic, the state was gradually centralized, clan structures were eroded and, in contrast to the androgynous gender roles in Minoan Crete, women were pushed out of the prestigious roles they had formerly played, and subordinated in the household. Thereafter children were socialized into a gender hierarchy which also prepared them to accept the class hierarchy.[13]

In ancient Sumer we see full-blown the militaristic, patriarchal state which could survive only by creating a chasm between women and men. This is the prototypical dystopia, against which peoples everywhere rebelled whenever possible, leading to the creation of utopias in fact and in fiction.

NOTES

1. Colin Renfrew, *Before Civilization: The Radiocarbon Revolution and Prehistoric Europe* (London: Cambridge University Press, 1973), p. 16.

2. Renfrew, p. 85.

3. Robert F. Spencer, Jesse D. Jennings, *et al.*, *The Native Americans* (New York: Harper & Row, 1965), p. 287.

4. Edward P. Dozier, *The Pueblo Indians of North America* (New York: Holt, Rinehart and Winston, Inc., 1970), p. 3.

5. Dozier, p. 19.

6. Ruby Rohrlich-Leavitt, Barbara Sykes, and Elizabeth Weatherford, "Aboriginal Woman: Male and Female Anthropological Perspectives," *Toward an Anthropology of Women*, edited by Rayna R. Reiter (New York: Monthly Review Press, 1975), pp. 110–126.

7. Martin B. Duberman, Fred Eggan, Richard Clemmer, eds., "Documents in Hopi Indian Sexuality: Imperialism, Culture, and Resistance," *Radical History Review* (Spring/Summer, 1979), pp. 99–139.

8. Paul Davies, *Other Worlds: A Portrait of Nature in Rebellion—Space, Super-Space and the Quantum Universe* (New York: Simon & Schuster, 1980), pp. 188–189.

9. Laura Thompson and Alice Joseph, *The Hopi Way* (Chicago: University of Chicago Press, 1944), p. 44.

10. Renfrew, p. 211.

11. Renfrew, p. 85.

12. Ruby Rohrlich-Leavitt, "Women in Transition: Crete and Sumer," *Becoming Visible, Women in European History*, edited by Renate Bridenthal and Claudia Koonz (Boston: Houghton Mifflin Co., 1977), pp. 36–59.

13. Ruby Rohrlich, "State Formation in Sumer and the Subjugation of Women," *Feminist Studies* (Spring 1980), pp. 76–102.

Rethinking Matriliny Among the Hopi

DIANE LEBOW

WHAT would a society be like in which women and men shared status, privilege, and responsibility in an equal and balanced manner? In the quest for answers to this question, much attention in recent years has focused on ancient matriarchies; however, much closer to home, societies continue to exist in which lineage is traced through the female line (matrilineal) and women own the residences (matrilocal: husbands move into their wives' homes). Noteworthy among these groups are the Hopi, the oldest of existing Native American cultures. They have lived on the mesas in northeastern Arizona for the past 1000 years.

Gender roles among the Hopi are egalitarian. Schlegel places them in a category among matrilineal kinship systems, in which neither brother nor husband exerts control over the woman, in contrast to other categories:

> I had gone to Hopiland assuming that brothers would exert a good deal of authority over the women, and husbands virtually none. What I saw, in fact, was a delicate balance of tactful suggestion and subtle pressure on the part of both while the women actually "ruled the roost."[1]

Neither sex is inferior. "The complementarity of the sexes is institutionalized."[2] Social responsibility, not privilege, is stressed. A Hopi saying goes: "Any time anyone may need help, so we all help one another."

In spite of the fact that women's status among the Hopi is respected and substantial, anthropological literature has tended to ignore or diminish women's political, economic, and social roles. Many anthropologists bring with them their own cultural stereotypes, biases, and expectations. Because the majority of anthropologists have been male, usually they cannot enter women's groups and observe women's behavior freely; so they focus on the males. What a person learns about a society depends upon the questions she or he asks. To date, few male anthropologists have looked closely at women's status and authority among the Hopi.

In reviewing the literature on the Hopi, we begin to see the emergence of a kind of primer for the exploration of equality between the sexes.

KINSHIP SYSTEM

The basic kinship unit is the clan with descent traced through the female line. Each of the twenty-one matrilineal clans is headed by a clan mother, usually the oldest woman, who is in charge of the household, the surplus, and problem solving. While she is the "real" head, the "ceremonial" head is usually her brother who is in charge of most of the religious ceremonies. The sacred property of the clan, such as the fetishes and ceremonial paraphernalia, are kept in the clan house under the custody of the clan mother.

Women have economic and social security independent of marital status. The houses are owned by the women, inherited usually through the youngest daughter (ultimogeniture).[3] In addition, house furnishings, crops, food stores, and seeds belong to the women of the clan under the charge of the clan mother. The springs, gardens, farmlands are also owned collectively by the clan and are distributed to the household groups by the female head. Most of the livestock and fruit trees belong to the men. The children also "belong" to the women in the sense that they remain affiliated with their maternal household. A man leaves his wife's house in the case of divorce, but the women have a fixed abode.

The household consists of a woman, her husband, her unmarried daughters and sons. Her married daughters and their husbands and children occupy a set of adjoining flat-roofed rooms, side by side or one atop the other, facing the pueblo court. Each household is an independent economic unit; each member works with others for the common good. After several children are born, if the pueblo becomes crowded, the husband will be pressured to build a house nearby for his family.

Women are in charge of all activities within the household. The women and girls care for the children, grind the corn, prepare and cook the food, haul water from the spring, care for the vegetable garden, and make pottery and baskets. The men and boys farm, herd, hunt, collect fuel and timber, spin, weave, tan leather, and, along with the women, conduct the ceremonial activities. Children call their biological mother and her sisters by the kinship term for mother, *inqu'u,* and sisters refer to all their offspring by the same term, *iti'i.* Sisters' children regard each other as siblings. When a woman dies, her sister adopts the children.

The care of children is shared by many members of the clan. The women of the father's house play important roles in the birth and naming rites and develop close, long-lasting relationships with the child. Children also have "ceremonial" mothers and fathers who sponsor them in various organizations.

Courtship, Marriage, and Divorce

Women play an active and direct role in courtship. To initiate marriage, the girl presents the boy of her choice with a loaf of *gomi,* a special cornmeal cake. The boy is obliged to receive it so as not to offend her. If he and his family decide to accept the proposal, the prospective bride moves temporarily into his mother's house for the ritual, three-day corn-grinding. While she grinds the corn, the young man's male relatives weave her wedding robes, which will later become the shroud which floats her spirit to the Spirit World. If divorced, she will keep these first marriage robes since she has paid for them with her labor, and her next husband will not need to provide them.[4]

Male and female anthropologists provide strikingly different emphases on courtship and marriage. Titiev[5] deemphasizes the fact that the girl takes the initiative and stresses the young man's wanderings around at night, wrapped in blankets as a disguise, calling into the girl's window. Well-documented by Schlegel[6] but omitted by Titiev are the psychological implications of matrilocality for the male. The boy often hesitates to leave the comforts of his mother's home for hard work, responsibility, and restrictions on his freedom and in numerous cases he does not go at all or only after a period of time. Schlegel's study[7] clearly counterpoints the emotional trauma experienced by brides in patrilocal societies, which are far less supportive of them than the matrilocal Hopi culture is of its males. In fact, a man's economic, social, and emotional security rests with his maternal extended family, not with his family of procreation. Although he eats and sleeps in his wife's house, on ceremonial and feast days he usually goes to his own clan household where he enjoys a higher status. He also acts as disciplinarian when the need arises, with his sister's children rather than his own.

Among the Hopi, a primary marital relationship is not necessary for a woman's economic security or for child-rearing. The divorce rate in matrilineal cultures tends to be quite high, often around fifty percent, and in the case of divorce, a woman and her children remain in their own home with their relatives. The social expectation is that a couple should make an effort to get along; the offending individual will be criticized, especially if the mate is "diligent and cooperative."[8] Divorce procedure simply involves the husband taking his personal possessions elsewhere or the woman placing his possessions outside the door. Remarriage is common and simple, especially since no gift exchange of corn and robes is required for a second or third marriage. Subsequent marriages must be between persons of the same marital status, e.g., both divorced once or twice.

In general, the Hopi woman feels that her husband is relatively unimportant to her life. She shows scorn toward the *ba-*

hana's (white woman's) emotional dependency in marriage.[9] Sometimes a woman will divorce her husband after having a girl child. "I don't need my husband anymore now that I have my baby girl. My family has some extra land, and my brothers will plant it for me."[10]

Titiev finds it hard to reconcile the "instability" of marriage and the "laxity" of divorce customs with the stable social structure. On the other hand, he does acknowledge that the nuclear family is not what gives permanence to Hopi society:

> The strength and durability of the household unit is scarcely affected by the *collapse* of limited families, and it is for this reason that the social structure of the Hopi has been unshaken by the widespread prevalence of *such disturbing factors as adultery and divorce.*[11] [my emphasis]

SOCIALIZATION

Hopi socialization patterns yield further evidence of egalitarianism between the sexes and cast light on the bases for the women's self-respect and dignity. "The Hopi's worlds of social interaction and ideological construction are based on the premise that the sexes, although different, are equal."[12]

Equality of treatment and emotional security seem to be the themes of children's early years. Boys and girls before adolescence are treated more or less similarly. At about four years of age both sexes begin to be trained for some responsibility. Both sexes experience the first initiation together at age six or seven and receive the same ceremonial instruction. Pre-adolescents play in mixed-sex groups and may, if they wish, enter sex-specific ceremonial societies, such as the Snake Society for men and the Mamzrau Society for women.[13] There is only mild discipline in the early years with much affectionate security. Children are "watched rather than restricted."[14] The intense dependency on the primary family, characteristic of Western culture, is absent among the Hopi.

"Children are socialized to be Hopi; it is at adolescence that girls are socialized to become women."[15] By puberty, girls feel the full weight of household responsibilities, whereas boys are not expected to take on their ceremonial responsibilities until their second initiation in their late teens or early twenties. Usually they do not have charge of a full herd or field until their marriage.

Matriarchal societies are often described as peace-loving, egalitarian, and reverencing life. The development of these characteristics is the goal of Hopi socialization. Hopi means "peaceful people." Aggression within the community is deplored. Between men, an occasional pushing bout will ensue until bystanders intervene; the rare fight will be talked about for years. Women are less rigidly socialized not to fight. Although still uncommon, fights between women are thought to happen more often than between men and are frequently caused by jealousy of a husband's affair.[16]

Individuals must take their part for the community to be effective. Private interests must be submerged to the interest of the group. The ethic of humility and non-competitiveness is paramount. People's first duty is to family and community and they are discouraged from striving for personal success. People should strive to portray themselves as worse than others. To be too clever or too prosperous is to risk being considered a witch, one whose heart has been sold for power and who must steal other hearts to stay alive.

Interestingly enough, coming from this supportive, non-competitive environment, Hopi children test higher on intelligence tests than other Native American children and most white children, and exhibit exceptional creative ability and talent for intense, extended concentration. Yet they dislike being singled out for praise. For example, a child who is quickest at completing board work in school will wait to sit down until another child finishes. A basketball game will continue for hours with no acknowledgement of scoring since what matters is the joy of the game, not the competition.[17]

People are expected to make their own decisions. *Pi um'i,* "it is up to you," is a common expression, indicating respect for individual autonomy. Hopi are quick to criticize but hesitate to give advice because a person must always take responsibility for the consequences.

Hopi are taught to kill only for food, to use the entire animal once it is killed, and never needlessly to pick or destroy anything, not even a weed, unless they intend to use it.[18] Sickness can be "willed" (prayed) away by concentrating on good thoughts, akin to the technique of visualization.

The main difference in the socialization of girls and boys is that the "expression of aggressiveness is felt to be natural for women," whereas men are expected to be more peaceable.[19] Adolescent girls are often impertinent toward their mothers, who tend to laugh off such behavior as natural childish thoughtlessness. Schlegel gives two main reasons for the higher tolerance of aggressiveness in women. First, women are mothers of the people and must develop their natural fierceness in order to protect their young. Second, female aggressiveness does not threaten community solidarity as much as male aggressiveness; with the major responsibility for the ceremonial cycles, men must maintain greater self-control for the good of the community. In contrast, female aggressiveness is encouraged as a natural aspect of Hopi women's autonomy. Fights between women are often caused by jealousy over a husband's affair.

Titiev has a totally different explanation for female aggressiveness. He says: "Boys have more tractable dispositions and better tempers than girls."[20] Girls tend to harbor resentments and frequently die out of self-pity. According to Titiev, girls put too high a value on themselves; they become vain because they are prospective mothers, responsible for the perpetuation of the clan. They even "disregard the instruction of their brothers and maternal uncles."[21]

An interesting note is that among the generally benevolent *kachinas* is one ogre *kachina,* a monster who is said to eat misbehaving children. This *kachina,* Soyoko, is a female!

A woman typically states: "You raise up a daughter for yourself; you raise up a son for someone else."[22] Girls are preferred because a girl will remain with or near her mother, whereas a boy will transfer his residence, labor, responsibility to his wife's household. "He moves over to her side" is a common expression describing the divided loyalties men will come to have after marriage. Daughters are as valuable to men as to women. An old man will live with his daughter who has inherited her mother's house; he has no right to live in his son's wife's house. "An old man without a daughter is in an unenviable position."[23] Couples without daughters will adopt them, often the child of a wife's biological or classificatory sister.

Even small girls are to be respected. They are not punished as severely as boys because "they will grow up and make *piki* [cornmeal wafer bread] for us."[24] Woman is seen as the social and spiritual source of life. She births people, nourishes them, and "feeds" the ceremonial objects. Even witches who steal hearts for additional years of life prefer a girl's heart which gives eight additional years while a boy's will only give four. Language illustrates the centrality of women to Hopi thought and culture. Many place names refer to female anatomy such as "Horse Vulva," "Clitoris Spring," and "Girl's Breast Point."

Women themselves claim they are more important than men, although they add that men are necessary, too. But the man's place is on the outside of the house, which is the social core.

Menstrual restrictions are the least severe in those matrilineal societies in which neither husband nor brother exerts control over the woman.[25] There are no taboos or feelings of shame about menstrual blood. Menstruation is simply referred to as "something women do."

The Hopi are relatively free and open about sexuality; it is good because it brings life. A distinction is made between sexuality in and out of marriage. For example, Hopi cannot marry distant clan relatives but they can have sex with them. There are no illegitimate children; any child is a full member of the mother's family. If the father is unknown or if his family refuses to perform the appropriate rituals, the mother's family will perform them. When the woman marries, her husband becomes the social father of her children.

RELIGION

The Hopi ceremonial system is "implicitly woven into the very fabric of Hopi life—into institutions, child-training patterns, customs, arts, values, character and mentality."[26] Although male anthropologists often refer to the "male-centered ceremonial system," it is virtually impossible to separate the religious system from the female-centered social order.

The twelve ceremonial societies cut across clan lines, with each society headed by a clan mother's brother. Nine of the societies are male and three are female; however, women play essential roles in the male societies and men play several major roles in the women's societies:

> The relationship between the kinship and the ceremonial systems gives a unique organic balance to Hopi social organization and tends to equilibrate the status of men and women in Hopi society. Each sex has its own unique and indispensable place and role. The complementary biological functions of male and female are institutionalized in a complex, correlatively balanced social order.[27]

Even though women's ceremonies are fewer, they occur at the crucial period of the year, harvest, and deal with subsistence, fertility and distribution of produce, certainly the central aspect of Hopi existence.

The religious society leadership is not the kind of heroic power base that most anthropologists have portrayed. Leadership is "unsought, self-effacing, fraught with heavy moral obligation."[28] The emphasis is on responsibility for tribal welfare, not on the prestige or power of the individual holding office. Since the chief is the clan mother's brother, she can exert a considerable amount of influence on him. Moreover, his successor is chosen from one of his sister's male children who shows special leadership potential.

The base of Hopi religion is the Earth, which is seen as a living entity, the mother. People are made from her flesh and suck at her breast; her milk is grass and corn. Two major religious figures are Mother Earth and the Corn Mother. The guardian of Mother Earth is Spiderwoman, who is one of the original creators in the Hopi origin myths and has the power to lead the people back to the Earth's womb. In fact, spiders, a female-dominant insect society, are revered among Hopi to this day. During the creation of the Four Worlds—part of the Hopi creation myth—it was the Ant People also female-dominant, in their underground homes, the prototype of the Hopi kivas, who saved the "good" Hopi each time a world was destroyed.

The symbol of the Emergence is known to the Hopi in two forms of the Earth Mother symbol which are carved on a rock near Oraibi, the oldest pueblo, and elsewhere. One symbol is square and the other circular; both are *Tá Púat*, Mother and Child, the unborn child within the womb of Mother Earth. Each labyrinthian symbol illustrates in its inside lines the fetal membranes and in its outside lines the mother's arms as well as the concentric boundaries of Hopiland. Similar labyrinthian symbols are associated with other female-centered societies, such as Minoan Crete.

The three women's ceremonies, the Lakón, the Márawu, and the Owaqlt, are staged by the women's societies in the autumn from September through early November. They are concerned with fertility, healing and hunting. In contemporary society both sexes participate in rabbit hunts. The women's ceremonies emphasize the need to prepare for germination, for the coming of the new year and life. Associated with the cycle is the Maraw Maiden carved on a rock in the desert, who sits with her legs outspread, her huge vulva ready for copulation and fertilization. This symbol, together with the women's fertility ceremonies, are integrated into the entire economic system of Hopi society.

Mother Earth Symbol

CONCLUSIONS

Among the Hopi, women enjoy an economically secure position regardless of marital status and participate fully in economic and political decision-making. Women's predominance in
the hereditary kinship system and men's predominance in the
system of voluntary secret associations afford both sexes stability
and balanced status.

Schlegel[29] predicts that matrilineal descent systems will continue to survive because of their flexibility and ability to change
in response to varying environmental conditions. Furthermore,
a variety of organizational forms is possible for these systems.
For example, even if the Hopi ceremonial system breaks down,
the matrilineage can continue. Matrilineal organization offers
security to subsequent generations, even under conditions of
colonialism and subjugation, such as those experienced by Native American peoples.

A comparison of the findings on the Hopi by female and
male anthropologists is instructive. In their data on kinship, socialization, and religion, the male anthropologists, Titiev, Fred
Eggan, and Euler consistently underplay the importance, participation, and authority of Hopi women while the female anthropologists, Schlegel, Dorothy Eggan, and Thompson, present more balanced material on female and male roles.

In their discussion of the kinship system, the male anthropologists de-emphasize Hopi women's initiating role in courtship, the importance of a female heir to female clan heads, and
they permit their preoccupation with the Euro-American nuclear family to bias their interpretation of Hopi marriage and
divorce customs. The male anthropologists omit or underplay
major aspects of socialization data such as the relatively greater
importance of female children to the clan structure, and salient
aspects of the mother-daughter relationship. The discussion of
women's participation in the religious sphere is severely limited,
giving the impression that the religious life of the Hopi is almost

totally male. The more balanced view of Hopi society by women anthropologists leads to the conclusion that matrilineal matrilocal kinship systems warrant further exploration in women's search for utopia.

NOTES

1. Alice Schlegel, *Male Dominance and Female Autonomy: Domestic Authority in Matrilineal Societies* (HRAF, 1972), p. 8.
2. Laura Thompson, *Culture in Crisis* (New York: Harper & Row, Publishers, 1950), p. 65.
3. Alice Schlegel, "Socialization of a Hopi Girl," *Ethnology*, 12, No. 4 (October 1973), pp. 451–2.
4. Schlegel, "Socialization," pp. 457–458.
5. Mischa Titiev, *Old Orabi: A Study of the Hopi Indians of Third Mesa* (Cambridge, Ma.: Peabody Museum, 1944).
6. Schlegel, "Socialization," pp. 457–458.
7. *Ibid.*, p. 458.
8. Dorothy Eggan, "Hopi Marriage and Family Relations," *Marriage and Family Living*, 6, No. 1 (Winter 1944), p. 2.
9. Dorothy Eggan, "Hopi Marriage," p. 6.
10. Frederick R. Eggan, *Social Organization of the Western Pueblos* (Chicago: University of Chicago Press, 1950), p. 35.
11. Titiev, *Old Orabi*, p. 43.
12. Alice Schlegel, "Women Anthropologists Look at Women," *Reviews in Anthropology*, 1, No. 6 (November–December 1974), p. 553.
13. Schlegel, "Socialization," p. 461.
14. Dorothy Eggan, "Hopi Marriage," p. 1.
15. Schlegel, "Socialization," p. 450.
16. Schlegel, "Women Anthropologists," p. 450.
17. Thompson, *Culture in Crisis*, pp. 92–95.
18. Laura Thompson, "Logico-Aesthetic Integration in Hopi Culture," *American Anthropologist*, 47, No. 4 (October–December 1945), p. 548.
19. Schlegel, "Socialization," p. 451.
20. Titiev, *Old Orabi*, pp. 23–24.
21. *Ibid.*, p. 24.
22. Schlegel, "Socialization," p. 453.
23. *Ibid.*

24. *Ibid.*
25. Schlegel, *Male Dominance,* p. 26.
26. Thompson, "Logico-Aesthetic Integration," p. 552.
27. Thompson, *Culture in Crisis,* p. 70.
28. *Ibid.,* p. 73.
29. Schlegel, *Male Dominance,* pp. 142–144.

SELECTED ADDITIONAL BIBLIOGRAPHY

Eggan, Frederick R., "The Hopi and the Lineage Principle," *Social Structure, Studies Presented to Radcliffe-Brown.* Edited by M. Fortes. New York: Oxford University Press, 1949.
Euler, Robert C. and Dobyns, Henry F. *The Hopi People.* Phoenix: Indian Tribal Series, 1971.
Goldfrank, Esther. "Socialization, Personality, and the Structure of Pueblo Society," *American Anthropologist,* 47, No. 4 (October–December 1945).
Marriott, Alice and Rachlin, Carol K. *American Indian Mythology.* New York: Thomas Y. Crowell, 1968.
O'Kane, Walter Collins. *The Hopis.* Norman, Okla.: University of Oklahoma Press, 1953.
Robinson, Ann O'Connor W. *Kachinas-Paone.* Austin: The Encino Press, 1976.
Schneider, David and Gough, Kathleen, eds. *Matrilineal Kinship.* Berkeley, Calif.: University of California Press, 1961.
Simmons, Leo W. *Sun Chief: The Autobiography of a Hopi Indian.* New Haven: Yale University Press, 1942.
Simpson, Ruth D. *The Hopi Indians.* Los Angeles: Southwest Museum, 1953.
Stephen, A. M. *Hopi Journal.* Vols. I and II. Edited by E. C. Parsons. New York: Columbia University Press, 1936.
Thomas, C. G. "Logico-Aesthetic Integration in Hopi Culture." *American Anthropologist,* 47, No. 4 (October–December 1945).
Thomas, C. G. and Joseph, Alice. *The Hopi Way.* Chicago: University of Chicago Press, 1944.
Udall, Louise, editor. *Me and Mine: The Life Story of Helen Sekaquaptewa.* Tucson: University of Arizona Press, 1969.
Waters, Frank. *Book of the Hopi.* New York: The Viking Press, 1963.
Witt, Shirley Hill. "Native Women Today: Sexism and the Indian Woman." *Civil Rights Digest,* 6, No. 3 (Spring 1974).

Women of the Celtic Tuath[1]

GERALDINE DAY MCNELLY

O, Don't you remember Sweet Betsy from Pike
Who crossed the wide prairies with her husband Ike,
With two yoke of cattle, and one spotted hog,
A tall Shanghai rooster, an old yellow dog.

>*Sing Too-ra-lee-oo-ra-lee-oo-ra-lee-aye*
>*Sing Too-ra-lee-oo-ra-lee-oo-ra-lee-aye.*

The Alkali Desert was burning and bare
And Ike cried in fear, "we are lost, I declare,
My dear old Pike Country, I'll come back to you."
Said Betsy, "you'll go by yourself, if you do."

>*Chorus*

They swam the wide rivers and crossed the tall peaks
They camped on the prairies for weeks upon weeks
They fought with the injuns with musket and ball
And they reached California in spite of it all.[2]

>*Chorus*

One helluva woman! Who is this Betsy? Where was she before this perilous western sojourn? Who are her people, her ancestors? Who is Betsy? She is as old as the hills. Betsy is Medb, Dierdru and Macha. Betsy is Danu and Scathach and Fedelm and Tailltiu. Betsy is woman, sorceress, and goddess. She has led her people, taught her people, and empowered them with life; she is the female half of the universe, the earth, the *tuath*. She not only fought in battle but she also taught the art of battle to the nation's great warrior, the giant Chuchullain. Her spiritual power gave healing magic to the fountains, mountains, and streams where her people came to be healed, blessed, or enspirited. Her power was equalled by her skill in the arts and survival crafts of tribal life. She created from the earth, and was of the earth. She lusted for life and sought out her lovers. She brought forth daughters and sons. Her appetite was at once tribal and personal.

She worked in the earth, a producer not only of human life but of the stuffs that maintain human life. Better than spinning straw into gold, she churned milk into butter, berries into sauce, corn into bread. She nurtured the calves, the lambs, the kids and, with her family, took the herds to the hills for summer grazing. She picked fruits and nuts to increase the larder and fished in the streams that were the home of spirits and goddesses.

She taught young children and heroes, sang the songs of her people, prophesied the future, recited the poetry of praise, and made deals with the goddesses. Myths and tales have been told of her, as well as jokes, poems, and songs. There she takes on many guises, fiction bearing witness to the truth.

Remembered in hills and streams, but also commemorated in stone and clay, the women/priestesses/goddesses have been found in the earth—in ancient buildings, graves and other underground sites. In the village of Vix, 120 miles southeast of Paris, is the grave of a young woman who was buried in 500 B.C. She is wearing a golden diadem, decorated with two tiny winged golden horses. At one side of her body is a bronze wine vessel, a yard in diameter, and at the other, a four-wheeled vehicle.[3] How comfortably this woman was guaranteed a safe journey to the other world—the transportation, the soothing sustenance.

For many years before this particular Vixen was buried, Europeans, including Celts, met in great collective burial places that were also sanctuaries for sacred ceremonies where the clan could establish *rapport* with their ancestors. All met together—the living, the dead, and the yet-to-be-born. The people thus celebrated the solidarity of the tribe in perpetuity, the collectivity equal in all things, in death even as in life.

During the two thousand years preceding the present era, as the great Urnfields beneath the earth have revealed, some

Celtic tribes were wealthy and artistically creative. Near their urnfields, the place-names of rivers, hills, and streams are Celtic.[4] In addition to highly stylized pottery, the beautifully worked items of bronze and gold bear evidence of their creativity, while their extensive trade routes brought them material wealth. The woman of Vix was of these people.

From time to time, the various Celtic tribes divided into small groups to migrate to new lands, or sometimes fled to avoid an enemy. They took their customs, their skills, and their beliefs with them. The customs that regulated their social relationships affirmed the reciprocal nature of rights and obligations among all tribal members. These customs were kept alive by word-of-mouth for hundreds and hundreds of years. In Ireland, where the conquering legions of Rome never appeared, these customs remained intact and eventually were written down by scribes in the monasteries. The so-called Brehon Laws detail the types of marriage and gift exchange, divorce, precise compensation for all types of misconduct, obligations for marital decision-making, child-rearing, land-sharing, and all other aspects of tribal life.

The individual was important in Celtic society. Every individual had an "honor price" according to his or her status within the group. All crimes against individuals were crimes against their honor and the kindred were responsible if the perpetrator could not pay for the crime committed.

Like other aspects of society, the marriage alliance was one of mutual obligation. A bride's maternal kin could exact vengeance if her husband neglected his duty, which included the education of the children and the payment of an honor price should a child be killed. Marriage was a contract and ten types of marriage or sexual-economic partnership were acknowledged.[5]

All contracts made by either spouse were the obligation of both; the fosterage, or socialization of children by another couple was planned by both; both man and woman provided food for festivals, bought household goods, pig litters, and breeding cattle jointly; sold useless oxen or horses and split the profit; decided together how to cooperate with others for tillage. These laws assumed not only equal rights for the woman but equal knowledge.

Legal separation could be obtained but, if adultery occurred, a woman had three days of total exemption from any penalties for offences she committed against her husband or the "other woman." During the ensuing month, she was exempt from half the penalties; after that, it was assumed she had cooled down. Of course, she forfeited these exemptions if she had her own "other man" on the side.

Divorce was available for many reasons, including illness, injury, barrenness, an "unarmed man" (impotent), or a man's disclosure of his woman's bed secrets.[6] The division of property at the time of divorce revealed women's status: their possessions and their work in herding, wool production, farming and food preparation were compensated.

Why have traditional historians ignored these facts and instead found barbaric women who were chattel in ferocious Celtic tribes? Why have archeologists emphasized weapon-swinging warriors? Has such historical and archeological interpretation merely reflected our own militaristic, male-dominated society?

Modern Westerners have seen themselves as direct descendants of the great civilizations, comprised of unique genius-people—at the top of a ranked order of less civilized and savage societies. This model of history was used as a rationale for Christianizing Africa, the Americas, Asia, and the Pacific, where "savage" people experienced the "benevolent" intervention of Christian missionaries bringing cultural and spiritual enlightenment while traders and merchants brought technology and armies to exploit the resources and labor of the "savages."

The belief in the superiority of civilization as the ultimate stage of cultural achievement included the concept of savagery to explain past and present tribal people—their low technology, magical beliefs, lack of political organization, and surly behavior. Western historians and archeologists have been primed to perceive axes only as battle weapons where they might have emphasized their utility in felling the hardwood forests and creating pastures and farmlands.

Status or prestige objects found in some graves have been designated as artifacts of class societies where the few ruled the many. The symbolic nature of chiefs has been ignored and the moral requirement that they share their worldly goods with the people through redistribution and adherence to the will of popular assemblies. In this way we are denied a true vision of the past and thus prevented from creating a just vision of the future. As anthropologist Stanley Diamond has pointed out, contemporary states

> forge or ignore history; create political myths which propagate the official version of human nature and an inevitable past that wholly justifies the present.[7]

Some contemporary scholars take issue with these historical interpretations and archeological analyses, and free our thinking for new discovery.[8] Thus, we now see among the Celts a variety of life-styles, revealing changes made according to environmental or political necessities. Regardless of the wide range of differences between a proto-state centered in the city of Bibracte[9] and the herding and farming life of Celts far from that urban center, in northern Europe, Brittany, Ireland, Scotland and Wales, certain tribal themes predominated according to the particular life-style. Tribal life was based on the integrated nature of all things—earth and sky, natural and supernatural, animal and human, male and female. The land was mother-earth, consort of a heavenly father, the sungod, symbolized by the male chief of the female *tuath,* and the male goat or ram. King and *tuath* were bound together in symbolic mating, the *feis,* to bring fertility to humans and beasts, in the ritual celebration of these values, the Feast of Lugnasud, traditionally celebrated in early August and still celebrated in County Kerry.

Motherearth-mothergod has survived. Ancient images of priestess, sorceress and goddess were bestowed upon the Magna Mater; mother of gods, genitor, progenitor and regenitor, and Christianized, as Holy Mary, Mother of God.

This goddess appeared to the women and children of Knock in 1879 when rotting potatoes and land evictions required an interceding hand and revitalization of identity and communality. Mary of Knock's priestess, the Poor Clare nun, Mary Cusak, was blessed by the great mother goddess and cured of her lameness, and in the tribal tradition of reciprocity, Sister Mary Cusak gave the gift back to the people: she fought evictions and starvation and struggled for the Land League, Home Rule, Women's Rights, and famine relief.[10]

Women in Northern Ireland now live behind wire fences in Divis Flats and stand behind the wire of Armagh Prison for Mother Ireland, Eire, the earth goddess, the *tuath*—the land and the people.

LED BY A WOMAN

Act I, scene i. Domestic, connubial love scene, the royal house of Cruachan. Medb and her husband, Ailill—"pillow talk."

AILILL: By the gods, Medb, I can't tell how it goes with you. You're laughing, you're weeping. Are we not great lovers?

MEDB: By the name of Danu, Ailill, you must have planted a great dynasty in me and I am full of love for you.

AILILL: Well then, it's good you told me, love, for the song you sing never quite announces whether this is a tragedy or a comedy.

MEDB: In that, then, dear Ailill, I sing a true song for how can I know whether love is a tragedy or comedy?

AILILL: In that you show the opposing sides of hot and cold and light and dark that mark the nature of woman, my Medb.

MEDB: Ahh no, that marks the nature of greatness, of the greatness of my people. It is a noble spirit that cries as it laughs and laughs as it weeps, comprehending the changing nature of the earth, the winds, the sea, all life.

AILILL: Then you're too great to clearly know there is a great bull in this earthly pasture.

MEDB: A great bull needs no reminder other than his horns. Why should he need praise?

Act I of a play adapted from *The Tain*, translated by Thomas Kinsella, from the Irish epic *Tain Bo Cuailnge*, Oxford University Press, 1977 (1969), Oxford, England. The phrases in quotation are directly from *The Tain*.

AILILL: Well then, I am content and know it must be well for you to have such a bull as I.

MEDB: It seems rather that you should be content to have a heifer such as I.

AILILL: But, "it is true what they say, love, it is well for the wife of a wealthy man."

MEDB: "True enough, what put that in your mind?"

AILILL: "It struck me, how much better off you are today than the day I married you."

MEDB: I was very well off indeed before I ever met you.

AILILL: Why had I not heard of such wealth? Why didn't I know?

MEDB: Why am I called Medb of Cruachan? The province is mine. My father gave me the province. And I was desired by kings from all over Ireland, who came to woo me. I didn't want any of them. I demanded a wedding gift greater than any other . . . absence of meanness, jealousy or fear. How could my husband be mean if I am generous? "It would be an insult if I were more generous than my husband but not if the two of us were equal in this." We must be equal in spirit, too, because "I thrive, myself, on all kinds of trouble." Nor could my husband be jealous for "I never had a man without another waiting in his shadow." So I got the kind of man I wanted, Ailill, for you have no meanness, jealousy or fear. I brought you a wedding gift worthy of my position and yours—apparel enough for many seasons, a chariot worth more than that, the weight of your arm and leg in gold. So let no one ill treat you. It will be my right to be compensated, for "you're a kept man," Ailill.

AILILL: Not at all. I'd be king of Leinster but I acceded to my brother—because he's older not because he's more generous. And since I never heard of a province run by a woman, I came here where a king was needed.

MEDB: Whatever you say, Ailill, my wealth is greater than yours.

AILILL: How can you say that, Medb? No one has more jewels or valuable properties than I do. I can prove it. It will all be brought here for display.

MEDB: We shall see, my dear Ailill, for I'll have my messengers bring here all that is mine and the truth will be in the count.

The tale continues. When the count is in, Medb and Ailill were equal except for one bull, which chose to belong to Ailill. Although born of Medb's heifer, he ran to the other side, refusing to be led by a woman. Medb, short a bull, tried to borrow, or trade the great bull of Ulster for a tryst. When she was refused, she decided to raid Ulster, formed an army, and attacked. Although her prophet, the woman Fedelm, predicted a rout, Medb remained confident. After all, the Ulstermen would be late to battle because of the curse of Macha that brought them labor pains each time they needed their energy the most, just as she had been seized with labor pains when forced by the King of Ulster to race while pregnant. But Medb had not foreseen the new strength that was Ulster's—the giant Cuchulainn. After a long battle, Medb, Ailill, and their allies were forced to retreat. Their friend Fergus was heard to say, "It is the usual thing for a herd led by a mare to be strayed and destroyed."

The tale reflects great changes among the Irish tribes: the accumulation of wealth, the increase in warring, and male domination. Accumulation of wealth and cattle as private property among an upper rank of chiefly families still retained the obligation of generosity on the part of the chiefs, and Medb brags about her own generosity to prove her queenliness. The expansion of war from ritualistic tribal raiding or retribution was bemoaned by Cuchulainn himself as he begs his "foster brother" and battling enemy to desist to save his life. The once egalitarian relationship between the sexes has devolved into a bitter struggle, the female fighting for her equality. To Medb it is worth risking all. Even at her moment of defeat, however, her basic generative power is acknowledged as she stoops in the bushes to relieve herself of her menstrual blood—this becoming three great rivers bearing her name. But her creative power is offset by the destructive super power of the giant Cuchulainn, the Hound of Ulster—watchdog, protector of male property (the bull of the King of Ulster). Cuchulainn is bigger than life as befits a bearer of incipient patriarchy. But Medb and her men and women warriors give him a run for his money. They have announced to us that the struggle is on.

NOTES

1. The research for this paper evolved from my participation in a group studying Irish ethnicity that included Vincent Corrigan, Ed O'Higgins, Greg Ryan, and most valuably, Elizabeth Sheehan.
2. Many versions of this song exist. I learned this one from Miss McCumber, my music teacher, Mayo Jr. High School, Paris, Illinois, 1948.
3. John E. Pfeiffer, *The Emergence of Man* (New York: Harper & Row, 1969).
4. E. G. Bowen, *Britain and the Western Seaways* (New York: Praeger Publishers, 1972).
5. See Patrick Power, *Sex and Marriage in Ancient Ireland* (Dublin: Mercier, 1976) and *Ancient Laws of Ireland,* printed for H.M. stationery office (London: Longman, Green, Longman, Roberts & Green, 1865–1901).
6. *Ibid.*
7. Stanley Diamond, *In Search of the Primitive: A Critique of Civilization* (New Brunswick, N.J.: Transaction Books, 1974), p. 209.
8. Colin Renfrew, *Before Civilization: The Radiocarbon Revolution and Prehistoric Europe* (London: Cambridge University Press, 1973).
9. Presently being excavated. See Robert Rodden, "Europe North of the Alps," in R. Stigler *et al.,* eds., *Varieties of Culture in the Old World* (New York: St. Martin's Press, 1979).
10. Edith Turner, "Piety and Patriotism: The Sacred and the Secular Images of Women in Irish Culture." Paper presented at the panel on Women in Irish Religion at the Berkshire Conference on the History of Women, 1978.

Women in Transition: Crete and Sumer

RUBY ROHRLICH

THE contrasting social structures of Minoan Crete and Sumer had a radically different impact on women. In urbanized Crete, peaceable trade led to the wide dispersion of political power, allowing the persistence of kin-based clans in which women predominated. In Sumer, inter-city competition for scarce resources led to chronic warfare, political centralization, the erosion of clan structures, and the decline in women's status. Both these Bronze Age civilizations emerged from similar egalitarian societies in which women had high status. But with the systematic subordination of women, beginning about 5,000 years ago, in class-stratified, militaristic Sumer, we first see utopian society transformed into a full-blown dystopia. Patriarchal states that became increasingly imperialistic gradually arose throughout the Old and New Worlds, culminating in the modern nation-states, global imperialism, and the threat of planetary destruction. But the patriarchal state societies have flourished for less than one percent of our time on earth and are now on the decline.[1] In this transitional period, we can learn much by looking at the earlier forms of social organization, and can avoid

This is an amalgamation of my two articles: "Women in Transition: Crete and Sumer," in Renate Bridenthal and Claudia Koonz, eds., *Becoming Visible: Women in European History* (Boston: Houghton Mifflin, 1977), and "State Formation in Sumer and the Subjugation of Women," *Feminist Studies* (Spring 1980).

My thanks to the National Endowment for the Humanities for their grant, Summer, 1976, at the University of Illinois, Urbana-Champaign, and residential fellowship, 1977–78, at the University of California, Santa Cruz, which enabled me to do much of the research for the two articles on which this paper is based. Copyright © 1984 Ruby Rohrlich.

much by analyzing the sources of their transformation. Ancient Crete and Sumer allow us to view both stages.

Seafaring pioneers settled Crete more than 8,000 years ago, beginning life there at a relatively advanced stage of Neolithic culture. They cultivated grains, fruit and olives; raised cattle, sheep, goats and pigs; and hunted the wild animals that roamed the island. Already in Neolithic times, long sailing voyages were organized for overseas trade.

The transformation of Neolithic society into the cultural stage we term "civilization" first took place, according to the archeological record, in Sumer, the ancient name for southern Mesopotamia, now known as Iraq and Iran, situated between the Tigris and Euphrates rivers. Here city life had emerged by about 3500 B.C., and about 500 years later, Crete also began to undergo urbanization.[2] The factors that gave rise to the brilliant and original civilization of Crete also account for the central position of Minoan women; the factors responsible for the decline in women's status in Sumer also brought about its eventual decay.

Crete was situated in a most fortunate position for travel to all parts of the ancient world—at a point where the great trade routes crossed. The island flanks the southern entrance to the Aegean basin and forms a bridgehead from Asia and Africa to the Greek mainland and so to Europe. Long before the Bronze Age, Cretans traded manufactured goods, such as ceramics, metal products and textiles, for the raw materials—gold, silver, tin, lead, copper, ivory and lapis lazuli—they needed for their industries. Minoan goods were traded in Egypt, Anatolia, Syria, Cyprus and the Greek mainland, and, in time, Crete achieved economic and cultural hegemony in the Aegean.

Cretan civilization developed out of trade and commerce, both local and long-distance, strong links with its tribal systems, and indigenous craft traditions. While these processes were also basic to the emergence of the other Bronze Age civilizations, in Minoan Crete trade was not superseded by military conquest as the primary means of gaining access to important resources. The island remained at peace both at home and abroad, and Minoans in the several social strata continued to be relatively autonomous within the clan system, in which women played crucial roles.

The character of the Minoan urban economy militated against the type of political centralization characteristic of the Sumerian cities and deriving from their internecine strife, as evidenced by the walls that began to surround them from around 3000 B.C. Cretan towns developed primarily around the harbors, with the market-place the center for the exchange of commodities and the hub of religious and social activity. Minoan cities were unfortified; the approach to the palace of Knossos, for example, was a great bridge, a viaduct, without a drawbridge or high defensive walls.

In the *Iliad*, Homer speaks admiringly of "Crete of the Hundred Cities." The rapid growth of the towns prevented the concentration of power in the hands of large landowners who, in Sumer, were both the religious and secular leaders and in control of commerce. There were shrines in the Minoan palaces, but no temples in the towns:

> The typical Minoan town clustered round an open space adjoining the palace of a prince, one who was high priest as well as governor, but primarily a merchant prince, with other merchants living close by in mansions only less rich . . . and with nothing to segregate . . . them from the rest of the community:[3]

The towns surrounding the palaces were well designed for "civilized" living, with the streets paved and drained. The haphazard cellular growth of the towns, their very planlessness, testifies to the lack of central control and the correspondingly greater freedom in Minoan Crete than in the other Bronze Age civilizations.

The nature of agricultural production in Minoan Crete also inhibited political centralization. Since military conquest and defense were not considerations, the farmers were neither heavily taxed nor drawn into military service and forced labor, as were the Sumerian peasants. Moreover, the palaces depended much more on industry and commerce than on agricultural production, and agriculture was left to skilled specialists, with an independent social tradition, who favored a form of garden tillage.

The surplus produced by the Mediterranean polyculture maintained the noble class, the merchants and sailors, artisans and artists, and swelled the cargoes of the merchant ships.

The communal land tenure of the clan was reflected in the communal burials that persisted through much of Minoan history. A whole community shared the same burial place sometimes for 500 years or more—the large, circular, vaulted stone tomb, the *tholos,* modeled on the dwelling place of the clan, and filled with the bones of a whole clan rather than of a ruling dynasty. The cemetery of the Sumerian city of Ur also contained communal burials, but of a vastly different nature:

> The burial of the kings was accompanied by human sacrifice on a lavish scale, the bottom of the grave pit being crowded with the bodies of men and women who seemed to have been brought down here and butchered where they stood.[4]

Minoans created a system of pictorial hieroglyphs, which by about 1900 B.C. had developed into a cursive script, Linear A, not yet deciphered, that was used for the palace records. Linear A was also found in numerous graffiti, indicating that literacy was not limited to the elites, as in the other Bronze Age civilizations, where writing adorned the palaces and tombs of the kings, and was used to record as history the events that perpetuated their rule.

An important class in Crete comprised the artisans and artists who provided goods and services for the aristocracy and the merchants, as well as for the towns and countryside. Construction and hydraulic engineers built networks of paved roads, aqueducts, viaducts, irrigation channels, and harbor installations that were among the best in the Bronze Age. Sanitation engineers constructed drainage systems that anticipated the most modern scientific methods. Architects built palaces that outshone those of the Orient. Metalworkers alloyed metals of great strength and were particularly skilled at molding bronze. Minoan sculptors were the first to use gold and ivory for statues; the potters invented faience; the fresco painters were unrivaled. Using a great variety of media, painters, jewelers and seal cutters created masterpieces in miniature, important sources of information about Minoan life.

Minoan art was realistic, yet imaginative and exuberant, and drew on every aspect of the natural environment and social life, both everyday and ritual. Artists showed women and men, animals and plants, in free and close communion with each other. Their works also demonstrated that the female figurines prevalent in the Neolithic had been transformed into images of the impressive and pervasive goddess, as well as of queens and priestesses.

The artifacts provide clear evidence that the status of women in this first European civilization, this rich and relatively free society, was very high. Women were the central subjects of the arts and crafts. And they are shown mainly in the public domain. On the Ring of Minos, a woman is shown steering a ship. A gold signet ring, found in a grave on Mochlos, shows a woman disembarking from a ship, carrying a tree. Was she a merchant prince trading in timber? In Sumer, even after it became patriarchal, women also carried on long-distance trade in their own names.

Again and again women are shown, on rings and seals, tending fruit trees. Crete was renowned for its fruit, and orchard cultivation became increasingly important as olives, grapes and fruit were traded abroad, as well as consumed locally. Using plants to heal and cure, as well as for food, women were the midwives and probably the general practitioners as well. The lily, poppy, crocus, and iris, favorite subjects of Minoan painters, potters, and seal cutters, were especially sacred, associated with the goddess in her aspect as deity of vegetation. The lily was used to check menstruation, and the poppy seed was used for both religious and medical purposes. A late figurine shows a woman wearing three poppy-seed heads, cut as for the extraction of opium, in a crown on her head.

Minoan women had equal access to the arts and crafts, particularly pottery. Minoan ware was famous throughout the ancient world, especially after the potter's wheel was introduced, about 2000 B.C., and a statue of a woman potter dates from this period. The pottery was as thin as porcelain and decorated with dynamic geometric patterns of flowers and leaves, shellfish and flying fish, birds and animals, and dancing women.

The Minoans had a passion for dancing, and the artists reveal that women did most of the dancing. Again and again, on the frescoes, seals, and signet rings they are shown dancing in meadows and groves, before the goddess and her altars, in front of large audiences, singly and in groups. Women were also expert tumblers and musicians, playing the flute and the lyre. The Minoan chorus consisted only of women, led by a priestess.

Minoan women also hunted, and are shown sometimes with bows and arrows, sometimes driving chariots. Above all, women and men together, entrusting their lives to one another, hunted the wild bull with staves and nooses, and played a most dangerous game, that of bull leaping, in public arenas. In one fresco, a young girl is shown hurling herself upon a bull's head. A scene on a gold Vapheio cup shows a male hunter thrown by a bull while the other hunter, a woman, grasps the animal's horns in an effort to bring it down.

Androgynous attire accompanied the role sharing in Minoan society. While both male and female bull leapers wore the loincloth and codpiece, during funerary rites women and men wore identical sheepskin skirts. In other ceremonies in which both sexes took part, men donned long, flounced robes, initially the garb of the priestess and usually worn by women. Both wore metal belts around their slim waists; both used a great deal of jewelry—bracelets, armbands, collars, and headbands. Both wore their hair the same way—falling down the back, with locks hanging in front of the ears. Clothes accentuating female breasts and the penis were equally revealing.

But it was above all their roles in religion, the institution that integrated Bronze Age life, that attests to the predominance of women in Minoan Crete. By about 2000 B.C., the Minoan goddess and her votaries were pictured in almost every aspect of the natural and social ambience of Crete:

> With animals, birds and snakes, with . . . the pillar and the sacred tree; with the sword and the double-axe. She is a huntress and a goddess of sports; she is armed and she presides over ritual

dances; she has female and male attendants; she has dominion over mountain, earth, sky and sea; over life and death; she is household-goddess, vegetation goddess, Mother and Maid.[5]

The one religious shrine found in the palace of Knossos contained faience figures of the Snake Goddess, with snakes wreathed around her wrists, waist and head. In Crete, as elsewhere, nonpoisonous snakes were a symbol of protection, since they exterminate vermin, and Minoan houses contained tubes into which snakes could crawl.

The men are also depicted in various roles and activities. They are the farmers on the Harvester Cup; they are acrobats, boxers and wrestlers, bull hunters and bull leapers, artisans and artists. But when they are associated with the goddess or her representatives, they are shown in worshipping and respectful postures. These are evident on a fresco in Knossos, where two lines of men, some carrying vases, are depicted advancing from both sides toward the central figure, the queen or priestess. Painted on a plaster relief in the Great Corridor of the palace of Knossos is a picture of a long-haired youth, unarmed, naked to the waist, wearing a headdress of peacock plumes and walking among flowers and butterflies. He has been dubbed the Young Prince or the Priest-King, but no indubitable representation of a king or male god has yet been found in Crete.

Who, then, occupied the one throne, placed between a pair of griffins painted in brilliant colors on a wall of the throne room in the palace at Knossos, the center of Minoan civilization? Many scholars are convinced that Crete was a matriarchy, ruled by a queen-priestess. The absence of portrayals of an all-powerful male ruler or god, so widespread in the other Bronze Age civilizations, confirms this belief, as does the social and religious prominence of women.[6]

But if queens occupied the Minoan throne, who was Minos, the king for whom this society was named? Increasing evidence indicates that he was a member of the dynasty established at Knossos by the Achaeans from Mycenaean Greece, who invaded Crete after its coastal towns had been devastated by tidal waves and earthquakes, floods and fires, sometime between 1500 and

1400 B.C. The Mycenaeans overran the weakened Cretans, colonized most of the fertile areas of their island and enslaved many of the people. Thus, "Minoan" is a misnomer for the period before 1500 B.C., the period of the matriarchal Cretan civilization. As Thomson puts it:

> Behind the work of the humane poets who composed the *Iliad* and *Odyssey* lies an age of brutality and violence, in which the bold pioneers of private property had ransacked the opulent, hieratic, sophisticated civilization of the Minoan matriarchate.[7]

In Sumer, as in Crete, the Neolithic era was marked by the prevalence of female figurines and an almost complete absence of differentiation in grave-wealth, reflecting the centrality of women in an egalitarian society. The impetus to urbanization in Sumer seems to have occurred when the Neolithic villages and towns drew together into larger territorial and political units in defense against raids by nomadic herders; thus, incipient militarism was associated with the beginnings of Sumerian civilization.

From the outset, the concomitant of urbanization was a managerial class that emerged not only out of the need for defensive measures, but also because reserves of foodstuffs, seed, and herds had to be accumulated to contend with environmental contingencies such as droughts, floods, and famines. Those who were already influential in the Neolithic, the ritual leaders, became the managers, and the temple—a complex of sanctuary, warehouses and workrooms—was the hub of the expanding city. The priesthood retained a considerable proportion of the surplus wealth contributed by the farmers, artisans, and artists, whose surplus labor was also appropriated for the building and maintenance of the temple complex. By about 3500 B.C., the farmers had lost their autonomy as they were forced to cultivate the temple lands. By this time, the demands of the priesthood for resources to embellish the increasingly elaborate temples led to the expansion of commodity production and to a great increase in long-distance trading. Another class arose, of merchants, that also acquired wealth, power, and land.

The competition of the Sumerian cities for land and water,

and for timber, stone, and metal, led to armed conflict, with walled cities a feature of the Sumerian landscape. As military matters became paramount in economic and political decision-making, successful generals eventually became the rulers, usually after a power struggle with the priesthood. But the priests maintained a secure place in the hierarchy as they carried out their principal function of validating the status of the rulers. A major consequence of militaristic conquest was the emergence of another new class, slaves, taken as war prisoners. In due time, slavery was extended to include those who could not pay their debts, or who committed offenses against the state. Thus, human beings, as well as land and commodities, came to be regarded as property.

Around 2500 B.C., all the city-states in Sumer were joined under a single ruler, and a century later Sargon the Great "unified" Sumer with Akkad in the north, becoming ruler of all Mesopotamia. Thenceforward, deities who had been patrons of agriculture became celestial warriors; Enlil, the "lord of the plow," became "lord of all lands." And under the far-flung empire of Hammurabi, who established his dynasty at Babylon around 1790 B.C., the history of Sumer came to an end.

When Babylon inherited Sumerian art, it had long since become static and stereotyped, in contrast to its florescence in the late Neolithic. Artists had been compelled to glorify the military exploits of the rulers, and the decline in artistic imagination is particularly marked when Sumerian art is compared with the creative exuberance of Minoan Crete. The alienation of Sumerian artists was only one symptom of the erosion of the egalitarian clan structures. The autonomy and cohesiveness of the corporate kin groups were sapped as land, formerly inalienable, was sold; as communal resources and labor were expropriated by the elites; as clan leaders became part of the hierarchy when clan structures were used to organize craft guilds, corvée squads, and militias. But the basic subversion of the clans occurred when the egalitarian relations between women and men, central to the democratic process, were destroyed. This occurred in the context of chronic warfare, which became a male occupation and a significant factor in the emergence of male supremacy, and in the development of private property and its transmission in the male line.

The changeover to a patrilineal, patrilocal system led to the creation of the patriarchal family, which reflected and confirmed the divisions throughout society. Women were wrested from their own clans and from the solidarity of the clanswomen, gradually ousted from prestigious economic roles, deprived of a voice in political decision-making, and made dependent on men. Analysis of the archeological artifacts and of the religious, literary, and economic documents indicates that the subordination of women was integral to the emergence of a rigidly stratified, militaristic society.

In the early Sumerian city-states "matriarchy seems to have left something more than a trace."[8] And in the early Sumerian myths the female deities, like those in Crete, were the creators of all life.[9] Initially, the goddess Inanna was associated with the date, one of the earliest domesticated plants in Mesopotamia, and with the communal storehouse,[10] symbolizing the authority of women as producers and distributors of staple foods and clothing. Later, she assumes multiple roles, all in the public domain. But as the city-states became dominated by militaristic male rulers, Inanna's roles change; she becomes the goddess of war, after women have been pushed out of political decision-making, and of prostitution. In Mesopotamia, prostitution was not the "oldest profession"; it emerged after the professions of priest, scribe, merchant and warrior had become predominantly male, when women were made legally and economically dependent on men. In a myth inscribed on a tablet dated around 2000 B.C., but probably referring to a much earlier period, "sexual intercourse and prostitution" are linked with priestly office, heroship, power, and warfare as "fundamental to civilization."[11]

Initially, women priests were administrators and officials in the temples, and were very active in the arts, especially in music and literature. They composed music and organized choirs and orchestras, in which women of all classes performed.[12] But with increasing male dominance, priestesses also played sexual roles which were defined primarily in relation to the male hierarchy. High-ranking women, wealthy in their own right and very independent, were still "the women of the god's harem,"[13] while at the bottom of the female hierarchy were the very many common temple prostitutes. But even when women were deprived of their public roles, they retained their religious prestige because of "the continuing power of the goddess the women served."[14]

The earliest patron of the scribes, of accounts, science, and education, and inventor of the alphabet, was Nisaba, female deity of the reeds, which were used both as a building material and writing instrument. The Sumerian Academy, over which Nisaba presided, was the center of literary creation. Scribes and scribal schools attached to the palaces and temples developed many specialized bodies of knowledge, including medicine, and medical texts record the change from the earlier beliefs in an empirical, rational system that relied on plants and other natural products, under the aegis of the goddess Gula, to a system in which magical mystification predominated when medicine became a male profession.

In early Sumer both girls and boys were trained to be scribes, and the services of street scribes were freely used by both women and men in a variety of business activities. But as the society became more stratified, the street scribes and the women scribes disappeared. By the time of Hammurabi, about 1792–1750 B.C., the patron deity of the scribes was Nabu, son of the war god Marduk. And by this time, mainly upper-class students, all male, attended the schools.[15] The exclusion of women from education in Sumer marks the beginning of a five-thousand-year period of male-dominated and male-centered educational institutions which still prevail throughout the world.

Writing was used mainly by the elites, for whom it became an "ideological instrument of incalculable power." "An official, fixed and permanent version of events can be made. . . . Those people who *could* write, the scribes and priests . . . were rarely disposed to record the attitudes of those they taxed, subordinated and mystified."[16]

The codification of the laws was a crucial factor in the centralization of the state, and laws were codified when a state had the police power to enforce them. Thus the earliest law code so far discovered was enacted by the high priest Urukagina, around

2415 B.C., after he had defeated another high priest in battle, installed himself as king, and reduced the status of the queen, his wife, to that of consort, at the same time taking possession of her wealth. Urukagina's Code contained a regulation imposing monogamy on women only, converting polyandry, a practice that had apparently been common when clans were matrilineal, into the crime of adultery, punishable by death.[17] The laws became increasingly restrictive for women. Compared with the Sumerian laws, Hammurabi's Code, enacted 1750 B.C. in the name of Marduk the war god, tended "to exact severer penalties for certain offences, especially for offences against the sacredness of the family tie."[18] And the later Assyrian laws "make no mention of a number of legal rights the mother of a family possessed in the much earlier epoch of Hammurabi."[19] With the legal establishment of the patriarchal family, children were socialized to accept gender and class hierarchy.

Thus was utopia transformed into dystopia in the very first civilization, the state society of Sumer.

NOTES

1. Hazel Henderson, *The Politics of the Solar Age* (Garden City, N.Y.: Anchor Press, 1981), p. 364.

2. Colin Renfrew, *Before Civilization: The Radiocarbon Revolution and Prehistoric Europe* (London: Cambridge University Press, 1973), p. 29.

3. George Thomson, *The Prehistoric Aegean* (New York: Citadel Press, 1965), p. 28.

4. Sir Leonard Woolley, *The Sumerians* (New York: W. W. Norton & Co., 1965), p. 39.

5. R. F. Willetts, *Cretan Cults and Festivals* (New York: Barnes & Noble, 1962), p. 20.

6. Jacquetta Hawkes, *Dawn of the Gods* (New York: Random House, 1968), p. 76; Sinclair Hood, *The Home of the Heroes: The Aegean before the Greeks* (New York: McGraw-Hill, Inc., 1967), p. 81; C. G. Thomas, "Matriarchy in Early Greece: The Bronze and Dark Ages," *Arethusa,* 6 (Fall 1973); Leonard Cottrell, *Lion Gate* (London: Evans Brothers, 1963), p. 199; Thomson, *The Prehistoric Aegean*, p. 450.

7. Thomson, *The Prehistoric Aegean,* p. 450.

8. *Ibid.,* p. 160.

9. Samuel Noah Kramer, *Sumerian Mythology* (New York: Harper Torchbooks, 1961), p. 39.

10. Thorkild Jacobsen, *Treasures of Darkness* (New Haven: Yale University Press, 1976), p. 26.

11. Kramer, *Sumerian Mythology,* p. 66.

12. Sophie Drinker, *Music and Women* (New York: Coward-McCann, 1948), p. 81.

13. Woolley, *The Sumerians,* p. 146.

14. Elise Boulding, *The Underside of History* (Boulder, Colo.: Westview Press, 1976), p. 185.

15. Sir Leonard Woolley and Jacquetta Hawkes, *Prehistory and the Beginnings of Civilization* (New York: Harper & Row, 1963), p. 662.

16. Stanley Diamond, *In Search of the Primitive* (New Brunswick, N.J.: Transaction Books, 1974), p. 304.

17. Samuel Noah Kramer, *The Sumerians* (Chicago: University of Chicago Press, 1963), p. 322.

18. Woolley, *The Sumerians,* p. 92.

19. Georges Contenau, *Everyday Life in Babylon and Assyria* (New York: St. Martin's Press, 1954), p. 18.

Al Dente

FRANCE BURKE

women are experienced
    as caves
    by men
not that which surrounds
    the cave
    the whole
as she experiences herself
    but only
    the hole
possibly equipped with teeth
    hard rows
    biting
in that soft, moist anatomy

BE A PEARL DIVER, PUT YOUR FINGER IN A MOUTH, LIFT UP THE
FRAGILE CHEEK—IS THAT FRIGHTENING?

with the magic of altered emphasis
enter the realm of the Goddess
the remembered golden age that never was
and you will never cease to seek

enter by the avenue of the Sphinxes
worship at the horseshoe-shaped lake
revel in the Temple and do not withdraw
at the sight of a vulture or a lion-head

if the Goddess is alive
God is not dead
and never believe the Temple is empty
because you are not there

Part Two

THE RECENT PAST

Introduction

ELAINE HOFFMAN BARUCH

SINCE the early days of European settlement, the New World has been the testing-ground for utopian ideas, which have often been transplanted from other countries. Especially in the nineteenth century, people carved out spaces for intentional communities which were designed to eliminate the political, social, religious, sexual, and economic inequities of the outside world. The nuclear family was replaced by a larger group tied together not by blood but by common ideals. In some cases, marriage itself was rejected. Whether women felt more at ease in these spaces than at home is a subject that is just beginning to be explored.

One of the most extraordinary of these communities was founded by a Scottish-born woman, Frances Wright. Wright's Nashoba (the Chickasaw Indian word for "wolf"[1]) in Tennessee was established initially to free slaves. However, as Bensman notes Wright did not want Nashoba to stand alone. She believed her plan would provide the peaceful transition to the slaveless American society that everyone desired. This plan and the liberation of American women, who she felt were caught in a legal system which made them virtual slaves, became her major life's work.

Like Mary Wollstonecraft, Wright believed that true freedom would not be achieved until all human beings were free to develop their intellectual and physical powers. This could only occur, she felt, if the family were abolished and if child rearing were collectivized. Like Fourier and Owen, but going much further, Wright sought to demonstrate that new roles were possible among the sexes, races, and classes.

Though the Shakers, who were founded earlier, had interracial communities, as Rohrlich points out, these were celibate. In contrast, sexual relations prevailed between blacks and whites, slaves and free, at Nashoba in the pre-abolitionist period. Condemned as a sexually free colony and stigmatized even more for being interracial, Nashoba lost some of its financial backing. With the best of intentions, intentional communities often become subject to the pressures of the larger society. Blacks ended up doing the heavy manual labor, since it was felt, as at Owen's New Harmony, that whites could not work effectively in the climate of Tennessee. Despite this blot, Nashoba remains one of the most daring and courageous experiments of the nineteenth century. The establishment newspapers dubbed Frances Wright "the Great Red Harlot," but according to Ehrenreich and English, "feminism, class struggle and the general social ferment of the twenties and thirties all came together in one figure, Fanny Wright."[2]

More central than racial equality was sexual equality in the minds of utopian thinkers in the nineteenth century—and indeed this remains the case up to the present day (as Gearhart points out in Part Four). Wollstonecraft's *Vindication of the Rights of Woman,* published in 1792 in England, had a great influence. Trailing after the rights of man came the rights of woman—at least in theory. "Utopian socialists—Owenites, Fourierists and religious communitarians—established dozens of experimental communities where communism was the rule for women's work as well as men's. They wanted to reform not only the kitchen and the laundry, but in some cases the conjugal bed as well."[3]

Barbara Taylor points out that "unlike many of the Socialist organizations which grew up after it, the Owenite strategy had at its center the abolition of *all* relations of power and subordination: Capitalist to worker, but also parent to child, old to young, and, above all, man to woman."[4] But for all of his criticisms of marriage, Owen became increasingly conservative, envisioning for the new moral order what was basically a middle-class family structure. In the Owenite experiments, though "endless schemes for the collectivization of housework were devised . . . most assumed that the responsibility for this communalized domestic labor would still remain with the women of the communities. . . .

At no point was male responsibility for childcare proposed."[5] In Harsin's words, ". . . Owen's utopian communities 'freed' women from the drudgery of domesticity by adding outside labor to their unpaid household tasks." The burden of the double day, formerly a burden of working-class women only, became one for all women in some of the intentional communities (and now seems to be the privilege of "liberated" career women as well). Such were the joys of utopian living for women in the socialist communities.

Who will do the housework remains a central problem for us. Fourier had one of the most original answers. He suggested that children do it—or at least clean up the garbage since they love dirt so much. Most of us haven't taken that route. We either do it ourselves or employ the labor of other women. "Women must transform the sexual division of domestic labor, the privatized economic basis of domestic work, and the spatial separation of homes and workplaces in the built environment if they are to be equal members of society,"[6] writes Dolores Hayden.

About a century ago, in *The Origin of the Family, Private Property and the State,* Engels wrote that the "first condition for the liberation of the wife is to bring the whole female sex back into public industry," and that this in turn demands the abolition of the monogamous family as the economic unit of society.[7] The Women's Commonwealth in Belton, Texas, a unique nineteenth-century community for women (and their children), made a start in this direction. On a small scale, these women overthrew the monogamous family—by leaving their husbands—but their professed reason was religious, not economic, even though they eventually ran a hotel as a profit-making enterprise.

Barbara Leslie Epstein, in her book *The Politics of Domesticity,* points out that by the mid-nineteenth century, men and women inhabited different cultural worlds that had different moral codes.[8] We might say that these different codes allowed the Belton women to refuse sexual relations and money from their unsanctified husbands. Along with the existence of women's networks and the example of other intentional communities, these codes enabled the Texas women to break out of customary roles.

Like the Beguines long before them and the twentieth-century women workers of the settlement houses afterwards (see Cook, Part Three), what the Belton Sanctificationists demonstrate is the efficacy of separatism under certain conditions. As Andreadis says, " . . . if men were absent, an intentional community might offer to women . . . a model for successful religious, economic, and emotional self-determination."

The middle-class Belton women were willing to do all kinds of manual labor to support their independent lives. It would seem that it is not just the nature of the work that is significant in developing a sense of autonomy, but also the matter of who makes the rules, and assigns the values and the wages.

The idea that women can do better in their own space, where they are free of the dominion and discouragement of men, continues into the twentieth century, both in utopian novels, as Farley and Gearhart point out (Part Four) and in women's communal experiments (Weinbaum, Part Three). The politics of physical space has not yet received as much attention as it deserves from twentieth-century feminists. And yet, spatial oppression is part of sexual and economic oppression. As Hayden and Wright say, "Physical settings help to organize the work we do and may thereby perpetuate the sexual division of labor, both functionally and ideologically!"[9] It is primarily men who design work settings, with their hierarchical divisions. And life in the home isn't arranged much better. What women need, according to Hayden and urban planner Jacqueline Leavitt, are alternative social spaces that take account of the multiple living arrangements that are now our reality and that consider our multiple needs—for areas of privacy as well as for shared living in dining, recreation, childcare, and work.[10]

The politics of another kind of space, that of our own bodies, has been a key element in the structure of multiple intentional communities, perhaps indeed of all utopian social experiments. Most utopias seek to minimize the demands of the body. They see dyadic love as subversive of the group and try to eliminate passion. The Shakers eliminated sexual activity altogether, probably to eliminate pregnancy. Because they couched their sexual prohibitions in religious terms, claiming that sex was the sin in the Garden of Eden, Ann Lee, their founder, was accused of being a witch, society's time-honored way of dealing with deviance in women and genius. In contrast, to insure loyalty to the community, the Perfectionists at Oneida played down "special love" (what we would call romantic love) and allowed "free love," to use the term of John Humphrey Noyes, founder of the community.[11]

While the Shakers sought to eliminate reproduction through celibacy, Oneida practised *coitus reservatus*. " 'The restoration of true relations between the sexes is a matter second only in importance to the reconciliation of man to God,' " claimed Noyes;[12] however, this did not prevent him from exercising the right of "first husband" for many years, in his system of "complex marriage," a right appropriated as well by Gilgamesh, king of ancient Sumer, the feudal lords of the Middle Ages, Russian nobles in the twentieth century and some capitalist masters.

Since all physical contact was prohibited among the Shakers and men and women ate at segregated tables and even passed through separate doors, one wonders why they joined together at all. The answer is that they still shared a sexual division of labor. ". . . each brother was assigned a sister, who looked after his clothes, took care of his laundry and mending, and otherwise kept a 'general sisterly oversight over his habits and temporal needs.' In return, the brother performed menial tasks for the sister, particularly those involving heavy manual labor."[13] Furthermore, even though women at Oneida cut their hair short and wore pants for greater comfort and efficiency and some did "men's work," men there did not perform traditional women's work. It remained for twentieth-century feminists to demand and experiment with the elimination of sex roles (see Sheer and Weinbaum, Part Three), something the Gnostic Christians had achieved centuries before.

In the nineteenth century, separatism, celibacy, and even "complex marriage" as at Oneida were ways of gaining reproductive control in a period that generally glorified motherhood. Indeed, perhaps the desire for this control was the main reason that communes altered the traditional structure of marriage.

In most intentional communities there are attempts to minimize the individual. Yet one person is almost always glorified—

the charismatic leader who becomes the repository for the group's ego ideal.[14] This is potentially dangerous, particularly when the leader is a male, as has been overwhelmingly the case, for his leadership symbolizes a return to the patriarchal father.

NOTES

1. Arthur and Lila Weinberg, eds., *Passport to Utopia: Great Panaceas in American History* (Chicago: Quadrangle Books, 1968), p. 16.

2. Barbara Ehrenreich and Deirdre English, *For Her Own Good: 150 Years of the Experts' Advice to Women.* (Garden City, N.Y.: Anchor Books, 1979), p. 51.

3. Carol Ellen DuBois, "Review of *The Grand Domestic Revolution*," *Signs* (Winter 1982), p. 359.

4. Barbara Taylor, " 'The Men Are as Bad as Their Masters . . .': Socialism, Feminism, and Sexual Antagonism in the London Tailoring Trade in the Early 1830's," *Feminist Studies* (Spring 1979), p. 9.

5. Taylor, p. 13.

6. Dolores Hayden, "What Would a Non-Sexist City Be Like: Speculations on Housing, Urban Design, and Human Work," *Signs* (Spring 1980), p. 187.

7. Friedrich Engels, *Origin of the Family, Private Property, and the State*, ed. Eleanor B. Leacock (New York: International Publishers, 1972), p. 66.

8. Barbara Leslie Epstein, *The Politics of Domesticity: Women, Evangelism, and Temperance in Nineteenth-Century America* (Middletown, Conn.: Wesleyan University Press, 1981).

9. Dolores Hayden and Gwendolyn Wright, "Architecture and Urban Planning," *Signs* (Summer 1976), p. 927.

10. Dolores Hayden, *The Grand Domestic Revolution: A History of Feminist Designs for American Homes, Neighborhoods and Cities* (Cambridge, MA: The MIT Press, 1981); see also Jacqueline Leavitt, "Planning and Women, Women and Planning," unpublished Ph.D. Dissertation, Columbia University, 1980.

11. William M. Kephart, *Extraordinary Groups: The Sociology of Unconventional Life-Styles* (New York: St. Martin's Press, 1982).

12. Lawrence Foster, *Religion and Sexuality: Three American Communal Experiments of the Nineteenth Century* (New York: Oxford University Press, 1981), p. 13.

13. Kephart, p. 217.

14. See Sigmund Freud, *Group Psychology and the Analysis of the Ego,* Standard Edition, Volume XVIII (1921), pp. 67–143.

The Shakers: Gender Equality in Hierarchy

RUBY ROHRLICH

SHAKER society is unique and paradoxical on several counts. With celibacy as their primary religious and organizational principle, the Shakers outlived by far most of the utopian communities that emerged in nineteenth-century North America. Committed to sexual and racial equality, they were hierarchically structured, and the sexes performed traditional gender-typed work.

The Shakers are among the most long-lasting communities in the United States. Founded in 1780, some 17,000 persons were at one time or another gathered into their fold,[1] and remnants still exist in New Hampshire and Maine. At the height of their prosperity, in the 1850's, eighteen Shaker societies, consisting of fifty-eight "families" or separate communes, owning about 100,000 acres of farmland, had been established in ten states.

The Shakers were a source of inspiration to many nineteenth-century social theorists, from Robert Owen to Friedrich Engels. In 1845, Engels argued that the Shakers, along with other American communal groups, showed that "communism, or life and work in a community where all goods are held in common, is not only possible but, . . . is already being practiced successfully in many communities in America . . ."[2] John Humphrey Noyes, who founded the Perfectionists, one of the "many communities in America," and himself a social theorist, described the success of the Shakers as "the 'specie basis' that has upheld all the paper theories, and counteracted the failures of the French and English Schools."[3] In fact, Noyes borrowed "the whole formal nature of his system" from the Shakers and, even when he drastically altered major Shaker doctrines, presented a clear counterpart to them.[4]

The Shakers, or the United Order of Believers, as they called themselves, originated in England, "their prophecies often . . . the passionate utterances" of the women who led them.[5] Mother Jane Wardley, the leader of the English sect, was succeeded by Ann Lee, who, after the difficult delivery and death of four infants, fastened on "cohabitation of the sexes" as the cardinal sin. The wife of John Humphrey Noyes experienced five difficult deliveries and the death of four babies. What Mother Ann and Noyes illustrate is that the personal is indeed political: Mother Ann, the child-bearer, renounced sex altogether; Noyes, the husband of the child-bearer, advocated much more of it but sought to avoid reproduction.

Mother Ann's denunciations of "lust of the flesh," together with the shakings and speaking-in-tongues of the sect, brought on charges of heresy and witchcraft; she was thrown into jail, and the sect was violently persecuted. In 1774, Ann Lee and seven members of the group emigrated to North America. By 1780, the first Shaker settlement had been established in upstate New York, followed within the decade by the founding of the central society at New Lebanon, Massachusetts, and other communes in several New England, Southern and Midwestern states. But in the New World they were also threatened and persecuted. While the slave trade was still going on, the Shakers took a strong stand against slavery, and during the Revolutionary War their societies were hotbeds of pacifist agitation. Particularly offensive, especially in Harvard, were their vehement denunciations of heterosexual relations which, they claimed, brought "distress and poverty, shame and disgrace upon families and individuals, and filled the earth with wretchedness and misery."[6] Not only did the Shakers contribute to the break-up of marriages and the separation of children from parents, according to their opponents, but, even worse, they were led by a woman, "a woman whom many believers almost deified."[7] After Mother Ann's death, even loyal Shakers had difficulty accepting the institutionalization of female leadership.

As in the majority of the nineteenth-century communities, agriculture was the basis of Shaker economy. However, unlike the Owenites, Fourierists and other utopian societies, the Shakers were able to translate their concepts into "an efficient system of combined labor, in model farms and villages, in fine workmanship and a remarkably productive industry."[8] Prefiguring "the people who talk to plants" at Findhorn, Scotland, the Shakers maintained that "if you love the plant, and take heed of what it likes, you will be well repaid by it . . . a tree feels when you care for it."[9] Labor was a sacred commitment, the frequent change of occupations precluded monotony, and ingenious labor-saving devices were constantly invented. Their craft products, particularly their furniture, were in great demand, and artistic creation, expressed in songs and dances, paintings and drawings, was both spirited and spiritual. In the Shaker societies, individual was fused with group, and technology with art. The Perfectionists also became economically successful, but their distinctive sexual arrangements were ended in 1879, after only 33 years, compared with two centuries of Shaker existence.

Except for Catholics, members of all denominations, including some Jews, joined the Shakers, in contrast to the Oneida society, where "members were deliberately chosen on the basis of complete loyalty to Noyes's leadership."[10] Several of the Shaker communes were interracial, and one commune with only black members was "organized in Philadelphia by a remarkable black woman,"[11] Mother Rebecca Jackson, and lasted for many years. Some slaveholders who became Shakers set their slaves free, inducing forty to join them.[12]

A central Shaker principle was "power over physical disease"; the "salvation of the body" was no less important than the "health of the soul." Starting with Mother Ann, who was famous for her miraculous cures of diseases and injuries by the laying on of hands, the "healing gift" was practiced by many Shakers with reportedly great success. Their medicinal herbs, tended by the women, sold far and wide, and some of their health practices are recognized as scientifically valid by contemporary medicine, both traditional and alternative: they did not smoke and were mainly vegetarians, insisting that animal foods, especially fats, were harmful, and claiming that cancer disappeared among them when they stopped eating pork. Their age at death ranged from sixty years to over ninety, and this "longevity of Virgin Celibates" and their general good health they attributed to "sexual purity."

Shaker women and men led lives that were interdependent but separate, parallel but symbiotic; they are the link between heterosocial and homosocial communities. Living in the same houses, physical contact between the men and women was avoided, but both sexes attended the nightly gatherings and the religious festivals, and they "often traveled together by horseback, sleighs, or by coach for longer journeys."[13] Meetings of the whole commune ended with same-sex hugging and kissing. Unlike the early Christians whom they claimed as their model, governance was hierarchical for both the sisterhoods and the brethren, with obedience strictly enjoined to elders and "eldresses," deacons and "deaconesses," foremen and forewomen, who were appointed by the ministers, without consultation with or vote by the members.

With celibacy the central tenet, Ann Lee reproved young men for seducing young women, young women for artfully ensnaring young men, and parents for "building up" their children "to allure the eyes of the different sex."[14] The Shakers claimed that other communities failed chiefly because they permitted marriage, "which is inextricably involved in the institution of private property."[15] Noyes also rejected marriage in "communist" terms, for its exclusiveness in persons as in property, decrying monogamous marriage because of its "scanty and monotonous" fare.

Like the Gnostic Christians who were sexually egalitarian, the Shakers regarded God as a male/female duality, who had first appeared in the person of Jesus, the male element, and later (the Second Coming), in the body of Ann Lee, the "female Messiah." The "sacred parentage" of Father Jesus and Mother Ann underlay their strong belief in sexual equality, and they looked forward "to the day when women shall, in the outer world, as in their own societies, hold office as well as men."[16] Ann Lee was convinced that heterosexual relations forced women into an extremely unjust role, and she "developed an intense concern to correct the imbalance that she perceived in the relations between the sexes."[17] Noyes, on the other hand, explicitly believed in the "natural" superiority of men over women,[18] and men were his closest associates at the top of the hierarchy he established. By contrast, the Shakers maintained that among them the women were "just as able as men in all business affairs, and far more spiritual."[19] Elder Frederick Evans, official spokesman for the New Lebanon community, "wanted to apply Shaker ideas by making the Presidency and governorship dual offices, limiting the national and state senates to women, and the lower houses to men, and confining leadership to a class of 'intellectual celibates,' male and female, who would be married only to the state."[20]

Gender roles among the Shakers were differentiated and traditional, women generally working indoors, and men doing the heavy work outside. However, since Shaker women and men participated equally in religious doctrine, governance and political decision-making, equality for women did not depend on doing exactly what men did.[21] Among the Perfectionists at Oneida, few occupational possibilities were formally closed to women, and some women did construction work while some men participated in child-rearing. But women typically gravitated toward traditional female occupations, and they were excluded from the upper administrative and ideological echelons.

Group marriage at Oneida was triggered by Noyes's attraction to Mary Cragin, to the great dissatisfaction of her husband; notwithstanding, Noyes and his wife and Mary and her husband were the first to give each other "full liberty" within the group.[22] Since sexual relations at Oneida were subject to strict regulation by Noyes, "sexual privileges" were suspended or limited as a method of disciplining recalcitrant individuals.[23]

Shaker women consistently outnumbered the men, women in the childbearing years (20–45) predominating "by a 2:1 or even 3:1 ratio."[24] The Shaker communes were havens for women with marital and economic problems:

> The rule of celibacy was a selective agent, attracting not only those
> who believed in the principle on doctrinal grounds but those
> others, chiefly women, who were drawn in because of their desire
> to escape from marital difficulties and broken homes. For persons
> oppressed by . . . economic ills the Shaker community, like the
> cloister, offered the opportunity for a renewal of life in useful
> service.[25]

The Shaker communities welcomed both women and men
from broken families, and before the 1840's they functioned as
community orphanages and later as old people's homes. Another
example of their commitment to the poor and the oppressed was
the "thousands of dollars of specie, livestock and produce" given
by two communities in 1803 "to help feed the starving poor suffering from cholera in New York City."[26]

The separation of the sexes in the Shaker settlements was
also "an integral part of . . . the larger American society" in the
nineteenth century. As Smith-Rosenberg points out, the "rigid
gender-role differentiation within the family and within society
as a whole, leading to the emotional segregation of women and
men" also led to the development of a specifically female world
"built around a generic and unself-conscious pattern of single-
sex or homosocial networks."[27] The diaries of Shaker women
were filled with expressions of strong emotion for their sisters in
each settlement as well as in the settlements they often visited.
Although there were extensive denunciations of heterosexual
love, Campbell points out that in the material she researched she
never "encountered a single explicit reference to or condemna-
tion of homosexual behavior": On the contrary,

> Shaker sisterhood must have substantially strengthened the
> Shaker network and have helped the separate settlements main-
> tain a unity of human affection and purpose.[28]

By the 1850's the decline in the number of men accelerated;
submission to authority, self-abnegation and communal ownership had little appeal in a country "glorifying liberty" and the
accumulation of private property.[29] Dissension and disunity increased particularly between the Eastern and Western societies,

Western youth objecting most of all to the rule of strict obedience, especially to Eastern leaders.

The sisters replaced the brethren in key industries, and expanded the output of their own shops, making regular tours to distant markets, such as mountain and seaside resorts, to peddle their wares. Eventually, small farming replaced stock raising, with men hired to till the fields. But then the sisters, too, began to insist on the "self-governing power of the individual," and their numbers also began to decline, along with the dwindling of their enterprises. Nevertheless, during their two hundred years and more in America, the Shakers were never divided by a successful schism.

NOTES

1. Edward Deming Andrews, *The People Called Shakers* (New York: Dover Publications, 1963), p. 201.

2. Lawrence Foster, *Religion and Sexuality: Three Communal Experiments of the Nineteenth Century* (New York: Oxford University Press, 1981), p. 266, fn. 7.

3. John Humphrey Noyes, *History of American Socialism* (Philadelphia: J. B. Lippincott, 1870), p. 670.

4. Benjamin D. Warfield, "John Humphrey Noyes and His 'Bible Communists,' " *Bibliotheca Sacra*, 78 (1921), pp. 346–347.

5. Andrews, p. 6.

6. *Ibid.*, p. 22.

7. Foster, p. 32.

8. Andrews, p. 95.

9. *Ibid.*, p. 119.

10. Foster, p. 103.

11. *Ibid.*, p. 277, fn. 97.

12. Charles Nordhoff, *The Communistic Societies of the United States* (New York: Dover Publications, 1966), p. 207.

13. D'Ann Campbell, "Women's Life in Utopia: The Shaker Experiment in Sexual Equality Reappraised—1810–1860," *New England Quarterly* (March 1978), p. 32.

14. Andrews, p. 22.

15. *Ibid.*, p. 103.

16. Nordhoff, p. 166.

17. Foster, p. 25.

18. *Ibid.*, p. 105.

19. Nordhoff, p. 166.

20. Andrews, p. 233.

21. Campbell, p. 27.

22. Foster, p. 100.

23. *Ibid.*, p. 107.

24. Campbell, p. 28.

25. Andrews, p. 178.

26. Foster, p. 22.

27. Carroll Smith-Rosenberg, "The Female World of Love and Ritual: Relations between Women in Nineteenth-Century America," *Signs* (Autumn 1975), p. 9.

28. Campbell, p. 31.

29. Andrews, p. 228.

Frances Wright: Utopian Feminist

MARILYN BENSMAN

THE nineteenth-century feminist ideology engendered
by Mary Wollstonecraft's vindication of women's rights represented a radical assault on cherished institutions of Western society, a fact which did not escape its critics. Yet, few feminists of
the past century were inclined to divulge their visions of the
future or to draw plans for the nonsexist society they wished to
bring about. For this reason, it is illuminating to review the life
and work of Frances Wright, an early nineteenth-century radical
feminist who made her visions public and attempted to put them
into practice.

Initially, Wright founded a "utopian" community, Nashoba,
in Tennessee, to demonstrate the feasibility of bringing about an
orderly end to slavery. On a visit to the United States in 1824,
she was struck by the anomalous institution of slavery in what
she regarded as an otherwise exemplary democratic nation. But
Nashoba increasingly became, for Wright, more than a pilot
project for the manumission of slaves. It came to demonstrate
new roles and relationships possible among the sexes, races and
classes.

Wright's utopian visions, like those of her nineteenth-century Romantic radical peers, Fourier, Saint-Simon, Owen and
their respective followers, were based on ideas of social evolution and progress. She, too, believed the creation of just, harmo-

This article is based in part on a section on "Frances Wright," in Marilyn
Bensman, "Feminism and Family Ideologies: Dilemmas and Conflict in the
American Women's Movement to 1870," submitted in partial fulfillment for the
Ph.D. degree, Department of Sociology, Graduate Faculty of the New School for
Social Research, April 1981. Marilyn Bensman, "Frances Wright: Utopian Fe-
minist," copyright © 1984 Marilyn Bensman.

nious and integrated societies was within the realm of possibility. Wright viewed herself as both a prophet and a practical reformer, who was not above participating in the arduous work of building a community from scratch.

Nor was Nashoba meant to stand alone as an isolated monument to her charity and good will, or a refuge from the larger world. Wright believed her plan could provide a peaceful transition to a slaveless American society. She continually reorganized Nashoba according to principles alternately stressing cooperation, communism, democracy, and strong leadership, as well as free sexuality and racial amalgamation. In time, the idea of rehabilitating slaves gave way to the idea of settling blacks in an interracial community. Two principles alone she never compromised: the right of women to equality and independence, and the right of all to public education.

Despite an inclination to "free the passions" by decree, which she shared with Fourier, Wright believed in the democratic process, the persuasive power of reason, and the need for social and economic planning. Slavery should not be abolished over the objections of slaveholders and without preparing the slaves for freedom. When slaveholders were informed of the economic wastefulness of slavery and were assured of compensation for their losses, they would voluntarily cooperate in its abolition. The slaves, for their part, Wright wrote, must be allowed to "labor with dignity" to buy their freedom and be helped to acquire the culture, knowledge and work ethic necessary for citizenship. For this, a benign environment would have to be provided in a community such as Nashoba, with proper models of industry, morality and civility.[1]

Wright was not content to wait for her ideas to attract attention, nor, like Fourier, to advertise in vain for wealthy patrons. She sought advice and support for her proposals from such eminent statesmen as Jefferson, Madison, Monroe, and Jackson. She was aided in receiving introductions to these people by her friend and travelling companion, General Lafayette, who was being honored, at the time, by the United States government for his role in the Revolutionary War. Despite the great difference in their ages, Lafayette and Wright were close friends, as well as political allies. He had been impressed with her book describing her travels in America in 1818.[2] Wright subsequently made extended visits to the Lafayette household in LaGrange and served as an international courier for his revolutionary organization, the Carbonari. Thus, Frances Wright, like Mary Wollstonecraft before her, combined all the traits of the quintessential "natural feminist": she was self-assured, adventuresome, and intellectually accomplished, though largely self-educated. In a note to Lafayette, she explained her sexually anomalous independence in this way:

> I dare say you marvel sometimes at my independent way of walking through the world just as if nature had made me of your sex, instead of poor Eve's. Trust me, my beloved friend, the mind has no sex but what habit and education give it, and I, who was thrown in infancy upon the waters, have learned as well to struggle with the elements as well as any child of Adam.[3]

As her note suggests, Frances Wright, born in Scotland in 1795, was orphaned at an early age. She came from a family of wealthy landowners and businessmen, and was raised as a member of the aristocracy. She was dressed, coiffed, and waited on. Yet, she was an avid reader from childhood on, and developed a great curiosity about America. When she reached her majority, Wright left the aunt with whom she had been living to reside with her uncle, James Milne, a professor of Moral Philosophy at the University of Glasgow. There Wright gained the use of a library and a community within which her intellectual interests could expand. She wrote plays and poetry which expressed her Byronic romanticism and interest in Epicurean and Utilitarian philosophy. At the same time her long-standing interest in America became a virtual obsession. Finally, in 1818, she was able to visit the land across the sea which so fascinated her, accompanied by her sister Camilla, and armed with letters of introduction provided by a family friend. The book she wrote based on her travels indicates she was not disappointed, particularly as she had yet to encounter slavery in the South.

On her second trip to the United States, she traveled up the

Mississippi River and witnessed slavery first-hand. From then on, its eradication became her obsession. She consulted with Thomas Jefferson about the economics of slavery and with Robert Owen about alternative systems of labor. She traveled to Albion, Illinois, to meet with George Flower, who had founded his own colony for poor English immigrants, and who was also opposed to slavery.

The idea of founding a similar community began to crystallize. Flower helped her to draw up detailed plans. After consulting with General Andrew Jackson and the governor of Tennessee, she decided to purchase a tract of land only recently claimed from the Indians, about fifteen miles from what is now Memphis. It was an almost totally undeveloped, virtually inaccessible, malaria-ridden site in the midst of the wilderness.

Initially, Wright expected to buy enough land on which to settle between fifty and one hundred slaves, who would work to pay off their purchase price. The productivity of family members would be calculated jointly, so they could be kept together, with subtractions made to defray the cost of their upkeep, the education of their children, and their eventual relocation outside of the United States. She estimated it would take five years for an industrious slave family to purchase its freedom.

Once at Nashoba, however, Wright was forced to reduce the scope of the operation. She purchased eight slaves, and a Mr. Wilson donated a slave woman and her five daughters. Other members of the colony consisted of her sister Camilla; George Flower's family; James Richardson, a former Scottish medical student; and Richeson Whitby, who had lived in a Shaker colony and functioned as Nashoba's resident expert on communalism. Whitby later married Camilla. A "quadroon" woman, a "free person of color," whom Frances had met earlier, sought refuge at Nashoba from the social snobbery and discrimination she encountered in New Orleans. And, from time to time, other, not always welcome, curiosity seekers and prospective members wandered into the remote community. Few, however, were prepared to withstand the hardships they encountered there.

A particularly virulent form of malaria struck down most of the white inhabitants almost immediately, forcing Camilla and the Flower children to depart for the north. Frances, too, was stricken. Believing her death was imminent, she named a Board of Trustees and deeded them the property, "to be held in perpetual trust for the negro race . . ." Wright specified that a school be built at Nashoba and that the slaves be freed when their "labor shall have paid a clear capital of $6000, plus interest of six per cent on the capital . . ." Once freed they were to be placed outside the United States because she feared for their safety.

Then, convinced that whites were incapable of laboring in Tennessee's inhospitable climate, Wright remodeled the community after Robert Owen's colony in New Harmony, Indiana, with slaves doing the heavy work. To avoid the inter-personal conflicts she had observed at New Harmony, Wright insisted that in the future family members apply as individuals, and each be subject to the approval of the resident members of the Board after a six-month trial period. All members, regardless of color, sex or status, were to be entitled to receive, to the best ability of the community, food, clothing, lodging, medical care, and protection in old age. The community would also attempt to raise and educate each child until the age of twenty, at which time he or she could either apply for membership, or be helped to settle elsewhere. Wright wrote:

> It will be seen that this community is founded on the principle of community property and labor; presenting every advantage to those desirous, not of accumulating money, but of enjoying life and rendering services to their fellow-creatures; these fellow-creatures, that is, the blacks here admitted, requiting these services, by services equal or greater by occupations, which their habits render easy, and which to their guides and assistants might be difficult, or unpleasing. No life of idleness, however, is proposed for the whites. Those who cannot work, must give an equivalent in property.[4]

The white members of Nashoba, she noted, could find suitable employment teaching school, tending gardens, or nursing the sick.

Over the next five years, Wright continued to attempt to

recruit members for Nashoba, though she herself rarely remained in residence. Upon her return from a long sea voyage in the company of Robert Dale Owen, son of Robert Owen, Frances fround that Nashoba had become notorious as a "free-love" colony, after the publication of James Richardson's personal diary, describing his sexual exploits and relationships with the slaves. Her sister Camilla's private letters in which she defended Richardson's diary, were also made public. In these letters Camilla expressed her hatred for the "laws of matrimony" and noted that Nashoba's residents were encouraged to seek sexual gratification with whomsoever they pleased, provided they received the consent of the other.

Under pressure from her friends, Frances wrote a public retraction in which she gently chastised her sister and Richardson for their views; but she succeeded only in fanning the flames of scandal by publishing her own "Explanatory Notes,"[5] addressed to the more liberal minded "Friends of Human Improvement" around the world. In this tract, Wright offered a critique of the ills of American society. Nashoba, she wrote, would no longer attempt to rehabilitate slaves, but would seek to demonstrate the "moral beauty" and "utility" of a truly free society. At Nashoba women who "shrink equally from the opprobrium stamped upon unlegalized connexions," and the "servitude of matrimony" would no longer be forced into a life of celibacy which was unhealthy for the women and not in the best interests of society. The "best class of women" would thus be able to contribute their potentially superior offspring to enhance the human race.

Wright's new proposal for Nashoba was never put into effect, as its white members one by one left the community. She returned only long enough to accompany the slaves to Haiti, a journey which proved so dangerous and arduous that it is a saga unto itself.

Wright then moved to New Harmony to help Robert Dale Owen publish *New Harmony Gazette,* and finally to New York to found *The New York Enquirer.* She discovered around this time that she possessed great skills as a lecturer, and, in the interest of promoting adult public education, she established a Hall of Science in New York as a forum for progressive ideas. At the same time, the staff of the *Enquirer,* impressed by the militancy and advanced ideas of the burgeoning labor movement, organized a Workingman's Party, among other things, to push their new radical plan for the nurturance and education of children at public expense. The plan, known as "State Guardianship Education," again honored Wright's commitment to the idea of the free and independent woman. Each parent would be taxed separately according to his or her ability to pay. Girls would be educated together with boys in residential schools where, she explained, "no inequality must be allowed to enter." Wright once again drew up detailed plans, complete with cost estimates, for which she sought approval in such high places as the New York State Legislature. She believed the new school system would not only promote the education of children, but would presage a new social order:

> . . . fed at a common board; clothed in a common garb; . . . raised in the exercise of common duties, in the acquirement of the same industry, varied only according to individual taste and capabilities; in the exercise of the same virtues, in the enjoyment of the same pleasures; in the study of the same nature; in the pursuit of the same object—their own and each other's happiness—say! would not such a race, when arrived at manhood and womanhood work out the reform of society—perfect the free institutions of America?[6]

The Workingman's Party, after having achieved some success in the election of 1829, ultimately split over the State Guardianship Education issue. Nevertheless, the plan contributed to the development of universal, publicly-financed education in New York State and the nation; and Wright's Hall of Science and her lectures helped to promote adult education.

In aiding the development of the Workingman's Party and the public education movement, Frances Wright abandoned the communitarian movement. As alternatives to isolated communes, her schools entailed the construction of residential educational establishments within the boundaries of an increasingly urban society. Yet, they could become the models for a new system of public education, which would provide the moral and intellectual foundations for a democratic society. As Wright continued her efforts to create the practical basis for a just society, she became more the reformer, and less the utopian.

In Paris, in 1831, Frances married Guillaume Sylvan Casimiar Phiquepal D'Arusmont shortly after she gave birth to their first child, who did not survive. She had been openly living with D'Arusmont for some time. He was a physician and educator, sixteen years her senior, whom she met at New Harmony, where he had helped to organize the schools. The marriage and unconventional household they maintained in Paris reflected their independent natures. After 1835, Frances spent most of her time in the States, where she continued for several years to lecture publicly on the philosophy of Auguste Comte. Although she embraced his elitist, positivist brand of reformism, she continued nonetheless to advocate the extension of democratic principles to women, the state, and the society of the future.

NOTES

1. Frances Wright, "A Plan for the Gradual Abolition of Slavery in the United States without Danger of Loss to its Citizens of the South" (Pamphlet, 1825).

2. Frances Wright, *Views of Society and Manners in America in a Series of Letters to a Friend in England during the Years 1818, 1819, 1820, by an Englishman* (London: Longman, 1821).

3. Wright MSS, Frances Wright to General Lafayette, February 11, 1822; quoted in William Randall Waterman, *Frances Wright* (New York: Columbia University Press, 1924), pp. 74–75.

4. Wright MSS. Deed of the Lands of Nashoba, West Tennessee; quoted in Waterman, p. 108.

5. A. J. Perkins and Theresa Wolfson, *Frances Wright, Free Enquirer: A Study of a Temperament* (New York: Harper & Bros., 1939), p. 193. Wright's defense of Nashoba was published in the *Memphis Advocate* and in the *New Harmony Gazette,* January 30, 1828.

6. Francis Wright, *Course of Popular Lectures,* 4th. edition (New York: Office of *The Free Enquirer,* Hall of Science, 1829); quoted in Perkins and Wolfson, p. 166.

A Song of Sojourner Truth

JUNE JORDAN

The trolley cars was rollin and the passengers all white
when Sojourner just decided it was time to take a seat
The trolley cars was rollin and the passengers all white
When Sojourner decided it was time to take a seat
It was time she felt to rest a while and ease up
on her feet
So Sojourner put her hand out
tried to flag the trolley down
So Sojourner put her hand out
for the trolley crossin town
And the driver did not see her
the conductor would not stop
But Sojourner yelled, "It's me!"
And put her body on the track
"It's me!" she yelled, "And yes,
I walked here but I ain walkin back!"
The trolley car conductor and the driver was afraid
to roll right over her and leave her lying dead
So they opened up the car and Sojourner took a seat
So Sojourner sat to rest a while and eased up on her feet

REFRAIN:

Sojourner had to be just crazy
tellin all that kinda truth

Dedicated to Bernice Reagon

I say she musta been plain crazy
plus they say she was uncouth
talkin loud to any crowd
talkin bad insteada sad
She just had to be plain crazy
talkin all that kinda truth
If she had somewhere to go she said
I'll ride
If she had somewhere to go she said
I'll ride
jim crow or no
she said *I'll go*
just like the lady
that she was in all the knowing darkness
of her pride
she said *I'll ride*
she said *I'll talk*
she said *A Righteous Mouth*
ain nothin you should hide
she said she'd ride
just like the lady
that she was in all the knowing darkness
of her pride
she said *I'll ride*

They said she's Black and ugly and they said she's
really rough
They said if you treat her like a dog
well that'll be plenty good enough
And Sojourner said
I'll ride
And Sojourner said
I'll go
I'm a woman and this hell has made me tough
(Thank God!)
This hell has made me tough
I'm a strong Black woman
and Thank God!

REFRAIN:

> Sojourner had to be just crazy
> tellin all that kinda truth
> I say she musta been plain crazy
> plus they say she was uncouth
> talkin loud to any crowd
> talkin bad insteada sad
> She just had to be plain crazy
> talkin all that kinda truth

Housework and Utopia: Women and the Owenite Socialist Communities

JILL HARSIN

"THE working man's wife is also his housekeeper, cook, and several other single domestics rolled into one," wrote an English workingman around the middle of the nineteenth century. "Even the poorest man," observed a London clergyman about the same time, "wants a servant to cook, to wash, and provide for his comfort."[1] It was an unquestioned assumption in Victorian society that women would fulfill their domestic responsibilities, in addition to any work they might do outside the home, just as it was long assumed that women in socialist societies would be freed from this narrow servitude. Yet recent work has revealed that the promises of socialism have not been fulfilled. Women work longer hours for less money, and one of the most persistent barriers to full equality for women has been the unequal burden of housework.[2] The link between women and housework has maintained itself under capitalism, under communism, and, frequently, in utopia as well, as illustrated by the experience of the Owenite utopian communities in the early nineteenth century.

The Owenite movement, one of the first socialist movements in Britain, was inspired by the writings and activity of the manufacturer-philanthropist Robert Owen. A self-made man with little formal education, he based his utopia on Enlightenment concepts. Nature and natural law were to replace the "priestly" laws which had governed man throughout recorded history. The idea that man was primarily a product of his envi-

ronment suggested the means for effecting social change. The proper education could create a new kind of human, one fit to inhabit the New Moral World.[3]

Women were to be fully equal in this world. The Eleventh Law in Owen's Universal Code of Laws stated that "Both sexes shall have equal education, rights, privileges, and personal liberty."[4] Unlike most utopian plans, the Owenite New Moral World had to stand the test of practical experience in a number of trial communities; the four most completely documented experiences are examined here.[5] The results were illuminating, for with all his grandiose plans for the future and for women, Owen did not deviate from the traditional assumption that women would do the cleaning up.

Owen's utopia was first outlined in 1817 and 1820 in two brief essays;[6] the finished utopia, *The Book of the New Moral World*, was published in 1842. Despite surface differences, the guiding principle behind all three plans was the same. Cooperative labor, both in agriculture and in manufacturing, would prove far more efficient than capitalist competition. The result would be so much superfluous wealth that private property would disappear; "individual accumulation of wealth will appear as irrational as to bottle up or store water."[7] Owen left the arrangements for distribution rather vague, because he did not think they would be important. As it turned out, distribution problems became critical to these struggling communities; unequal distribution and the degree to which labor was actually communal proved to be particular problems for women.

Owen's list of the duties of women in his 1817 plan made them responsible for all domestic labor; their first responsibility was "the care of their infants, and keeping their dwelling in the best order." They were also responsible for all communal domestic duties, including the cultivation of the kitchen garden, the making of clothing, and service in the public kitchens, dining rooms, dorms, and schoolrooms. Finally, they were to spend "not more than four or five hours in the day" in the "various manufactures" which would be established.[8] Their domestic responsibilities would cut into the time they could spend in the production of visible products for exchange, and, thus, into their individual remuneration. And, though this was a plan for a transitional society, the apparently unbreakable bond between women and housework was to be transmitted to the next generation. According to Owen's educational plans for the working classes, all girls were to be instructed "in the best method of treating infants and training children, in all the usual domestic arrangements to make themselves and others comfortable,—in the practice and knowledge of gardening, and in some one useful, light, and healthy manufacture."[9]

In contrast to the busy women of the intermediate societies, the women of the New Moral World—the finished utopia—were to be ladies of comparative leisure. In Owen's utopia, which was based on material prosperity and mechanical invention the like of which has not yet been seen, the necessary productive activity was to require so little labor that it would be performed entirely by children or young adults. After the age of twenty-five, according to Owen, it would unnecessary for a member to labor directly or to instruct the others, unless he or she wished to do so. When the first generation of women had been raised in perfect equality with men, they would be qualified to take their places as equal members of society.[10] This equality was dependent on the educational process; more importantly, it depended on the ability of children, aided by as-yet-uninvented machinery, to support the community. When Owen's economic prosperity and mechanical innovations did not materialize, and when it became evident, in his communal experiments, that all members of these tiny communities would have to work very hard in order to make them survive, the Owenites simply fell back on traditional sex roles.

Orbiston (1825–1827) was the first British Owenite community. Its constitution guaranteed women the right to belong to the Committee of Management. More importantly, they were offered freedom from "domestic slavery"; cooking was to be communal, and it was promised that "the clothes, shoes, etc. will be cleaned by Machinery."[11] Despite these projected advantages, women apparently had a negative influence on the community. Abram Combe, the guiding spirit behind Orbiston, complained that "nothing but the refusal of their husbands to accompany them" prevented the wives from leaving the experiment.[12]

Women were not, perhaps, to be blamed for their lack of enthusiasm, for their political equality was undercut economically by the constitution itself. According to the Articles of Agreement, the profits were to be divided equally among the members, but their daily needs were to be met by their own labor; thus it was required "that each individual should prepare an estimate of the hourly value of his own labour, and this, when satisfactory, will be the amount of his claims on the general store."[13] The wage rates were judged according to the standards prevailing outside the community, a necessary compromise made to attract skilled laborers. Only the communal labor of women was counted, not that which they performed in their own homes, and their labor was valued by the lower outside rate. Moreover, the communal organization began to break down. The public dining rooms were "almost wholly deserted," according to Combe, and "everyone began to look to themselves in the old way."[14] The more they looked to the "old way," the more the private responsibilities of women increased. The encroachment of individualism in other areas further clouded the original goals of the community, and it was disbanded after the death of Abram Combe.[15]

The information for Ralahine (1831–1833), the next community, was only slightly less sketchy, but it suggested the same combination of political equality and economic inequality, two principles which were enshrined in the governing agreement. By Article Thirty-seven of the Ralahine constitution, women were given the right to vote for the nine-member governing committee. By Article Fifteen, women's wages were permanently fixed at a lower rate than those of the lowest-paid men in the community; specifically, the act resolved:

> That each agricultural labouring man shall receive eight-pence, and every woman five-pence per day for their labour, which it is expected will be laid out at the store in provisions, or any other article the society may produce or keep there; any other article may be purchased elsewhere.[16]

Skilled laborers, as in Orbiston, received higher wages than the "agricultural labouring men." At the same time, the wages of all women were fixed at the same low rate, regardless of what they did in the community. Although domestic labor was limited to women, women were not limited to domestic labor. A worksheet for the community revealed that only one woman was employed in "domestic arrangements"; the rest were "at dairy and poultry" or were engaged in agriculture.[17] Because of the presumably more efficient arrangements, all women were able, as one enthusiastic observer noted, "to keep their cottages clean and neat with very little labour."[18]

The pattern of inequality became more apparent in New Harmony, Indiana (1825–1828), and in Queenwood (1839–1845), the first and last of the Owenite communities. Men and women in Queenwood were equally subject to a strict central authority.[19] New Harmony, like the other communities, was self-governing, but the rights of women were rather precarious "privileges" which the male members could revoke at will. In September, 1825, it was decided that "wives of members are not members, and it was finally decided they they should not vote." By February, 1826, women of the main colony had the suffrage restored to them. However, those dissenters who had by this time founded the splinter community of Macluria had decreed that women could not vote in the assembly. Female suffrage was maintained but restricted in the constitution, adopted July 30, 1826, of the New Harmony Agricultural and Pastoral Society; it was declared that "females shall have a right to vote on the reception or dismissal of a female, but in no other case whatever, except in cases of business which more properly belong to female management."[20]

This vacillation among the possibilities of equal rights, less-than-equal rights, and no rights at all reflected the basic economic inferiority of women in the New Harmony community. Their economic sphere was strictly limited from the beginning in a way that the men's sphere was not. The constitution of the "preliminary society" (drawn up by Owen) guaranteed that, in assigning employment, the governing committee would "pay every regard to the inclinations of each." Article Twenty-one, which regulated employment for women, was much less flexible:

> The employments of the female part of the committee consist, in preparing food and clothing; in the care of the dwelling houses,

dormitories, and public buildings; in the management of the washing and drying houses; in the education (in part) of the children, and in other occupations suited to the female character. By the proposed domestic arrangements, one female will, with great ease and comfort, perform as much as *twenty* menial servants can do at present; and instead of the wife of a working man, with a family, being a drudge and a slave, she will be engaged only in healthy and cleanly employments, acquire better manners, and have sufficient leisure for mental improvement and rational enjoyment.[21]

Owen apparently felt the need to justify woman's supposedly new role. Moreover, Owen's explanation revealed an essential lack of respect for the theoretically equal work done by domestic slaves and "menial servants." The denigration of housework was widespread enough to arouse the concern of Owen's partner, William Maclure, who suggested rather unhelpfully that "the common occupations of women, such as Sewing, Cooking, Washing, etc." might be turned into an "amusement" by early training.[22]

The lack of respect for women's work (and the failure of communal organization) had tangible consequences for the economic and political standing of women in the community. Thomas Pears of New Harmony explained the intricacies of membership and voting rights, displaying a traditional blindness to domestic labor:

Women, not actively employed, are not considered as members, and can only receive credit for the amount of sewing, washing, etc., they may be able to do for the society, when not engaged in family concerns.[23]

Active employment, or full-time employment in communal concerns, did not excuse women from domestic labors. Sarah Pears, Thomas's wife, explained why Sunday was not a day of rest for everyone, noting that "Those ladies who are in regular employment, having no time allowed them, have some excuse for washing, ironing, and doing their own sewing on the Sabbath."[24]

The situation was the same in Queenwood, as testimony before the Owenite Congress of the Rational Society revealed. The elected representative from the community stated that all the members were free on Sunday to do as they wished except women, who could not be "altogether so"; they had to fix Sunday dinner. Moreover, the same representative admitted that women worked "more hours per day, or per week," than the men, "by a great deal." Such testimony could not go unchallenged by an organization which advocated equal rights for women. The matter was not allowed to rest until it was determined that women worked more, "simply in consequence of their avocations requiring it."[25]

Owen confessed that he was puzzled by women's complaints of overwork and placed the blame on the women themselves:

> He had been endeavouring to ascertain the real cause why so much difficulty is experienced by the females of this community [New Harmony] in the performance of their domestic duties. Female labor in a community would certainly under proper arrangements be lighter than it can ever be in individual society. Perhaps the true cause of the evil complained of, may be that, when females who have heretofore been strangers to each other meet together in order to cooperate in some domestic labor, they spend that time in talking, which should be devoted exclusively to work.[26]

The Owenite communities had numerous excuses for failure. They had chronic financial difficulties, and the inhabitants were imperfectly schooled in the virtues of cooperative labor. The physical structures which they inherited from previous owners were often ill-suited to communal purposes, and those who best understood Owenite principles were not necessarily those best prepared to get a struggling enterprise on its feet. In short, conditions were not ideal for a demonstration of woman's equality to man. Yet the difficulties for women in the Owenite communities stemmed more from theoretical than from practical grounds. Owen believed, along with his antisocialist opponents, that women were most concerned with matters closest to domestic life. With that idea as a starting point, he believed that he had taken care of "the new state of society relative to women" by his attacks on marriage.

Owen's denunciation of marriage in the 1830's was in many ways merely an extension of his attack on society as a whole. Private households perpetuated economic inequality. Economic considerations often dictated the choice of a marriage partner and inhibited the "natural" desire to have many children. Of special relevance to the wife was the fact that religion and law declared that she belonged to her husband; if he insisted upon complete obedience, he merely forced her to learn the "common hypocrisy" of the wife.[27]

Owen complemented his attack on middle class domesticity with an historical analysis which linked the rise of private property with the development of monogamous marriage. Religion had contributed the sacrament of marriage, which cast an aura of divinity over naked property relations. Owen's interpretation reads today like a distorted echo of Engels' later work *The Origin of the Family, Private Property and the State,* not least because both works tended to imply that the entire social system would have to be scrapped before a substantial change could be effected in the position of women. Unfortunately for Owen's followers, the attack upon marriage quickly became mired in controversy over divorce. Owen was said to be the apologist of "universal and indiscriminate prostitution"; one anti-Owenite pamphlet purportedly revealed "The dark scenes and midnight revels that were carried on, in a Male and Female 'co-operative society.' "[28]

Attacks such as these led Owen and his followers away from the analysis of woman's role in society and the family and into a series of increasingly conservative "clarifications" of the marriage issue. In the end, the denunciation of marriage amounted to little more than anti-clerical rantings against "priestly" marriages performed according to the sacraments of the Old Immoral World. The Owenites boldly declared themselves to be opposed to marriages "of interest and sordid motives," of marriages "proceeding from other motives than pure affection." It was asserted that "the *permanent* union of affectionate and sympathising individuals, is the aim of all the projected arrangements of the New Moral World."[29]

Owen was able to convince himself that marriage in the New Moral World would be qualitatively different, however greatly it resembled conventional marriage. Women would benefit because their domestic situation would be more pleasant; that would be the extent of their equality. As his later statements revealed, Owen wished to transplant an essentially middle-class family structure with all its traditional obligations and responsibilities (now purified by its severance from religion) to the New Moral World.

The carryover of traditional domesticity into communal society served to incorporate the inequalities of the old world into the new. Its effects were felt in the choices of work open to women, in the payment (or lack of it) received for that work, and indeed, in political power within the communities, since that power was based to some degree on economic strength. The fact that labors formerly done individually would now be done communally did not change the nature of women's limited participation. Children would be cared for communally in the transitional societies, but entirely by women; food would be prepared communally, by women; laundry would be done communally, by women. The time saved by all these cooperative endeavors would leave women free to clean their homes, and the rest of their free time could be filled by communal work. Or rather, the communal work came first; a woman's domestic chores were done on her own.

In short, Owen's utopian communities "freed" women from the drudgery of domesticity by adding outside labor to their unpaid household tasks. The Owenites held an essentially conservative view of women; even their propaganda efforts aimed at "ladies" tended to define women according to their relationships with men. "Woman has never yet estimated her true position," stated an address from the Rational Tract Society. "She has never correctly appreciated her influence for good or evil; whether she is looked upon as the wife or the mother, the friend or the sweetheart, the consideration is no light one."[30] Yet it is simply too easy to blame the innate conservatism of the Owenite utopians for woman's limited role and greater burdens in the communities. The difficulties of redistributing the domestic role have thus far proved to be almost insurmountable.

NOTES

1. Thomas Wright, *The Great Unwashed* (London: Tinsley Brothers, 1868; rpt. New York: Augustus M. Kelley, 1970), p. 31; Thomas Beames, *The Rookeries of London* (London: Thomas Bosworth, 1852; rpt. London: Frank Cass, 1970), p. 150.

2. See, for example, Hilda Scott, *Does Socialism Liberate Women?* (Boston: Beacon Press, 1974).

3. The basic tenets of Owenism are explained in Robert Owen, *The Book of the New Moral World*, 7 pts. (London: The Home Colonization Society, 1842); rpt. New York: Augustus M. Kelley, 1970).

4. *Ibid.*, part 6, p. 38.

5. Harrison has counted 16 Owenite communities in America and 10 Owenite or Owenite-influenced colonies in Britain. J. F. C. Harrison, *Quest for the New Moral World* (New York: Charles Scribner's Sons, 1969), p. 163. See also R. G. Garnett, *Co-operation and the Owenite Socialist Communities in Britain, 1824–45* (Manchester: Manchester University Press, 1972) for a detailed discussion of the three largest British communities: Orbiston in Scotland, Ralahine in Ireland, and Queenwood in England.

6. These were the "Report to the Committee of the Association for the Relief of the Manufacturing and Labouring Poor," in 1817, and the "Report to the County of Lanark," in 1820. Both are in Robert Owen, *A New View of Society and Other Writings* (London: J. M. Dent, 1927).

7. Owen, "Report to the Committee of the Association for the Relief," *A New View of Society*, pp. 161–162; and Owen, "Report to Lanark," p. 287.

8. Owen, "Report to the Committee of the Association for the Relief," *A New View of Society*, p. 163.

9. Owen, "Letters on Poor Relief," *A New View of Society*, p. 195.

10. Owen, *Book of the New Moral World*, part 5, pp. 66–78.

11. Mary Hennell, *An Outline of the Various Social Systems* (London; Longman, Brown, and Green, 1844), p. 134; Garnett, *Co-operation and the Owenite Socialist Communities*, p. 75.

12. Abram Combe, "Lessons from the Past," *New Moral World*, 5 August 1837.

13. Hennell, *Outline*, p. 134.

14. Combe, "Lessons," *New Moral World*, 5 August 1837.

15. Garnett, *Co-operation and the Owenite Socialist Communities*, p. 87.

16. "Laws of the Ralahine Agricultural and Manufacturing Co-operative Association," cited by E. T. Craig, *The Irish Land and Labour Question, Illustrated in the History of Ralahine and Co-operative Farming* (London: Trubner & Co., 1882), p. 49; p. 47.

17. *Ibid.*, p. 165.

18. John Finch, cited by William Pare, *Co-operative Agriculture: A Solution of the Land Question, as Exemplified in the History of the Ralahine Co-operative Agricultural Association, County Clare, Ireland* (London: Longmans, Green, Reader, and Dyer, 1870), p. 73.

19. Lloyd Jones, *The Life, Times, and Labours of Robert Owen* (London: Swan Sonnenschein & Co., 1900), p. 394.

20. Thomas Pears and Sarah Pears, *New Harmony: An Adventure in Happiness, Papers of Thomas and Sarah Pears, Indiana Historical Society Publications*, vol. 11, ed. Thomas C. Pears, Jr. (Indianapolis: Indiana Historical Society, 1933), p. 31; p. 66; George B. Lockwood, *The New Harmony Movement* (New York: D. Appleton & Co., 1905), p. 133; and "Constitution of the New Harmony Agricultural and Pastoral Society," *New Harmony Gazette*, 9 August 1826.

21. Robert Owen, *Robert Owen in the United States*, ed. Oakley Johnson (New York: Humanities Press, 1970), p. 58; p. 60.

22. Arthur E. Bestor, Jr., ed., *Education and Reform at New Harmony: Correspondence of William Maclure and Marie Duclos Fretageot, 1820–1833*, in *Indiana Historical Society Publications*, vol. 15 (Indianapolis: Indiana Historical Society, 1949), p. 379.

23. Pears and Pears, *New Harmony*, p. 13.

24. *Ibid.*, p. 83.

25. "Proceedings of the Eighth Session of the Annual Congress of the Rational Society," *New Moral World*, 27 May 1843.

26. *New Harmony Gazette*, 30 August 1826.

27. See Robert Owen, *Lectures on the Marriages of the Priesthood of the Old Immoral World* (Leeds: J. Hobson, 1840). These ten lectures were published at weekly intervals in the *New Moral World*, beginning in December 1834.

28. "Women and the Social System," *Fraser's Magazine* (June 1840), p. 690; and Harrison, *Quest*, p. 390.

29. "Clerical Calumnies Refuted," *New Moral World*, 31 August 1839.

30. "Address of the Committee of the Rational Tract Society," *New Moral World*, 2 March 1844.

What's that smell in the kitchen?

MARGE PIERCY

ALL over America women are burning dinners.
It's lambchops in Peoria; it's haddock
in Providence; it's steak in Chicago
tofu delight in Big Sur; red
rice and beans in Dallas.
All over America women are burning
food they're supposed to bring with calico
smile on platters glittering like wax.
Anger sputters in her brainpan, confined
but spewing out missiles of hot fat.
Carbonized despair presses like a clinker
from a barbecue against the back of her eyes.
If she wants to grill anything, it's
her husband spitted over a slow fire.
If she wants to serve him anything
it's a dead rat with a bomb in its belly
ticking like the heart of an insomniac.
Her life is cooked and digested,
nothing but leftovers in Tupperware.
Look, she says, once I was roast duck
on your platter with parsley but now I am Spam.
Burning dinner is not incompetence but war.

The Woman's Commonwealth: Utopia in Nineteenth-Century Texas

A. HARRIETTE ANDREADIS

IN 1837, Harriet Martineau, an English visitor to the United States, remarked of the American woman that "indulgence is given her as a substitute for justice."[1] "She hears," Martineau wrote,

> oratorical flourishes on public occasions about wives and home, and apostrophes to woman: her husband's hair stands on end at the idea of her working, and he toils to indulge her with money: she has liberty to get her brain turned by religious excitements, that her attention may be diverted from morals, politics, and philosophy; and, especially, her morals are guarded by the strictest observance of propriety in her presence.[2]

As Martineau observed, religion became for many middle-class women "a substitute for the public life society foreclosed."[3] One group of middle-class women in Belton, Texas, were, however, able to turn the religious license allowed them into a way of living independently in what was in essence a separatist commune.[4]

During the last third of the nineteenth century, the unique phenomenon of a group calling themselves the Woman's Commonwealth came into being in Belton, a small-sized town in central Texas, sixty miles north of Austin, and forty miles south of Waco.[5] The commune, for this is what it eventually became, was

A more extensive treatment of this article appears in *Frontiers* VII: 2 (1983). A. Harriette Andreadis, "The Woman's Commonwealth: Utopia in 19th Century Texas," copyright © 1983 A. Harriette Andreadis.

made up of anywhere from thirty to fifty adult women and some children from eleven of the most respected families in town. Because their husbands and families were horrified and enraged by their behavior, and therefore unwilling that their disgrace be known, available records of the existence and activities of these women are rather scanty. For the most part, we must rely for information about them on court depositions from the legal battles in which they were involved, on some contemporary newspaper accounts, on the recorded accounts of their contemporaries, and on the folklore which their behavior generated.[6]

The women who joined the Woman's Commonwealth were regarded by their contemporaries as at best eccentric, as at worst fanatical and dangerous to the community. More recently, they have been rediscovered and hailed as a model for separatist feminism.[7] It is the intention of this essay to show that—even though they were unique—the shape that their quest for independence finally assumed was a consequence of the acceptable social forms available to them rather than a deliberate flouting of social convention.

The Woman's Commonwealth began in 1866 with Bible-study groups and prayer meetings. Their impetus was the sanctification first experienced by Martha McWhirter, who, with her husband, was one of the leaders of Belton's Methodist non-sectarian Sunday School movement. This sanctification was to be the women's own brand of non-sectarian Pentecostal Wesleyanism and held to the spiritual, rather than literal, truth of the Bible. As their community grew during the 1870's, these respectable middle-class women turned increasingly to celibacy, refusing to have sexual relations with their unsanctified husbands, and to the discovery of an independent economy, refusing to take money from unsanctified hands. These women, who were accustomed to having their household needs taken care of by servants, began to make money by selling butter and eggs, letting themselves out for household work, taking in laundry, chopping wood and selling it for a profit. By 1879, they had forged a communal economic system and several of the women were living at Martha McWhirter's house, her husband having moved out.[8] They were able to buy a productive farm outside

Belton and, by 1886, to begin building the Central Hotel, in which they eventually lived, and which was to be their major economic enterprise until they moved to Washington, D.C., in 1899. The Hotel flourished, was a major boon to travellers between Austin and Waco, and finally regained for them the lost respectability which had exacerbated their separatism. With their communal wealth they were able to travel and see something of the rest of the world, to have leisure to educate themselves in necessary skills—there were a dentist and a blacksmith among them—and to buy another farm and a hotel in Waco. Martha McWhirter died in 1904, but the women stayed together in Maryland, on a farm they had bought there, until at least 1918. Thus, their sanctification brought them together, set them apart, and enabled them to create their own full spiritual and economic independence.

Why did a group of middle-class women in the middle of Texas in the latter third of the nineteenth century do heavy manual labor to support themselves? Why wasn't it impossible for them to develop the system of living that they did? I believe that the answer to this question lies in the prevalence at the time of three social possibilities in the United States at large which also obtained in Belton. First, Women's Moral Reform Societies and Women's Voluntary Associations were an important social force throughout much of the United States. These organizations developed out of the tradition of private networks, Bible-study groups and prayer meetings which were a means of solidarity and cohesion for women, particularly in rural, semi-rural, and small-town areas. As we have seen, such was the case in Belton: women came together through their spiritual affiliations. Second, and most important to the Belton Woman's Commonwealth, Wesley's anti-Calvinist Methodism was strongly social reformist in its Evangelical Arminianism. This was the particular form of Pentecostal Protestantism which was called sanctification in Belton as well as in other parts of the country where revivalism had taken hold.[9] Third, utopian communities were rife during the nineteenth century both as a form of intellectual and social experiment and of religious belief; in all of these, the economy was communal and women shared in production.

The growth and influence of female moral reform societies and of voluntary organizations in the mid-nineteenth century have been documented by Mary P. Ryan, Barbara Berg, and Carroll Smith-Rosenberg.[10] Ryan, using Utica, New York, as a model community, has shown how the more formal organizations evolved from the traditional informal house-to-house networks which constituted women's usual social interactions.[11] That these networks should have solidified into formal organizations which exerted moral, religious, and political power in their communities is a striking example in American social history of how powerless groups used the socially sanctioned means available to them to exert public force for political change. Because the prerogatives of the "woman's sphere"[12] included moral influence and religious activity, women channelled their resentment of both public and private male domination into religiously motivated moral-reform activities.[13] They exerted pressure to reform male sexual promiscuity, to better the lot of prostitutes and of girls who might be potential prostitutes, to provide homes for orphans, to curb alcoholic abuse, and to further temperance. Thus, respectable nineteenth-century women might find a public outlet in reform activities to assuage what might be personal grievances at home by extending the areas of influence allotted to them. Women turned their personal friendships into political connections and their private feelings into religiously-sanctioned public causes.[14]

Mid-nineteenth century American society was also shaped by waves of religious revivalism as Calvinism and the Old School theology gave way to the impact of the Second Great Awakening (1795 to 1835)[15] and the Arminian heresy—the doctrine of individual free will and the conditionality of predestination—of a Protestantism which was becoming increasingly nonsectarian, social reformist ("humanitarian reform" included abolitionism and woman's suffrage), egalitarian, and inclined to give the individual more and more powers of self-determination.[16] The revival movement led by mid-nineteenth-century preachers like the Perfectionists Charles Grandison Finney and William Arthur, with its "evangelical ideology of the millennium" and its commitment to "second blessing" or entire sanctification (the individual reception of the Holy Ghost), in the post-war period "merged

without a break into what came to be called the social gospel."[17]
During the 1850's, a growing impulse for church union and
non-sectarianism consolidated the infant awakening of the first
decades of the century, so that by the late 1850's the Methodist
evangelical crusade for holiness was spreading westward.[18] The
reissuance of Finney's 1835 *Lectures on Revivals of Religion* in
1868, which "clearly marks the end of two centuries of Calvinism
and the acceptance of pietistic evangelicalism as the predominant faith of the nation,"[19] attests to the continuing evocative
power of evangelicalism and sanctification by grace into the latter half of the nineteenth century.[20] The participation of women
in this revivalism and in the reform activities spawned by it reflected not only the social acceptability of religious involvement
for women (submission to God reflecting the social passivity offi-
cially exacted of women) but also the growth of lay activity in
gospel work which was encouraged in women by the apostle
Peter's words at Pentecost: "And it shall come to pass in the last
days, saith God, I would pour out of my Spirit upon all flesh:
and your sons and your daughters shall prophesy" (Acts 2:17).[21]
This was a crucial element in precipitating Martha McWhirter's
initial sanctification and the consequent emergence of the Belton Woman's Commonwealth.

The proliferation of intentional communities during the
mid-nineteenth century in the United States undoubtedly expressed the highly idealistic character of that era, its belief in the
perfectability of social and economic relations as well as of the
individual soul. The followers of Saint-Simon, Fourier, and Robert Owen established utopian socialist communities whose main
intention was economic egalitarianism; the followers of Étienne
Cabet attempted to carry out the ideals of the French enlightenment—*liberté, égalité, fraternité*—by actualizing his literary utopia, *Voyage en Icarie* (1840); the founders of Brook Farm tried to
put into practice the intellectual ideals of Transcendentalism.

Only the Shakers, followers of the English spiritualist Ann
Lee, and the Oneidans, followers of the Perfectionist John
Humphrey Noyes, combined religious zeal and deviation from
conventional family structure (as did the Woman's Commonwealth) with economic communalism: the Shakers practiced celi-

bacy and the Oneidans practiced "complex marriage" and "male continence."[22] The holding of goods in common and task rotation were practiced by all the intentional communities, and submission to authoritarian rule by almost all. The Shakers and Oneidans, in addition, practiced an exceptional conformity to a religiously-infused authority and conformed to an extreme austerity in matters of personal habit and physical comfort. Though some have wished to believe that women were accorded more or less full equality among the Shakers and Oneidans, this was not the case.[23] They were considered inferior to men by Noyes at Oneida and they were not full participants in crucial decision-making, despite the fact that, among the Shakers at least, there were on occasion strong female authority figures in charge. However, women did share fully in production and in task rotation, as they did in other intentional communities. They were relieved of the burdens of the individual childcare by communalism. They were celibate among the Shakers and accorded sexual pleasure with multiple partners among the Oneidans. Women in these communities did have some time to themselves and were to some extent liberated from the rigid sex-role divisions enforced on women outside. Thus, if men were absent, an intentional community might offer to women—as it did in the unique instance of the Belton Woman's Commonwealth—a model for successful religious, economic, sexual, and emotional self-determination.[24]

The Woman's Commonwealth in Belton is of special historical significance to feminists because it represents the coalescence of these three important nineteenth-century social forms, any two of which would not have been sufficient to make its emergence possible. This community would have been impossible were it not for the economic egalitarianism enjoyed by women in other intentional communities, the tradition of women's private networks, and the tenets of Wesleyanism evangelicalism.

If there had been available to the Belton women only the tradition of private networks which allowed them to meet regularly at each other's houses, and the belief in salvation through personal revelation, or sanctification, and there had not been the possibility for developing complete economic self-sufficiency

through a communal arrangement, the Woman's Commonwealth could not have come into being. The prospect that, as
respectable middle-class wives and daughters of mostly well-to-
do citizens, they would have to humble themselves to such tasks
as selling eggs and butter to their neighbors, felling trees and
selling wood, doing laundry and providing domestic services,
was satisfying to their religious sense; but even these tasks could
not have provided an independent living wage to the women as
individuals. However, the formulation of the idea that economic
independence could be achieved through the sharing of work
and income was possible only because the intentional religious
community was already in existence (there were, in fact, several
in Texas) and because women, in particular, played crucially
productive economic roles in the most successful of these communities. The communal economy was the only available and
viable social form for the achievement of economic independence by women who were, individually, not trained to labor,
and who had no means or talents for economic self-sustenance.
Without economic communalism, they would have had to stay
with their husbands or starve.

The traditional Bible-study groups and prayer meetings enabled Martha McWhirter and the first of the "Sanctified Sisters"
to explore the meaning of their dreams and private revelations
and pursue their sanctification. The traditions of Bible-study and
prayer meeting made it possible for these women to meet safely
and regularly in their different homes for intimate discussion of
the state of their souls. The network was a forum for spiritual
expression, support, and exchange. It was here that they shared
the revealed truth that the sanctified should separate from the
unsanctified, both sexually and economically. In its critical initial
stages, the group began to emerge from the safe and intimate
environment of a women's house-to-house network.

If there had been available to the Belton women only the
tradition of women's private networks and the economic notions
of intentional communities, and there had not been available the
tenets of social reform and personal revelation embodied in
John Wesley's religious doctrines, there would have been no
necessary catalyst to convert a traditional women's private net-

work into a successfully functioning and stable communal economic enterprise. That they should have appropriated the power necessary to convert their women's network into an economically self-sustaining institution is unthinkable; they would have had to acknowledge to themselves, to their families, and to their community, what it would have been socially, psychologically, morally, and culturally impossible to admit: that emotional and financial dependence on their husbands was degrading and debilitating. The private revelations of sanctification provided an experience these women could share in their network—and, conversely, a motive for continuing to meet—and provided a mission which would explain their rejection of their husbands' sex and money as "unholy." The belief that was crucial in separating them from their husbands was revealed to them in the form of a prohibition against sharing the beds and finances of the unsanctified. Thus, personal revelation in the form of sanctification (as well as the implicit permission embodied in the social reformism of Wesley's doctrines) was the catalyst that transformed an informal network into an independent, economically viable, social unit that could be legally incorporated. Sanctification provided a religious justification for their economic vision.

As feminists, it is at our peril to view these women, as did their contemporary townspeople, as religious fanatics or, from our own vantage, as visionary feminists, as crypto-lesbians. They did not represent a historically deviant phenomenon. Rather, they were ordinary women committed to the amelioration of their daily lives who brought together into a unique synthesis the social forms available to them.

NOTES

1. *Society in America* (London, 1837 [rpt. New York, 1966]), III, 106.

2. *Ibid.*

3. Henry F. Bedford and Trevor Colbourn, *The Americans: A Brief History* (New York, 1976), p. 184.

4. The existence of these women was first called to my attention by Carol Shakeshaft in her brief description of them in

South Central Women's Studies Association Newsletter (Vol. 1, no. 3, p. 3) and in further personal conversations. I would also like to thank Lena Armstrong of the Belton Public Library for her generous assistance in locating pertinent documents. Terry Winant contributed invaluable suggestions for the argument which follows.

5. In 1871, Belton numbered 777 inhabitants; this figure more than doubled by 1880 to 2,000 inhabitants and, by 1900, there were 3,700 people in Belton. The 1975 U.S. Census gives the population as 10,989.

6. The summary historical account which follows has been compiled from these sources and from conversations with residents of Belton: A. L. Bennett, "The Sanctified Sisters," in *The Sunny Slopes of Long Ago*, ed. William M. Hudson and Allen Maxwell ([n.p.], [n.d.]), pp. 136–145; George Pierce Garrison, "A Woman's Community in Texas," *The Charities Review*, III (November, 1893), 26–46; Margarita Spalding Gerry, "The Woman's Commonwealth of Washington," *Ainslee's Magazine*, X (September 1902), no. 8, 133–141; Eleanor James, "The Sanctificationists of Belton," *The American West*, II (Summer 1965), no. 3, 67–73; Aline Roth, "Texas Women's Commonwealth," *The Houston Chronicle Magazine*, 19 November 1950; George W. Tyler, *The History of Bell County* (San Antonio, 1930); Records of the County Clerk in Belton: proceedings before the District Court of Bell County concerning E. J. Rancier vs Josephine Rancier (March 30, 1880); B. W. Haymond vs Ada McWhirter Haymond (December 1887); the appeal of Ada Haymond before the Supreme Court of Texas (June 15, 1891); insanity proceedings of Matthew and David Dow before the District Court (February 17, 1880); Gwendolyn Wright, "The Woman's Commonwealth," *Architectural Association Quarterly* VI, Nos. 3–4 (London, 1974), pp. 37–43.

7. See Shakeshaft, *SCWSA Newsletter*, and Wright, *AAQ*.

8. George McWhirter's "faith in his wife remained unshaken to the last" (Garrison, p. 40). Though he did not share her views, he always affirmed her honesty and sincerity. This is in striking contrast to the resentment, anger, and violence expressed by the husbands of other women who joined the Commonwealth. Visitors to Belton still go by the McWhirter house to see the bullet-hole in the front door made by a posse of angry husbands who came, unsuccessfully, to reclaim their wives.

9. The term *sanctification* was used with varying degrees of theological nuance by all the evangelical denominations.

10. See Mary P. Ryan, "The Power of Women's Networks: A Case Study of Female Moral Reform in Antebellum America," *Feminist Studies*, 5 (Spring 1979), no. 1, pp. 66–85; Barbara J. Berg, *The Remembered Gate: Origins of American Feminism, The Woman and the City, 1800–1860* (Oxford and New York: Oxford University Press, 1978), especially chapters 8 and 9; Carroll Smith-Rosenberg, *Religion and the Rise of the American City: The New York City Mission Movement, 1812–1870* (Ithaca and London: Cornell University Press, 1971), and "Beauty, the Beast, and the Militant Woman," in *A Heritage of Her Own*, ed. Nancy F. Cott and Elizabeth H. Pleck (New York: Simon and Shuster 1979), pp. 197–221.

11. See above n. 10.

12. Nancy F. Cott, *The Bonds of Womanhood: "Woman's Sphere" in New England, 1780–1835* (New Haven and London: Yale University Press, 1977), explores the parameters of women's power.

13. In a different context, Nancy F. Cott observes that "Conversion set up a direct relation to God's authority that allowed female converts to denigrate or bypass men's authority—to defy men—for God" ("Young Women in the Second Great Awakening," *Feminist Studies*, 3 [Fall 1975], nos. 1 and 2, p. 21).

14. See Ryan, "Women's Networks," pp. 80–81.

15. These dates are approximate.

16. William G. McLoughlin, ed., *Lectures on Revivals of Religion* [1835] by Charles Grandison Finney (Cambridge, Mass.: Harvard University Press, 1960), p. xiv, gives an especially incisive account of the popular appeal of the new revivalism. See also Timothy L. Smith, *Revivalism and Social Reform in Mid-Nineteenth Century America* (New York: Abingdon Press, and Nashville: University of Tennessee Press, 1957) for the complexities of church history at this time, particularly chapter 8, "Sanctification in American Methodism." Wesley had, of course, bequeathed to Methodism 100 years earlier the tenets of social reformism.

17. Smith, *Revivalism*, p. 235.

18. *Ibid.*, p. 83 ff., p. 118ff.

19. McLoughlin, Introduction to Finney, p. vii.

20. Robert Mapes Anderson, *Vision of the Disinherited: The*

Making of American Pentecostalism (New York and Oxford: Oxford University Press, 1979) gives a complete account of the Holiness Movement in the twentieth century, in which Pentecostal thought has set revivalism and social reform in opposition to each other.

21. Quoted in Smith, *Revivalism*, p. 82.

22. Maren Lockwood Carden, *Oneida: Utopian Community to Modern Corporation* (Baltimore: The Johns Hopkins University Press, 1969), and Peyton E. Richter, ed., *Utopias: Social Ideals and Communal Experiments* (Boston: Holbrook, 1971), pp. 137–147, provide relatively unbiased views of these controversial practices.

23. Mary P. Ryan, *Womanhood in America; From Colonial Times to the Present* (New York: New Viewpoints, 1975), pp. 175–176. Barbara Welter, *Dimity Convictions* (Athens, Ohio: Ohio University Press, 1976), pp. 83–102, and Barbara Brown Zigmund, "The Feminist Thrust of Sectarian Christianity," in *Women of Spirit: Female Leadership in the Jewish and Christian Traditions*, ed. Rosemary Reuther and Eleanor McLaughlin (New York: Simon and Schuster Touchstone Books, 1979), pp. 205–224, regard the situation of women in these communities, particularly among the Oneidans, as quite liberated. However, Carden concludes that, on the contrary, "There was no more attempt to define women as equal to men . . . than there was to assert that all the men were equally talented or equally spiritual. . . . The *Handbook* of 1875 is quite specific . . . even if given equal opportunities, women would do a task less well than men" (*Oneida*, p. 67).

24. Gerry records the following: " 'Oh, yes, we have had men among us,' they say; 'they are welcome if they are willing to live the life we do. But they never stay very long. You see it is in the nature of men to want to boss—and—Well, they find they can't' " (*Ainslee's*, p. 139).

❧ *Part Three*

CONTEMPORARY DIRECTIONS

Introduction

RUBY ROHRLICH

I N the twentieth century women figure prominently and passionately in both communal experiments and large-scale social movements and transformations. As documented by the papers in this section, women invented a variety of strategies to transcend their circumstances, in the United States, Spain, Denmark, Israel, and Scotland. Urgently conscious of the links between their liberation and the threat of planetary devastation, women have devised ingenious alternatives, on local, national, and international levels, to the patriarchal pathologies of both capitalist and socialist nations.

"The feminist critique of industrialism, socialist and capitalist, is the only fundamentally innovative analysis available," according to the French Marxist Roger Garaudy as quoted by the futurist Hazel Henderson.[1] She points out that feminist theory has incorporated much of the "libertarian-anarchist-utopian tradition," and has produced a rich synthesis infused with "anthropological and archaeological studies of matrilineal, matriarchal and polyandrous traditions." This has led to "innovative concepts of social organization characterized by androgynizing human behavior and social roles and liberating both sexes from their current roles as prisoners of gender."[2] Women's analyses of the use of language as an instrument of domination and, conversely, as a wellspring of revitalization, are also revolutionizing the field of linguistics as well as everyday speech; and their poetry, telling us of their discontents and fears, their strengths and visions, affirms the concept "the personal is political." In their endeavors to create the good life, women sometimes join

with men, but much more frequently now with other women.
Each way is replete with contradictions, frustrations, failures
and successes. So it goes in utopia.

A strategy that is increasingly occupying the attention of
feminist scholars is the use of women's culture by separatist
groups to gain political leverage and autonomy, as illustrated by
United States social workers and Spanish anarchists in the early
twentieth century, and by intentional communities in the United
States and Denmark in the 1960's and 1970's.

In "A Utopian Female Support Network" Blanche Cook
writes: "It becomes increasingly clear that women acting together to create institutions of their own have had by far the
greatest influence on civic life." The community formed by social workers and nurses in the Henry Street Settlement House,
for example, provided the emotional support and strength they
needed to overcome the "poverty and wretchedness" of New
York City's Lower East Side, and to work miracles in a corrupt
and brutal public arena. Working, living and travelling together,.
this first generation of twentieth-century United States feminists
was able to transform "their relationship to a society that validated women only as wives and mothers," and to withstand the
harassment and vilification that their suffragism and anti-impe-
rialism brought upon them. Branded as "asexual, lonely spinsters," these women-loving women, lesbians, hated injustice in
every form.

Like the settlement houses in New York and Chicago, *Mujeres Libres* ("Liberated Women") was founded before the turn of
the century within the Spanish anarchist movement, and by
1938, had 20,000 members throughout the Republican sector of
Spain.[3] Spanish anarchist women have a history of militancy,
particularly in their female unions in both rural and urban
areas. Despite the opposition of the male anarchists, *Mujeres
Libres* were convinced that only through their own autonomous
groups could they end the "triple enslavement of women to
ignorance, to capital and to men," as Ackelsberg points out.
"Ironically, women in *Mujeres Libres* and in many of the less
well-known female syndicates and associations went further in
implementing anarchist ideals than most sexually-integrated

anarchist institutions were willing to go";[4] and they were able to provide Spanish women with a community that was just as powerful emotionally and economically as the Church, "if only for a little while."[5] The truncation of *Mujeres Libres* was one of the major tragedies in the defeat of the Spanish Republic in 1939.

In Israel "the Zionist dream of a Jewish utopia has been overlaid with the dream of creating a socialist and humanist utopia, in which democracy and equality would flourish" (Pladott's essay on Broner's *A Weave of Women*, Part Four). But like women throughout the industrialized world, Israeli women rarely rise above the middle levels of all occupations; they are notably absent in national and local political life and, restricted to auxiliary roles in the armed forces, rank low in the military hierarchy. "When men are planning war," says a character in Broner's novel, "they are also planning the subjugation of women."[6]

Utopia within utopia, the kibbutz was to bring about, as one of its goals, a crucial change in gender roles. But men on the kibbutz dominate agriculture and industry, the mainstays, while women work mainly in education and services, and are additionally responsible for the household chores. However, during my fieldwork at Kfar Blum in 1970, I observed that while women and men performed different tasks in the family apartments, they did about the same amount of labor. Unlike the situation among the Hopi, differentiated gender roles in Israel give men central decision-making power, but have much less of an impact on kibbutz women than on city women with children who may suffer great hardship if they are divorced or widowed. Women are members of the kibbutz in their own right, and, like the Hopi, are economically independent of their husbands. Their economic returns do not depend on type of occupation. Moreover, the increasing mechanization of collective services has professionalized the work, and occupations within the communal educational system "are among the most respected and sought-after" in the kibbutz.[7]

Children of God (COG) was founded in 1968 in southern California, and spread throughout the U.S.A. and other areas of the "free world," reaching a peak membership of about 5,000 youth by 1978. COG cosmology blended Pentecostalism with criticisms of the "system," particularly of its sexual repressiveness and materialism. Of the three communities under discussion here COG alone made the so-called sexual revolution the core of its preachment and practice; women were urged to be both sexy and motherly. Initially, motherhood ranked higher; children, pregnant women and mothers received good care, and ambitious women could become leaders in such traditional areas as supervision of child care. Men, of course, were the policymakers, and when finances ran short as donations, the major source of income, dropped off, the middle-aged polygamous patriarch and founder of the group invented "flirty fishing," which required women (and sometimes men) to lure prosperous "fish" into the fold by having sex with them. In the process, motherhood became secondary, and some mothers were "abandoned and sometimes even turned away from colonies." By the 1980's, in the wake of the Jonestown tragedy, COG membership had largely dissipated.

Findhorn, a New Age spiritual community founded in Scotland in 1962, operates on principles diametrically opposed to those of COG, has little in common with any orthodox religion, and the many spin-off communities in Europe and the United States attest to its growing appeal. Findhorn seeks attunement with nature, and gained fame by growing huge vegetables in inhospitable soil (as noted in the movie *My Dinner with André*). Findhorn supports itself through a publishing plant, garden nursery, paying guests, and fees from the New Age conferences it holds. As at Twin Oaks, members express their affection for each other by "the embrace of hugging." Work is very important at Findhorn; it is "love in action," and "brings spirit into matter." Both women and men shovel manure, work in the kitchen, and fix the plumbing, so there are no gender roles. Most of the women are feminists, who respond sharply and negatively to manifestations of male chauvinism, especially in language. But, as Sheer discovered, sexism is not altogether absent; as sexual beings, older women are invisible. Few utopians, with the exception of Fourier and Noyes, have addressed themselves to the needs of older women.

Founded in 1966, Twin Oaks, near Louisa, Virginia, was

initially patterned on Skinner's *Walden II,* but it has long since veered away from behaviorism. "Equality and social justice are the commune's reigning values" and "since the advent of the women's liberation movement, the community interest in eliminating sex-role distinctions has risen."[8] Twin Oaks has a system of labor credits, which values all work equally, as at Findhorn; an hour of laundry earns equal credit with an hour of car repair or slaughtering cattle, and the unpaid labor of women vanishes, according to Weinbaum. Here, too, work is central, but there are no full-time jobs, and communal work allows plenty of time for leisure activities. The community supports itself primarily by the direct-mail sale of hammocks woven by the members.

Women's sexual preferences at Twin Oaks are diverse: heterosexual, lesbian, and bisexual. Motherhood and childhood experiences are community matters. The community decides how many births can be handled each year, finances artificial insemination when this is desired, and women earn labor credits throughout pregnancy. A father has as much contact with a child as a mother, and children receive much affection from other adults. Weinbaum notes that the lack of a primary "home/mother, working/father image" means that there is no "dependency upon a single source of love/hate/punishment/approval."

Members study the history of utopian societies and create networks with other intentional communities through publications and conferences. Twin Oaks is "developing its own culture and its own institutions through a slow and painful process of experiment and growth, and . . . shares in the utopian ideal of social reconstruction."[9]

Twentieth-century women's collectives are a direct offshoot of the contemporary women's movement, and began to emerge in the 1960's both in cities and rural areas. Many of the women who formed these collectives had initially tried living in mixed communities, but found them to be male-dominant. The collectives visited by Weinbaum during her year's quest for women's utopias in the United States were on rural farms which generally eked out a precarious existence based on economic exchange through barter and the sale of craft products. Socialization and economic discrimination have prevented these women from acquiring the business skills and financial resources necessary to create a viable economy. At Findhorn, too, "no woman member has the financial background and skills" needed to function in the executive branch of governance. The relatively few women who are now acquiring these skills in middle-level banking and industry are not those who are motivated to form collectives. But the farms that are exploring New Age spirituality and psychic phenomena provide important services, according to Weinbaum: they are a retreat where women who are "burnt out" may heal themselves, and they provide the opportunity to share with other women and to learn new skills.

In 1975, I visited women's collectives in Copenhagen, Denmark, and was introduced to their literature, particularly Phyllis Graber's paper, "Communities of the Heart: Women's Collectives in Denmark." The members of the Copenhagen groups, all comprising both lesbian and heterosexual women, had jobs or were students, and had joined together in collectives because of their common involvement in the women's movement, as well as for other reasons, as set forth below pretty much in their own words:

> The collective is part of the women's movement. We all speak the same language and are involved with the same problems. Living together means that we're putting our theories into practice, which forces us to adjust our theories.

> I was working in the front yard of our collective, sawing wood, chopping branches off the hedges, and ripping roots from the ground. I worked in a tank top, and you could see the strength of my shoulders and arms. Four neighborhood boys of about eleven looked on, very puzzled; they had never associated physical strength with women.

> Women are living in collectives to get the strength which most people, both male and female, deny them. When men are around, women often slip unconsciously into roles of dependence, physical and mental. Men have been taught to function as pillars of strength upon which women could lean, but the foundations of these pillars are crumbling as women learn to rely on themselves and on other women.

If you lose your job you're not really lost; you can get help from the people you're living with, and you get dinner every day. It cheers you up when you come home and see three or four of your close friends.[10]

Graber defines women's collectives as "communities of the heart, working together to realize shared goals." She is pessimistic about their future "because all society is against it." With increasing unemployment, the government is cutting day-care; "they want to get women back in the house, back in the nuclear family."

The time is long past when technological production is equated with progress. On the other hand, the view that technology is inherently alienating is anthropomorphic. As Baruch notes in the Introduction to Part Four, Mischa Adams' "Therrillium" "displays women's use of technology for the creation of art instead of the exercise of exploitative power. . . . It reveals a unity between performer and instrument, nature, technology, and art." Nor were technology and art separate and unrelated entities in the societies discussed in Part One; everyone was both artist and scientist.

In "Utopia in Question," Zimmerman urges us to evaluate the new technology in terms of whether it improves or further degrades women's status, both in the labor market and the home. She warns us that already it is being used to downgrade the work of secretaries; that, as computers become more widely used in the household women may be doing without pay the labor done by women who get paid, and find themselves more tightly bound to the house in the process. In addition, the new biological industries may lead to even greater male control of reproduction. Thus, more girls and women should enter technical fields, and we must demand public hearings on the impact of technology on environment and health.

More women are now entering the fields of architecture and urban planning. At a conference entitled "The House of Women: Art and Culture in the Eighties," held at California State University at Long Beach, November, 1983, urban planner and socialist feminist theorist Dolores Hayden, in her keynote address on the future of housing, work, and family life, offered the following useful diagram:[11]

POLITICS OF SPACE AND SOCIAL REPRODUCTION IN THE WOMEN'S MOVEMENT

Spatial Scale	Social Scale	Women's Movement 1848–1930	Women's Movement 1960–1983
body	biological reproduction	"domestic feminism"	reproductive rights
dwelling and residential neighborhood	reproduction of daily life	"material feminism"	"room of one's own"; male housework
city	reproduction of social relations	"social feminism"	"take back the night"
nation	reproduction of national political economy	suffrage	E.R.A.

During the last two decades the women's movement has recognized that language, as the primary socializing mechanism, reproduces women's subordination, and the papers by Gershuny and by Thorne, Kramarae, and Henley review the studies analyzing the ways in which women scholars are using language to help create egalitarian and cooperative institutions. Thorne, Kramarae, and Henley point out that feminists have given us the gift of a new meaning for power; instead of defining power as domination, we now define it as "energy, effective interaction and empowerment." As Gershuny notes, feminist writers merge "poetry and philosophy, history and myth, psychology and religion, and the personal with the political" and thereby transcend the "dualism, opposition, difference and dominance" that "characterize "patriarchal myths and metaphors." Indeed, this merging of disciplines is a major aspect of women's studies in contrast to the fragmented traditional curricula we now term "men's studies."

In *From the Legend of Biel* (discussed by Pearson, Part Four), Mary Staton shows how language can engender despair and fear in human beings (p. 176):

> Hidden deep in the sounds of their words was despair and fear. Repeated use of the words and phrases only reinforced those feelings. The essential thrust of their language was control and ownership [of land, animals, mates, progeny, emotions, ideas] where control and ownership was not possible.

And Wittig in *Les Guérillères* (as discussed by Farley, Part Four) insists that women must use the force of language to crack male history and to create their own culture (p. 134):

> They say that there is no reality before it has been given shape by words rules regulations. They say that in what concern them everything has to be remade starting from basic principles. They say that in the first place the vocabulary of every language is to be examined, modified, turned upside down, that every word must be screened.

Women writers are creating utopian fiction that offers us a multitude of alternatives to patriarchal society. They write about the murderous revenges we plan in the kitchen (Piercy's "What's that smell in the kitchen?"); the bloody agonies of sheer survival for black women, children and men (Lorde's "A Litany for Survival, and Shange's "Tulsa"); and the joy and excitement of using technology to repair and create (Whyatt's "The Craft of Their Hands").

NOTES

1. Hazel Henderson, *The Politics of the Solar Age* (Garden City, N.Y.: Anchor Books, 1981), p. 375.
2. Henderson, p. 370.
3. Temma Kaplan, "Other Scenarios: Women and Spanish Anarchism," in Renate Bridenthal and Claudia Koonz, eds., *Becoming Visible: Women in European History* (Boston: Houghton Mifflin Co., 1977), p. 415.

4. Kaplan, p. 419.

5. *Ibid.*

6. Esther Broner, *A Weave of Women* (New York: Holt Rinehart and Winston, 1978).

7. Dorit Padan-Eisenstark, "Image and Reality: Women's Status in Israel," in Ruby Rohrlich-Leavitt, ed., *Women Cross-Culturally, Change and Challenge* (The Hague: Mouton Publications, 1975), p. 503.

8. Rosabeth Moss Kanter, *Commitment and Community: Communes and Utopias in Sociological Perspective* (Cambridge, Mass.: Harvard University Press, 1972), pp. 22–23.

9. Kanter, p. 31.

10. Phyllis Graber, "Communities of the Heart: Women's Collectives in Denmark," [n.d., unpublished].

11. Published in Dolores Hayden's "The American Sense of Place and the Politics of Space," in Sylvia Lavin, ed., *American Architecture: Innovation and Tradition* (New York: Proceedings of a Columbia University Conference, 1983).

A Utopian Female Support Network: The Case of the Henry Street Settlement

BLANCHE WIESEN COOK

DICTIONARY choices offered for utopia include: "an imaginary and definitely remote place," "a place of ideal perfection," "an impractical scheme for social improvement." Of these choices, two relate to an actual experiment in living conducted by progressive women in the early years of this century. The Settlement House movement, created by Jane Addams in Chicago and Lillian Wald in New York City, may seem today "an impractical scheme for social improvement," but was then, for the women involved, a working situation or "place of ideal perfection." Under what circumstances and for whom might the *fin de siècle* settlements be seen as genuine centers of utopian living?

As we analyze women in relation to power, to force-fields of public influence, it becomes increasingly clear that women acting together to create institutions of their own have had by far the greatest influence on civic life. Some historical analysts have trivialized the settlement house movement by defining their contributions to the community as "social housekeeping." It would be far more helpful, I believe, to recognize these centers as institutions of influence and power that impacted on society in a variety of immediate, far-reaching, and permanent ways. Above all, they represented an entirely new way to organize social relations.

Whenever we think of a utopia, we think first of some kind

of community, a place where people who share ideas and sensibilities live and work together. Chicago's Hull House, founded in 1889, and the Henry Street Settlement, founded in 1895, represent a movement that enabled the first generation of twentieth-century feminists to transform their relationship to a society that validated women only as wives and mothers. Born daughters in a society that reared daughters to be dependent and servile, the female support network of the settlement house community enabled activist women to work with vigor, strength, and success in partisan and public arenas dominated by the corruption and brutality of big city bossism, laissez-faire capitalism, and misogynist politics that denied women the vote and access to opportunity and independence.

Public women, women who deal with politicians, financiers, professional philanthropists, and interest groups, depend on support from a wide variety of sources. Lillian Wald's profound friendship with Jacob Schiff secured a permanent base of financial security for the public work that she believed in. To insure that support she compromised whenever necessary to maintain his approval. It was not an equal friendship. He provided the support; she provided the services to the community of which he approved. Insofar as he shared her work, her vision, and her brand of social change, he supported her. For emotional sustenance, for a true community of interests and vision there was a more immediate network of alliances, the core of which lived in residence at Henry Street.

Wald's basic support group consisted of the long-term residents of Henry Street, notably Ysabella Waters, Annie Goodrich, Florence Kelley, Helene MacDowell, and Lavinia L. Dock. Except for Kelley, a social reformer best known for her work with the National Consumer's League, Wald's closest associates were the nurses who with her created the public health and university-trained nursing movement. They were her "steadies" and whatever special friend came or went in Wald's life, they were there—determining the hours, sustaining relentless schedules, expanding always the horizon of their social commitment. Daily they read the morning newspaper together over coffee. With each breakfast, they determined the course of each new struggle. Their plans were ambitious. Their success rate was remarkable.

They had built their utopia in the heart of an unacceptable environment of poverty and wretchedness that they sought to change fundamentally. When Lillian Wald first moved to the Lower East Side, it was as crowded as the most densely populated cities of India. In one neighborhood there were almost one thousand persons to the acre. Each apartment had its own heart-rending situation that required the work of the settlement house women. As Wald recalled:

> Bad as the streets were, the conditions of most of the houses were worse. Filth and grime accumulated on the stairs, sanitation was primitive and bathtubs were scarce. Rear tenements in which there was no running water looked down on yards filled with debris; children played on heaps of offal, while families of six or more were herded together in one or two rooms. . . .

Lillian Wald and her circle determined to correct every one of these outrages. They did so not in terms of charity, which they correctly perceived reinforced poverty and humiliating circumstances, but in terms of institutional change that would be permanent and public. With the creation of each new playground, public health program, or child welfare bureau they urged that the continuance of their effort be taken over by the government. They insisted that the state was responsible for social welfare. In 1940, on the eve of her death, Lillian Wald commented contentedly that she was satisfied with her work: Not only had it brought her much pleasure and love, but it was now insured by the New Deal. The Roosevelt government had fulfilled the vision of her utopian community during an era of national depression and suffering. Today, as each of these programs is being truncated or abandoned entirely, it is helpful to recall the victories.

By 1897 the Henry Street nurses and reformers had persuaded New York City's Health Department to assign a team of 150 physicians to spend one hour a day in New York's public schools. Wald assigned Nurse Lina Rogers to make regular school visits and subsequently founded a school nurse program. Eventually the Bureau of Child Hygiene was formed to insure a visiting nurse for each public school. At the same time, they introduced the "penny lunches," a program to insure a hot, nutritional mid-day meal for each public school child. (Today, this program is under severest attack. With rare, perhaps unparallelled, antagonism to the health and well-being of the nation's children President Ronald Reagan has called for an end to subsidized, nutritious lunches for school children and in the interim has designated ketchup a "vegetable"). Concerned with the emotional life of the young people of their neighborhood, the Henry Street workers created the Social Halls Association, and built auditoriums for public lectures, concerts, political meetings, dining halls, ballrooms, pool rooms, and social centers as well as study halls for children who had no private space to study or to practice musical instruments. The entire CRMD program for teachers of handicapped and retarded children originated at Henry Street under the sponsorship of Lillian Wald and Elizabeth Farrell. New York's first public playground was the backyard at Henry Street, equipped with flowers, sand piles, swinging hammocks, parallel bars and overhead ladders. The movement for public playgrounds and swimming pools was institutionalized by Wald and her coworkers through the National Playground Association and the Outdoor Recreation League in 1898.

Lillian Wald's most abiding contribution to the health of New York City and to the nation was the creation of the Visiting Home Nurse Service. By 1932, the Service made over 600,000 visits a year. Over 250 nurses toured the city, traveling from borough to borough by trolley and ferry, visiting sick and needy people who, prior to the existence of this corps of nurses who charged only a nominal fee, had customarily suffered and frequently died needlessly of preventable and curable diseases. The existence of the Visiting Home Nurse Service remains a challenge for public health care in the United States, the only industrial country besides South Africa where nationally-insured public health care is still not guaranteed.

The Visiting Nurses who set off each day from Henry Street 80 years ago were radical practitioners, as well as radical politically. They gave advice on nutrition and on disease prevention. Their vision was holistic, and bore no resemblance to the medical engineering that dominates and limits so much of Western medicine today.

As Lavinia Dock explained in a 1907 speech, in which she discussed the "great, urgent, throbbing, pressing social claims of our day and generation":

> Of old the nursing sisters of the religious orders, closely confined in shackles of mental subjugation and social renunciation, consciously withdrew from all participation in things of the world, had no idea of preventive or constructive reforms, held no radical hopes of remaking the social order about them, but gave their lives to an unquestioning service of reparative and ameliorative devotion. . . . We have cast off their shackles, because we refuse to be cut off from the world about us. We have declared our principles to arise from another basis than theirs. We belong to an age which rejects the theory that misery and sickness are unpreventable— which is learning to place prevention before amelioration, which is responding to the thrill of the discovery that the human race, as well as raw materials, is capable of construction, of indefinite development and improvement; that human society can be voluntarily and consciously built into nobler and fairer forms than those of the past. . . .

Who were these women and how did they live? Their own words tell us that they lived fully and they lived well. They lived together, travelled together, and worked together. The networks of love and support that they created were the very sources of strength that enabled them to function. Their living arrangement was a positive choice in a society that offered little access to freedom or economic independence for women. These companionate women who lived together all their adult lives have been branded, by traditional historians, on no evidence whatsoever, "lonely, asexual spinsters." Homophobia, a bigotry that declares same-sex friendships an evil before God or a mental disease or both, continues to erase the sexual aspects of the relations of some of these women, who because they appear in history as moral and ordinary, if not exemplary and extraordinary, have had the basic elements of their lives trivialized and ignored. Our prejudices are such that it has been considered less critical to label a women "asexual" rather than "lesbian." As recently as 1977 Anita Bryant's "Save Our Children" campaign against homosexuals was aimed at public women and men— social workers, teachers, nurses and attorneys—who choose to live together and to love each other.

But the residents of the settlement house utopias were also criticized and reviled in their own time. During the suffrage struggles they were harassed and jailed. During World War I, their anti-imperialist and anti-militarist activities subjected them to vile epithets, mountains of hate mail, and significant losses of funds so needed for the continuance of their public works. During the Red Scare of the 1920's and 1930's, they were red-baited. Both Lillian Wald and Jane Addams, and most of their co-workers, were listed as part of the red web of traitors who threatened America with subversion and upheaval. In 1935, the year of her death, Jane Addams was called the most dangerous woman in the U.S. by self-proclaimed "patriots."

Supported by the loving energy and loyalty of their own communities, the settlement house workers remained steadfast and visionary through decades of criticism and anguish. They did their work as they had to do it—compromising when necessary, boldly advancing when possible. Their interests were as wide as the world, and their passions ran deep—passion for justice, passion for social change. They helped to found the National Women's Trade Union League to promote safe and healthful industrial conditions, an eight-hour day, and decent wages. They created the federal Children's Bureau to campaign against child labor, and to work for the educational and economic needs of children in a systematic way. The first meetings of the National Association for the Advancement of Colored People (NAACP) were held at Henry Street, the only public facility in New York City where an integrated meeting was possible. They founded the Woman's Peace Party, the American Union Against Militarism, and a variety of organizations that sought to avoid war, and to create world-wide conditions of social, political and economic order that would guarantee international stability, and peace.

In 1937, Lillian Wald was widely honored on her seventieth birthday. In response she said:

> If you look about you will find the settlement, for one thing, a demonstration of what can be accomplished in a comparatively short time by people who believe in one another and have learned to work together, who worked well and worked hard. The opportunity of accomplishing this is the greatest gift. . . .

But, Lillian Wald insisted, it was just the beginning. Her goal, to end war, poverty, unemployment, to establish freedom, security, and global harmony depended on the "organized action" of future generations who would commit themselves with as much vigor and vision as she and her friends had committed themselves. For Lillian Wald and her co-workers the journey had been utopian. She died surrounded by love and content in her belief that the future would fulfill the insignia she had designed for Henry Street Nurses on her trip to Japan in 1910. It signified "we are all one family."

NOTES

For a more detailed analysis of the lives of Lillian Wald, Jane Addams and the settlement house community see B. W. Cook, "Female Support Networks and Political Activism," *Chrysalis* 3, reprinted by Out and Out Books (1979), and in Linda Kerber and Jane DeHart Matthews, eds., *Women's America* (New York: Oxford University Press, 1982).

I am grateful to Clare Coss for her essay on Lillian Wald and to Teresa E. Christy for her series on nursing pioneers, "Portrait of a Leader," in *Nursing Outlook*. See especially Christy's "Lillian D. Wald," *Nursing Outlook* (March 1970), pp. 50–54; "Annie Warburton Goodrich," *Nursing Outlook* (August 1970), pp. 46–50; "Lavinia Lloyd Dock," *Nursing Outlook* (June 1969), pp. 72–75. See especially Bea Siegel's biography of Lillian Wald.

Other quotations in this essay are from S. J. Woolf, "Miss Wald at 70. . . ," *New York Times Magazine*, 7 March 1937; "Nation Honors Lillian Wald on 70th Birthday," *New York Herald Tribune*, 11 March 1937.

Mujeres Libres *and the Role of Women in Anarchist Revolution*

MARTHA A. ACKELSBERG

A REVOLUTIONARY movement which attempts to establish a new society must reflect an understanding of the life experiences of those who participate in it as a first step to engaging them in the revolutionary process. The need is particularly acute—and the failures singularly striking—in the case of women, whose daily life experiences are often quite different from those of men. While many revolutionary movements have attempted to incorporate women and have even made commitments to overcome their subordination, most have floundered over the differences between men's and women's lives. Where the subordination of women is severe, or when the context in which women live their lives is substantially different from that in which men live theirs, separate organizations will often be necessary.

In May, 1936, a group of anarchist women founded *Mujeres Libres,* the first autonomous, proletarian feminist organization in Spain.[1] They had as their goal to end the "triple enslavement of women, to ignorance, to capital, and to men." The struggles they

*Research for this paper was funded, in part, by a fellowship from the American Association of University Women and, in part, by a grant from the Andrew W. Mellon Foundation to the Smith College Project on Women and Social Change. I am grateful to Kathryn Pyne (Parsons) Addelson, Anne Balazs, Donna Robinson Divine, Temma Kaplan, and Robin Stolk for helpful comments on earlier drafts of the article. A more extensive version of this article appears in *Feminist Studies.*

confronted highlight the problematic role of women in revolutionary movements.

The experience of anarchists should be of particular interest to those concerned with the place of women in utopian visions, since anarchists, in theory at least, are committed to equality and oppose hierarchies of any sort. Equality implies that the experiences of one group cannot be taken as normative for all and that, in a fully egalitarian society, there can be no institutions through which some exercise social, economic, or political power over others. The anti-hierarchical perspective has important implications for the process of social revolution as well as for the model of a new society. Anarchists argue that revolutionary activity must begin with the concrete realities of people's lives and that the process itself must be a transformative one. Means are inseparable from ends. People can establish, and learn to live in, a non-hierarchical society only through non-hierarchical, egalitarian forms of revolutionary activity. In opposing claims that hierarchy is essential to order, anarchists argue that coordination can be achieved either through "propaganda by the deed," which brings adherents by the power of the positive example it sets, or by "spontaneous organization," which implies that both the form and the goals of an organization are set by the people whose needs it expresses.

Finally, anarchists recognize that people whose life circumstances keep them in positions of subordination and lack of control cannot easily transform themselves into self-confident, self-directed people. Extensive "preparation" for such participation is an essential part of the process of personal transformation. But such preparation, if it is not to take a hierarchical form, can take place only through people's experience of new and different forms of social organization. To be effective, such preparation has to respond to the different life experiences of the people whose needs it attempts to address.

In Civil War Spain, women constituted a special group, with their own particular needs. Their subordination—both economic and cultural—was much more severe than that of men. Rates of illiteracy were higher among women than among men.

Those women who did work for wages were relegated to the lowest-paid jobs in the most oppressive work conditions. Men and women lived their lives in very different ways, in some areas almost as members of separate societies.

Nevertheless, although those differences should have provided striking evidence of the need for a revolutionary organization to address the specific subordination of women, the mainstream of the Spanish anarchist movement refused to acknowledge either the specificity of women's oppression or the legitimacy of separate struggle to overcome it. Only *Mujeres Libres* actively articulated a perspective which recognized, and addressed, the particularity of women's experience.

While committed to the creation of an egalitarian society, Spanish anarchists exhibited a complex attitude toward the subordination of women and what would be necessary to overcome it. Some argued that women's subordination stemmed from the division of labor by sex, from women's "domestication" and consequent exclusion from the paid labor force. To overcome it, women would have to join the labor force as workers, along with men, and struggle in unions to improve the position of all workers. Others insisted that women's subordination flowed from broad cultural phenomena, and reflected a devaluation of women and their activities mediated through family and church. That devaluation would end, along with those institutions, with the establishment of anarchist society.

But the subordination of women was at best a peripheral concern of the anarchist movement as a whole. Few men were willing to give up the power over women they had enjoyed for so long.[2] Probably reflecting the majority position within the movement, some denied that women were oppressed in ways that required particular attention. Federica Montseny, for example, the anarchist intellectual who later served as Minister of Health in the Republican Government during the War, while acknowledging that "the emancipation of women" was a "critical problem of the present time," insisted that the appropriate goal was not the accession of women to positions currently held by men, but the restructuring of society, which would liberate all.

"Feminism? Never! Humanism always!"[3]

A small minority within the movement recognized that women faced sex-specific forms of subordination which needed particular attention. But many of these insisted that the struggle to overcome this subordination, whether in society at large or within the anarchist movement, must not take place in separate organizations. They found support for their position in the anarchist perspective on social change, particularly the emphasis on the unity of means and ends,[4] and on a strategy of direct action. This perspective justified opposition to "separate struggle" on the ground that, since the aim of the movement was the creation of a non-sexist society in which men and women would interact as equals, struggle to achieve that end could take place only in organizations in which men and women participated equally. According to this view, direct action, the strategy of basing organization on people's lived experience, did not extend so far as to justify an independent organization oriented to the needs of women.

In short, while some groups within the organized anarchist movement recognized the specific oppression of women and the sexism of men within the anarchist movement, mainstream anarchist organizations devoted little attention to issues of concern to women, and denied the legitimacy of separate organizations to address those issues.[5] Those women who insisted on the specificity of women's oppression and on the need for separate struggle to overcome it, created an organization of their own: *Mujeres Libres.*

The insistence on a separate organization reflected their analysis of women's subordination.[6] First, *Mujeres Libres* devoted specific attention to the problems that were of particular concern to women: illiteracy, economic dependence and exploitation, ignorance about health care, child care, and sexuality. Second, they insisted that engagement in struggle requires a changed sense of self, which could be developed by women only if they acted independently of men, in an organization designed to protect new self-definitions. Finally, a separate and independent organization was essential to challenge the masculinist hierarchy of the CNT (the anarcho-syndicalist labor confederation) and of the anarchist movement as a whole. The organization addressed each dimension of women's "triple enslavement": ignorance, economic exploitation, and subordination to men within the family.

Programmatically, the organization focused most of its attention on "ignorance," which the founders believed contributed to women's subordination in every sphere of life. *Mujeres Libres* mounted a massive literacy drive to provide the foundation necessary for an "enculturation" of women. Literacy would enable women better to understand their society and their place in it, and to struggle to improve it.[7] *Mujeres Libres* insisted that "cultural backwardness" prevented many women from active engagement in the struggle for revolutionary change. The tools of literacy were also important for the development of women's self-confidence.

To address the roots of subordination in economic dependence, and, in particular, the extreme sexual division of labor which relegated women to the lowest-paid work, under the most oppressive conditions, *Mujeres Libres* developed a comprehensive employment program with a heavy focus on education. They worked closely with CNT unions, and organized support, training, and apprenticeship programs for women entering the paid labor force. In rural areas, they sponsored agricultural training programs.[8] In addition, they set up and supported child-care facilities, both in neighborhoods and in factories. And they fought for equalization of salaries between men and women.[9]

However, they directed little attention to the sexual division of labor itself. Much recent feminist analysis has examined the relationships among monogamy, childbirth, child-rearing, and a differential labor-force participation and the subordination of women. Neither *Mujeres Libres*, nor any other anarchist or feminist organization in Spain at the time, questioned that primary responsibility for child-rearing and domestic activities would remain with women.

While Amparo Poch y Gascón, a founder of *Mujeres Libres*, criticized both monogamy and the assumption that marriages could be "contracted, in practice, for always,"[10] the majority of women in *Mujeres Libres* probably disagreed with her rejection of marriage and monogamy. But the organization did criticize extreme forms of male dominance in the family.

There was greater agreement within the organization on other manifestations of women's "cultural" subordination. Prostitution expressed the connections between economic and sexual subordination most clearly. *Mujeres Libres* set up *liberatorios de prostitución*, centers where former prostitutes could be supported while they "retrained" themselves for better lives. The organization also issued appeals to anarchist men not to patronize prostitutes, and pointed out that to do so was to continue patterns of exploitation they were, presumably, committed to overcome.[11]

Mujeres Libres also directed attention to health care. They trained nurses to work in hospitals and replace the nuns who had previously monopolized nursing care.[12] They mounted extensive educational and hygiene programs in maternity hospitals, especially in Barcelona, and attempted to overcome women's ignorance about their own bodies, and their sexuality, an ignorance which was yet another source of women's sexual subordination.[13]

Educational programs to eliminate cultural subordination extended to children as well as to adult women. *Mujeres Libres* sponsored child-rearing courses for mothers to enable them better to prepare their children for life in a libertarian society.[14] They also developed new forms of education for children, which would challenge both bourgeois and patriarchal values and prepare children to develop a critical conscience of their own.

Nevertheless, *Mujeres Libres'* activities and propaganda reflected some ambivalence about women's role in society, in revolutionary struggle, and even in their challenge to traditional family roles. At least some of the appeals to women to go to work outside the home and to take advantage of the day-care facilities set up at the factories suggest that this "sacrifice" was to be only temporary.[15]

But whatever the limits of *Mujeres Libres'* analysis and program, its propaganda was different from that of other women's organizations at the time. Most of these were merely the "women's auxiliary" of various party organizations, and urged women to play a supportive role in the struggle against fascism.

Mujeres Libres, however, argued consistently that women's emancipation need not await the conclusion of the war, and that
women could best help both themselves and the war effort by
insisting on their equality and participating as fully as possible in
the ongoing struggle.[16]

To overcome woman's subordination and make possible her
full participation in revolutionary struggle required more than
an attack on the sources of subordination, however. Women's
consciousness had to be changed, so that they could begin to see
themselves as independent, effective actors in the social arena.

Mujeres Libres' program reflected their belief that most
women were not prepared to take a fully equal role in the ongoing social revolution. They could best prepare for that role by
participating in a libertarian but explicitly women's organization
which had, as its major function, the empowerment of women to
overcome the ignorance and lack of self-confidence which accompanied their subordination. "Consciousness raising" was,
therefore, an essential aspect of the program. Through talks
and discussion groups, the organization attempted to overcome
women's reluctance to participate, by providing them with information and with opportunities to speak out and take action.

Finally, *Mujeres Libres* challenged the sexism of anarchist
organizations. Unless the masculinist atmosphere were challenged, they argued, no anarchist strategy or program could
hope to be successful—especially not in appealing to women.
Too often, women who attended discussion and study sessions
were ignored or ridiculed.[17] If women were not treated with
respect, then informal educational gatherings became just one
more arena for the subordination of women.

Mujeres Libres' challenge to the anarchist movement was organizational in another sense, as well. In October, 1938, it re-
quested recognition as an autonomous branch of the libertarian
movement, equivalent to such organizations as the FAI or the
FIJL.[18] The response of movement spokesmen was negative.
They refused to recognize the credentials of members of *Mujeres
Libres* (as an autonomous organization) at a conference of the
libertarian movement, and insisted that "a specifically women's
organization would be an element of disunity and inequality

within the libertarian movement, and that it would have negative consequences for the development of the interests of the working class."[19]

The women of *Mujeres Libres* were puzzled by this response. They did not understand why the movement accepted an organization for young people, but not one for women. For some of these women, the explanation was sexism: the unwillingness of male anarchists to take seriously the issue of women's subordination.[20] Others interpreted it more as an indication of the lack of understanding on the part of male anarchists of the dimensions of women's subordination. Members of *Mujeres Libres* who met with leaders of the CNT reported, for example, that CNT leaders agreed to "accept" *Mujeres Libres* as part of the movement—even to *fund* its activities—on the condition that *Mujeres Libres* would allow the *movement* to determine its programs and set its priorities. But it was precisely that autonomy that the women refused to cede.[21] Their experiences with this Congress confirmed the necessity of a separate organization which would confront such issues on a continuing basis.

The claim that an organization specifically devoted to the needs of women was inappropriate to an anarchist movement seems to contradict the movement's explicit commitment to direct action. Specifically, it negates the policy that organization derives from people's lived experiences and perceived needs. Leaders of the movement seemed willing to accept this conclusion in the case of young people. Why were they unwilling to do so in the case of women?

The crucial difference between the two cases seems to be the *focus* of the organization, rather than the nature of its membership. Although the youth organization, FIJL, addressed itself only to young people, its project was the anarchist project, in both the short and the long term. *Mujeres Libres*, as an autonomous women's organization, was different. Not only did it address itself specifically to women, it also set up a separate and independent set of goals. Its challenge to male dominance within the anarchist movement threatened, at least in the short run, to upset the structure and practice of existing anarchist organizations. That difference may well account for a substantial amount of the opposition to a separate organization for women.[22]

CONCLUSIONS

The women of *Mujeres Libres* found support for their anti-hierarchical goals and their strategy of direct action within the anarchist tradition. But their advocacy of separate struggle stemmed from more than a commitment to direct action and to meeting people's needs on their own terms. It developed, as well, from an analysis of the particular nature of Spanish society and the place of women in it. Members of *Mujeres Libres* insisted that, within the context of Spanish society, joint action would only perpetuate existing patterns of male dominance. Women's subordination had to be confronted directly if women were to be able to participate equally with men.

Mujeres Libres shared with mainstream anarchists an egalitarian vision—both of the society they hoped to create and of the movement which would create it. They agreed that truly revolutionary change would require alliances of women with men. But they insisted that unless equality emerged within that coalition, there was no guarantee either of an egalitarian revolutionary process or of an egalitarian society. The women of *Mujeres Libres* defined themselves not as women who were struggling against men, but as one of many potential groups participating in a vast coalition for social change. In their view, the only way to enable women to overcome their subordination was to struggle through an organization which built on the particular experience of women. Sometimes, a recognition of diversity is the most effective route to change and unity.

NOTES

1. Many of the founders were professional or semi-professional women. Still, the vast majority of its members (who numbered approximately 20,000 in July 1937) were working-class women, and its goals were different from those which were

characteristic of bourgeois feminist organizations, e.g., access to higher education and professional occupations.

2. See, for example, the comments of the national secretary of the CNT in 1935, in response to a series of articles on the woman's issue: "We know it is more pleasant to give orders than to receive . . . That is reality. And, in the face of that, to ask men to give up [their privileges] is to dream." Mariano R. Vazquez, "Avance: Por la elevación de la mujer," *Solidaridad Obrera* (October 10, 1935), p. 4.

3. "Feminismo y humanismo," *La revista blanca* 2 (October 1, 1924).

4. See, for example, Martha A. Ackelsberg, "The Possibility of Anarchism: The Theory and Practice of Non-Authoritarian Organization" (Ph.D. diss., Princeton University, 1976), chapter 5; John P. Clark, "What Is Anarchism?" in *Nomos XVIII, Anarchism,* ed. J. R. Pennock (New York: New York University Press, 1978), pp. 3–28; Ackelsberg and Parsons, "Anarchism and Feminism," (Northampton, Mass.: Smith College, 1978): Daniel Guerin, *Anarchism* (New York: Monthly Review Press, 1970); Colin Ward, *Anarchy in Action* (New York: Harper Torchbooks, 1973).

5. For a more complete account of these debates, see Mary Nash, "Dos intelectuales anarquistas frente al problema de la mujer; Federica Montseny y Lucía Sanchez Saornil," *Convivium* (Barcelona: Universidad de Barcelona, 1975), pp. 73–79; and *Mujer y Movimiento obrero en España, 1931–1939* (Barcelona: Editorial Fontamara, 1981), especially chapters 1 and 2.

6. The analysis to follow relies heavily on interviews and conversations I have had with Spanish anarchist women who were engaged in these debates and activities at the time of the Civil War. The interviews were conducted in Spain during the spring of 1979, August 1981, and winter of 1981–82.

7. " 'Mujeres Libres': La mujer ante el presente y futuro social," *Sídero-metalurgía* (Revista del sindicato de la Industria Sídero-metalúrgica de Barcelona) 5 (November, 1937), p. 9; also Pilar Grangel, interview with author, Montpellier, France, December 31, 1981.

8. Mary Nash, ed., *"Mujeres Libres" España 1936–39,* Serie Los Libertarios 1 (Barcelona: Tusquets Editor, 1976), pp. 29–30; and F. N. de Mujeres Libres, *Actividades de la Federación Nacional, Mujeres Libres* (Barcelona, 1937).

9. Temma Kaplan, "Spanish Anarchism and Women's Liberation," *Journal of Contemporary History* 6, no. 2 (1971), pp. 106–8; Kaplan, "Other Scenarios: Women and Spanish Anarchism," in Renate Bridenthal and Claudia Koonz, eds., *Becoming Visible* (Boston: Houghton Mifflin Co., 1977), pp. 400–21; and Nash, *"Mujeres Libres."*

10. "La autoridad en el amor y en la sociedad," *Solidaridad Obrera* (27 Septiembre 1935), p. 1; see also *La vida sexual de la mujer*, Cuadernos de cultura: Fisiología e higiene, no. 4 (1932), p. 32.

11. For an example of an appeal, see Nash, *Mujeres Libres*, pp. 186–87. On the campaign in general, see Carmen Alcalde, *La mujer en la Guerra civil española* (Madrid: Editorial Cambio 16, n.d.), pp. 161–63 and Kaplan, "Spanish Anarchism," pp. 108–9.

12. Suceso Portales, Interview with author, Móstoles, Madrid, June 29, 1979; also Luzdivina Parera, interviews with author, Sitges, July 15 and 22, 1979; Lola Iturbe, interviews with author, Alella and Barcelona, August 3 and 4, 1981; and Azucena Fernandez, interview, August 15, 1981.

13. Poch y Gascón, *La vida sexual*, pp. 10–26; also Nash, *Mujeres Libres, passim*, and interviews with Mercedes Comaposada, Paris, January 5, 1982; Azucena Fernandez, August 15 and December 27, 1981; Enriqueta Rovira, Castellnaudray, December 28 & 29, 1981; Pepita Carpena, Montpellier, December 30, 1981.

14. "La mujer y su importancia en la sociedad proletaria," *Sidero-metalurgía* 1 (October 1937): 3; Federación Nacional de Mujeres Libres, *Actividades;* and Nash, *Mujeres Libres* pp. 191–230. See also interview with Pilar Grangel, Montpellier, France, December 31, 1981.

15. Nash, *Mujeres Libres,* pp. 86, 96, 205–6.

16. Alcalde, *La mujer,* pp. 142–3, 154.

17. Mary Nash, *Mujer y movimiento obrero en España, 1931–1939* (Barcelona: Editorial Fontamara, 1981), pp. 33–37, 70–76.

18. The "libertarian movement" was another, more general, name for the anarchist movement. The term came into common usage only in 1937–38. That larger movement included within its ranks the CNT (the anarcho-syndicalist labor confederation), the FAI (Iberian Anarchist Federation) and the FIJL (Libertarian Youth Organization).

19. See Nash, *"Mujeres Libres,"* p. 19.

20. Nash, "La Mujer en las organizaciones de izquierda en España (1931–1939)," Ph.D. Dissertation, Universidad de Barcelona, 1977, pp. 670ff; Portales, 1979.

21. Mercedes Comaposada and Soledad Estorach, interviews, Paris, January 4, 5, 6, 1982.

22. It should also be noted that the Spanish anarchist movement had never been free of what might be termed "organizational fetishism." The movement which had been split by controversy in earlier periods continues to be so today, between "pure anarchists" and "syndicalists." See John Brademas, *Anarcosindicalismo y revolución en España (1930–1937)*. Traducción Castellana de Joaquín Romero Maura (Barcelona: Ariel, 1974), pp. 76–86 on the "treintista" episode. A concern for "organizational loyalty," then, is not unique to the opposition to *Mujeres Libres*.

I wish to express my thanks to Paul Mattick and Molly Nolan and other participants in the study group on Women in European Societies of the Center for European Studies, Harvard University, with whom I discussed these and other issues at a seminar on May 9, 1980.

A Litany for Survival

AUDRE LORDE

FOR those of us who live at the shoreline
standing upon the constant edges of decision
crucial and alone
for those of us who cannot indulge
the passing dreams of choice
who love in doorways coming and going
in the hours between dawns
looking inward and outward
at once before and after
seeking a now that can breed
futures
like bread in our children's mouths
so their dream will not reflect
the death of ours;

For those of us
who were imprinted with fear
like a faint line in the center of our foreheads
learning to be afraid with our mother's milk
for by this weapon
this illusion of some safety to be found
the heavy-footed hoped to silence us
For all of us
this instant and this triumph
We were never meant to survive.

And when the sun rises we are afraid
it might not remain
when the sun sets we are afraid
it might not rise in the morning
when our stomachs are full we are afraid
of indigestion
when our stomachs are empty we are afraid
we may never eat again
when we are loved we are afraid
love will vanish
when we are alone we are afraid
love will never return
and when we speak we are afraid
our words will not be heard
nor welcomed
but when we are silent
we are still afraid.

But it is better to speak
remembering
we were never meant to survive.

Women in the Children of God: "Revolutionary Women" or "Mountin' Maids"?

RUTH ELIZABETH WANGERIN

IN January 1971, NBC-TV's "First Tuesday" featured a religious commune on a ranch called the Texas Soul Clinic. As the camera scanned a kitchen full of young women in long cotton-print dresses who were reciting Bible verses in unison while they cooked and washed dishes, the narrator commented, "There's no women's liberation in the Children of God." A few years later during my fieldwork for my dissertation in anthropology I asked the "food deacon" of another Children of God "colony" what she thought about women's liberation. "Actually," she replied, "I feel more free now than I ever did before."

The Children of God (COG) was founded in 1968 in southern California by a family of Pentecostal missionaries named Berg. After moving to the Texas ranch, and particularly after the showing of the TV special, the group attracted large numbers of American youth, hippies as well as religious people. The women I met in the group between 1973 and 1982 appeared very much like other young American women, except that they seemed to have been a bit more disillusioned about the possibilty of finding happiness somewhere along the life-path recommended by home, church, and school, and they believed that Jesus had given them a chance, with the Children of God, to try something really different.

"BYE BYE MISS AMERICAN PIE"

In December 1978, there were an estimated 5,000 Children of God, of whom 1,741 were children and about 1,000 were adult women. Most of the Children of God lived outside the United States, having emigrated during the early and mid-1970's to other parts of what politicians call the "free world." I interviewed one hundred or more women disciples between 1975 and 1978 in the United States, Italy, and Mexico, but this paper will concentrate on the largest group, the white North Americans.

In the early 1970's, a hit song by Don McLean, "Bye Bye Miss American Pie," spoke to the hearts of many young Americans. COG published a commentary on it as one of the earliest leaflets they distributed on the streets. Basically, the leaflet said that America had betrayed its youth and lost their trust. Most of the women I interviewed agreed. The "System" (the world outside COG, especially in the United States) was falling apart.

It turned out that many disciples came from "broken" or unhappy homes, and many had parents with drinking or drug problems. Women often told me that they had been pessimistic about ever meeting and marrying a nice man, or about being able to hold any marriage together in order to support children. Martha was a middle-class woman who had "run away with the hippies" to California instead of going to college, lived with a man and, for money, picked fruit. Then she had a disturbing dream: she was on welfare with three kids and no husband, just like many of the fruit-pickers from Arkansas. Eventually, Martha joined COG.

Few Americans realize how little our "pro-family" society does, compared with other "industrialized societies" or with "socialist countries," to encourage people to start families. Except for welfare, there are no child allowances in the United States. Pre-natal, pediatric, and gynecological medical care, baby-sitting and day-care all cost money, though some of the cost can be deducted from income taxes. Those with "good jobs"—and how many youth had "good jobs" in the 1970's, or do now?—might have health coverage. But that still leaves the problem of baby-sitting. With high geographic mobility separating women from their mothers and sisters, and with the rising cost of living forcing many households to have two wage-earners, many couples have had to deal with the dilemma of care for the children while the mother works. Increasingly, couples have postponed or forfeited having children because of this.

The Children of God was partly a product of the counter-culture of the 1960's and early 1970's, as well as of Pentecostalism and other religious traditions. On disciples' lips and in COG literature were found many of the criticisms of culture and politics that had been raised by the hippie, civil rights, ecology, and peace movements. The attorney general of New York State accused COG of aiding draft dodgers, and, in fact, many disciples I interviewed had opposed the draft and the Vietnam War. In some cases, clashes with politically conservative families had caused them to leave home. However, despite the prophet's early claim to have converted "the violent revolutionaries," few of the converts I met had been activists. What many early converts had been doing, though, was using marijuana, hashish, and LSD. And when they converted, they did not so much repent of that activity as give it up in favor of something more satisfying.

In the Children of God, hippies and Pentecostals together criticized American culture, and hoped for a change in people's "hearts." They said that children were brainwashed by TV, school, church, and home to accept violence, racism, sexual repression, and unquestioning obedience to the White House and "scientists." The evangelists who led COG combined the counter-culture's criticisms of the schools with their own pet peeve—that the public schools taught "Evolution" and had no prayer or Bible verse memorization. Children of God believed that Americans were socialized to value "things" above people and to long for more and more commodities. Frequently, disciples said that when they'd been in the "system" they had wanted to be "set free!" The break with the old way of thinking was symbolized by "forsaking all" belongings and social ties when they joined COG.

Interestingly, I rarely heard disciples complain about the high unemployment rate for their age group. In part, that was because they were trying to escape the world of jobs. The Canadian who said he had joined COG because none of the ten factories in his town had work for him was the exception. Usually, people told me they had converted because of unhappiness. They had been looking for love and for something meaningful to do with their lives. Young women who had been hoping to become homemakers and mothers, of course, did not think of themselves as unemployed, but as having a personal problem. Even some young people who had been studying education failed to mention that the bottom had dropped out of the teachers' market the year they joined COG. This lack of "working class consciousness" also made them susceptible to religious utopianism.

PATRIARCHAL TRIBALISM

"Moses David" (David Berg), COG's prophet and leader, said the group practiced "patriarchal tribalism" modelled on the Old Testament Hebrews. Like most Christian sects, disciples also claimed to be the reincarnation of the early Christians. In any case, Berg, who was in his fifties, was the patriarch—the "King," "Dad," and polygamous husband-lover. Berg said that he had suffered as a youth from the sexual repressiveness of the evangelical milieu, and that the early years of his marriage had been troubled because both he and his wife had been miseducated about sex. Now Berg, with a new young wife, was telling the world about his sexual activities, dreams, and fantasies. He urged young women to strive for sexual satisfaction and to act sexy for their mates. Some religious youth declined to join COG because it seemed too "sexy." COG totally rejected male homosexuality until about 1981, but accepted lesbian relations as long as these didn't interfere with marriage and motherhood. The male converts, a two-thirds majority, saw no reason to challenge Berg's male-fantasy definition of "sexual freedom," and the women seemed to accept it also. In COG, "Playboy" married the "Total Woman."

The influence of the women's liberation movement was less apparent in COG than the influence of other parts of the counterculture. In the early years COG women had avoided becoming sex objects by wearing long dresses and no makeup, and repressing sexuality outside marriage. However, they accepted the traditional sexual division of labor and the stereotypes about the intuitive, spiritual qualities of women and the natural leadership abilities of men. Though a married couple was the ideal image of the leadership team, there was a tendency to confine the woman's leadership to children and home-care concerns and to assign her secretarial tasks.

From my observations, women were rarely bossed around by men, though many of the younger women who were extremely shy deferred to men. Until Februrary, 1978, both male and female followers had to obey leaders without question, work hard, and usually live without luxuries. But since women were considered a rare and valuable resource, the men generally tried to keep them happy.

SOCIAL SECURITY FOR MOTHERS

All COG mothers interviewed said that they felt they were better off as mothers in COG than they would be in the "system." That was because the group put pregnant women, mothers and children first—supporting and honoring them in keeping with COG's pro-natalist ideology, making sure they had good diets, and assigning them child-care workers. A continuing group discussion focused on how best to raise and educate children, and mothers found this very helpful. COG opposed birth control, saying it showed lack of trust in God. Having lots of children was also seen as a way to enlarge the group. Men in COG, aware of the advantages the group gave mothers, told me they married the female converts and got them pregnant to keep them in the group. There is some evidence that women were sometimes coerced into marriages or "trial marriages."

In the early 1970's, the Children of God began to "flee Babylon" (the United States). Disciples I met overseas had often lost the apocalyptic fervor I had observed in the United States. Their leaders were living a comfortable life, and the group was expanding by reproduction as well as by conversions. Most COG children were born outside the United States. Teens from the United States and from the host countries served as child-care workers and fundraisers, and in most European countries and Australia, the state helped fund the costs of children. Having the baby at home, with the help of a midwife or family doctor, was also easier overseas than in the United States.

Mothers in COG also benefited from the fact that the fathers were usually very interested in children. Many fathers attended the natural childbirth classes with the pregnant women and were present at delivery. Some even learned to deliver babies themselves. The cost of a child to the father, as to the mother, was minimal, and, because they lived in an alternative society, they did not have to worry about planning or saving for education. Disciples lived like gypsies, and, like gypsies, found ways to use the children to get donations. Many men said that children were an economic asset.

WOMEN LEADERS

With all the help in the kitchen and nursery, many COG mothers were able to develop leadership and other skills, and to nurture networks among themselves. Pentecostalism, unlike most Protestant denominations, Judaism, or Roman Catholicism, has a tradition of women preachers and singers. "Grandmother" Berg, David Berg's mother, a former radio evangelist, was instrumental in founding COG and gave the group its first apocalyptic prophecy. All the women in the Berg family were important leaders and administrators in COG. They provided a variety of role models—from "super-mom" with ten children to star singer—for other ambitious women in COG.

"Mother Eve," Berg's first wife, was the mother figure for the young converts, just as Berg was the father figure. But her amibitions as a "come-to-Jesus" preacher led her to gather her own little group of disciples who were periodically criticized in the newsletter for not following Berg's instructions. Apparently, he wanted her to stick to writing recipes and devotions, while she wanted to travel around in Libya, for example. In 1977, an ex-lover of Berg, "Queen Rachel," who had converted as a teenager, was viewed by many as Berg's successor.

Most of the women who joined COG wanted to save the world. They chose for themselves the names of strong and famous women from the Bible, like Miriam, Sarah, Ruth, Martha, Naomi, and Esther. By no means were they going to be confined to the "private" as opposed to the "public" sphere. Women leaders sometimes travelled without husbands or children. Outsiders were often impressed, as I was, by their self-possession, assertiveness, and competence. And in the colonies, when the male leaders were not around, male and female followers deferred to these women.

The area in which the majority of women became prominent was child care. From 1974 to 1976, there were two COG newsletters, *New Nation News* and *Family News.* The latter was filled with stories by women about their experiences with natural childbirth, nursing, and infant and child care. Some women obtained certification as Montessori teachers through correspondence courses so that they could establish COG schools instead of sending the children to "System schools." The COG schools also provided a place for top women leaders to leave their children for days at a time or longer.

WOMEN'S LIBERATION?

COG eliminated the dichotomy between virgin and whore. All women were considered both sexy and motherly ("sexy madonnas," so to speak), sex was a pleasurable gift of God, and virginity was irrelevant. This *was* women's sexual liberation for many converts from Fundamentalist denominations and from

Roman Catholicism. And for many women who had already experienced so-called sexual freedom, COG's way of life was liberation from loveless sex.

However, women in the Children of God did not get everything their utopia was supposed to bring. Early on, they had to accept a middle-aged male prophet's fantasy-image of them: the soft-core pornography of the cover illustrations for the COG leaflets "Revolutionary Women" and "Mountin' Maids." Male disciples were portrayed, by contrast, as brave young "Mountain Men."

In 1978, Berg announced that God really only *used* the talk of "revolution" to attract a sexy young army to lure the businessmen of the world into the true fold. That luring was called "flirty fishing" because Jesus had urged his followers to become "fishers of men." Women's importance increased, but it was based even more than before on their anatomy. While the early "sexy madonnas" had posed nursing their infants for newsletter photos, the "flirty fishies" posed in low-cut dresses, or nude or semi-nude. While disciples had earlier been told to "love thy neighbor," now that love was to include meeting the neighbor's sexual needs. Sex as an alienating "sacrifice" was therefore a religious duty, one which fell most heavily on women because it was men who could be "fished" in bars and clubs, and men who had money to donate. The acceptance of gifts from "fish" quickly led to charges of prostitution, which COG denied.

Flirty fishing was, for some disciples, adopted in response to the difficulties of living in smaller households and supporting themselves in an increasingly hostile social environment. Flirty fishing also opened up new "mission fields," such as Moslem countries or Latin American dictatorships, where it was easier for disciples' households to live off lovers from the elite or the foreign community than to preach the Gospel to the native masses and risk deportation.

However, flirty fishing was not universally practiced. Berg had begun writing about it by 1975, but he did not really push it until 1977, when *Time* magazine and others "exposed" the practice in the Canary Islands. Even after that, some disciples ignored Berg's instructions. Some of the women I talked to said that for them "f-f-ing" was not "sacrificing," but going out and having fun while the men stayed home with the children. The "fish" sometimes joined COG, but more often were sought as friends and supporters. Some of them fathered COG babies.

Since male disciples also flirty fished, the sexual and marital arrangements in the homes became complex. Flirty fishing was gradually extended to formerly celibate, unmarried followers. Finally, all sexual restrictions were lifted, when Berg declared, in February 1978, that all leaders were deposed and all followers were set free. No longer could "little dictators" enforce celibacy, taxes, and hard work on the "sheep." Single disciples, whose future marriages and sex lives had once depended on remaining in good favor with leaders, were now free to start their own homes and elect their own "servants" and sleep with whomever they pleased.

A side effect of this freedom was that the mothers' security was lost. No longer were the men as eager to marry and to adopt women's children. COG dropped the rule that a couple should marry if the woman became pregnant. The men were free to wander in and out of homes, asking the women to "help" them with their sexual needs, but contributing little to the support of the children. As the younger women who had been helping the mothers became mothers themselves, the birth rate shot up. Distressed disciples of both sexes wrote to the newsletter that mothers were being abandoned and sometimes even turned away from colonies.

Attempts to remedy the situation included complex marriages in which one parent married the male or female child-care worker. "Fish" were also sometimes brought into the marriage. (As all the rules changed, greater tolerance for male as well as female homosexuality developed.) However, many disciples had to move back temporarily with their parents, live in camping trailers, resort to welfare, or, sadly, take jobs.

CONCLUSION

It is very important to point out that COG was not alone responsible for abandoning its young mothers to the cold cruel "realities" of life in twentieth-century America. Disciples had thought that by obeying their prophet and being religious missionaries who lived off donations they would be able to maintain a communal way of life longer than the hippies. But much of COG's financial support came from politically conservative religious people. The anticult, deprogramming movement tried to convince both large and small donors that the group was subversive and immoral. Leftists, meanwhile, suspected them of collusion with the CIA. One deprogrammer told me that her goal was to break up the large colonies so that recruits could not be "brainwashed" in isolation from the outside society. Yet it was the colonies that had supported motherhood.

This was by no means the first time in Western history that groups practicing "deviant" domestic and sexual patterns have been attacked. The Mormons and the Oneida community, for example, were both forced by outside pressure to conform to the monogamous "nuclear family" style of household. Like them, the Children of God who had to move from their utopia, flawed as it was, into the "best of all legally possible worlds" have suffered both psychic and material deprivation. What will become of them? Will they redefine being "saved" and "set free" to mean simply praying to Jesus and hoping to go to heaven? Or will they keep dreaming about and trying to make a better world here on earth?

Tulsa

NTOZAKE SHANGE

i tried to tell the doctor
i really tried to tell her
tween the urine test & the internal exam/
when her fingers were circling my swollen cervix
i tried
to tell her the baby was confused
the baby doesnt know
she's not another poem.
you see/ i was working on a major piece of fiction
at the time of conception
"doctor/ are you listening?"
had just sent 4 poems off to the *new yorker*
& was copy-editing a collection of plays
during those "formative first twelve weeks"
there were opening parties
all of which involved me & altered the poor baby's
amniotic bliss/
    "doctor/ the baby doesnt think she shd
    come out that way!"
i mean/ she thinks she shd come up not down
into the ground/ she thinks her mother makes up things
nice things ugly things but made up things nonetheless

From "Bocas: A Daughter's Geography"/A Performance Piece. I wrote this for my daughter, in an attempt to give her the planet, her culture, her lands, mythological & otherwise.

Tulsa & Conakry, the Cosmic Revolutionary Couple who parent all Third World People, are commited to our freedom in every sense.

Ntozake Shange, "Tulsa," from *Bocas: A Daughter's Geography*. Reprinted by permission of Russell & Volkening, Inc. Copyright © 1982 by Ntozake Shange.

unprovable irrational subjective fantastic things
not subject to objective or clinical investigation/
she believes the uterine cave is metaphor
    "doctor/ you have to help me"
this baby wants to jump out of my mouth
at a reading someplace/
that baby's refusing to come out/ down
she wants to come out a spoken word
but i have no way to reach her
no mere choice of words/ how can i convince her
to drop her head & take on the world like the rest of us
she cant move up til she comes out
    "whatever shall i do? i've been pregnant
    a long time"
i finally figured out what to say
to this literary die-hard of a child of mine
"you are an imperative my dear"/ & i felt her startle
toward my right ovary then i said/ "as an imperative
it is incumbent upon you to present yrself"

(DANCER *#3 enters on "to present . . ." as child, jumps into* CONAKRY's
arms as if looking for her mother and daddy. He puts her down; she exits.
CONAKRY *follows.*

SLIDE *#16 dissolve to* SLIDE *#17*)

    TULSA
    cuz she's black & poor
    she's disappeared
    the name was lost   the games werent played
    nobody tucks her in at night/ wipes traces
    of cornbread & syrup from her fingers
    the corners of her mouth
    cuz she's black & poor/ she's not
    just gone
    disappeared one day
    & her blood soaks up what's awready red
    in atlanta

no ropes this time   no tar & feathers
werent no parades of sheets fires & crosses
nothing/   no signs
empty bunkbeds
mothers who forget & cook too much on sundays
just gone/ disappeared
cuz he's black & poor   he's gone
took a bus/ never heard from again

CONAKRY (*entering*)
but somebody heard a child screaming
    & went right on ahead
children disappearing/ somewhere in the woods/ decaying
just gone/ disappeared/ in atlanta

TULSA
mothers are always at the window watching
caint nobody disappear right in fronta yr eyes
but who knows what we cd do
when we're black & poor
we aint here no way/ how cd we disappear?
who wd hear us screaming?

DANCER #3 *enters, crawling along wall slowly; she will exit other side of
stage by end of next "disappeared")*

CONAKRY
say it was a man with a badge & some candy
say it was a man with a badge & some money
say it was a maniac
cd be more n sticks n stones
gotta be more than stars n stripes
children caint play war when they in one.
    (*stops*)
caint make believe they dyin/ when they are
    (*gets stronger*)
caint imagine what they'll be/ cuz they wont

just gone/ disappeared
    (*intensely, to himself*)
oh mary dont you weep & dont you moan
oh mary dont you weep & dont you moan
HOLLAR i say HOLLAR

TULSA (*angry*)
cuz we black & poor & we just disappear
we cant find em   jesus cant find em
til they seepin in soil
father reekin in soil
they bones bout disappeared
they lives aint never been
they bleeding where the earth's awready red
dyin cuz they took a bus
& mama caint see that far out her window
the front porch dont go from here to eternity

CONAKRY
& they gone

TULSA
just disappeared

CONAKRY
but somebody heard them screaming
somebody crushed them children's bones
somebody's walkin who shd be crawling
for killing who aint never been
cuz we black & poor/ we just be gone

TULSA
no matter how sweet/ no matter how quiet
just gone
be right back ma
going to the store mother dear
see ya later nana

call ya when i get there mama
& the soil runs red with our dead in atlanta

CONAKRY (*to audience*)
cuz somebody went right on ahead
crushing them lil bones/ strangling them frail wails
cuz we black & poor & our blood soaks up dirt
while we disappearing

TULSA (*strong*)
mamas keep looking out the door
saying "i wonder where is my child/ i wonder
    where is my child"

CONAKRY
she dont turn the bed back cuz she knows
we black & poor
& we just disappear/ be gone

TULSA
oh mary dont you weep & dont you moan
oh mary dont you weep & dont you moan
    (*worried*)
i wonder where is my child
    (*angry*)
i wonder where is my child

(*she exits, repeating phrase*)

CONAKRY
nothing/ no signs
in atlanta

(DANCER *#3 skips on, kneels* DSLC; CONAKRY *exits, repeating phrase.*
MUSIC: *2 loops of* "NONAAH" *by Art Ensemble of Chicago, segues into
Gunter Hampel music.* SLIDE *#17 dissolves.*

   DANCER *#1 enters and begins solo dance.* SLIDE *#18 up.*

TULSA *enters half-way through dance*)

TULSA
we need a god who bleeds now
a god whose wounds are not
some small male vengeance
some pitiful concession to humility
a desert swept with dryin marrow in honor of the lord

we need a god who bleeds
spreads her lunar vulva & showers us in shades of scarlet
thick & warm like the breath of her
our mothers tearing to let us   in
this place breaks open
like our mothers bleeding
the planet is heaving   mourning our ignorance
the moon tugs the seas
to hold her/ to hold her
embrace swelling hills/ i am
not wounded i am bleeding to life
we need a god who bleeds now
whose wounds are not the end of anything

(SLIDE *#18 dissolves;* MUSIC *segues back to* "NONAAH" DANCER *#1 exits.* DANCER *#2 enters and begins a brutal dance as* TULSA *stands frozen;* SLIDE *#19 comes up*)

Findhorn, Scotland:
The People Who Talk to Plants

ARLENE SHEER

MY going to Findhorn was a leap of faith. I knew virtually nothing about the place. But my idea of community as a place where people, especially women, could grow and flourish, has become stronger over the past two years. To live and work in an atmosphere of love and support seems to me the only way to go. I knew, for me at least, it had to be a spiritual community, one based on the precepts of love and the acknowledgement of divinity within all people and things.

Findhorn means "white goddess" in Gaelic, a suitable name for this community in the northeastern part of Scotland, where the feminine energies run as clear and quick as the Findhorn River. The community functions on the principles of the love, support, and trust I was looking for and on the deep-rooted belief that god will provide and make manifest the means by which needs are met. With a little help from friends, of course. It works. For twenty years now what started in a dinky trailer park has grown into an energetic, bustling, spiritual community of about 200 permanent members who live together, work together, eat together, share thoughts, feelings and concerns. These members think of themselves as family and hold family meetings once a week.

The Findhorn Community is a spread-out affair; different parts in different places covering several miles. Cluny Hill, where I stayed for three months, is just outside the town of

Forres. It was originally a hotel and is used primarily for the guest program although many permanent members live there as well. Half the community consists of families living at the Findhorn Bay Caravan Park four miles away. Since some people at Cluny work at the Park and *vice versa,* two buses, Daphne and Henry, transport the commuters. All machines, from buses to vacuum cleaners, are named, the feeling being that if something has a name it will be treated with the care and respect due it; it won't just be a thing.

In 1962, Peter and Eileen Caddy, their three children, and Dorothy McLean, their friend, found themselves out of work and moved to the Findhorn Bay Caravan Park. They cleaned up the rubbish heap next to their trailer and began growing vegetables to feed themselves. Nothing unusual about that. What was unusual was that they began growing forty-pound cabbages in midwinter in soil that a United Nations expert described as "almost barren, powdery sand." The expert came to the conclusion that "there are other factors, and they are vital ones." The factors were the contact they made with nature (Devas—"angels of nature"). Co-creating, the Findhorn community calls it. The news of these marvels spread world-wide. If you have heard of Findhorn at all, it is probably in this context.

When I arrived at Cluny Hill on Saturday morning, the first sight that greeted me was a young man vacuuming the entrance hall carpet. A good omen, I thought. Maybe they've done away with sex roles.

As a guest member, I had registered for the Experience Week to be followed by a nine week Essence Program. My focalizers for the Experience Week, Marci and Sally (all names are fictitious), were waiting in the lounge to answer any questions I might have. A focalizer is a community member, part of the personnel department, who facilitates group sessions with a very light touch.

After unpacking, I went down to lunch. The dining room at Cluny extends almost the length of the building. It is large, light and airy. There was a serve-yourself assortment of vegetarian foods and breads. Every Saturday, Cluny kitchen turns out loaves and loaves of whole grain breads.

The Experience Week would meet in the BeechTree room at two-thirty that afternoon. All dated sections that follow are excerpted from my daily journal.

———————

Saturday, February 20, 1982. The Experience group, about twenty-four of us, went round the room telling how we'd first heard of Findhorn and why we decided to come. The lives are all different, of course, but the reasons for coming here are similar: need for new direction, change in the life, community support, need for deeper meaning.

Sunday, February 21. We did sacred dances this morning. Folk dances, really. The last dance was to be male-female partnering. Two men were left together as partners as well as two women. The women had no objections to partnering each other, but the men did.

Marie brought this point up during our evening meeting. She's a strong feminist, as are most of the young women here. She has that acute awareness that comes with being mentally up front all the time. Marci, the focalizer, admitted it was a problem for her; it had happened once before, and after that she simply did not play that dance again.

There is great affection among most of the younger people here, male-female, female-female, male-male, that is openly shown.

Monday, February 22. We chose our work experience for two days through the process of Attunement. A list is read of the jobs to be done. Then we hold hands, all of us, with the right palm up and the left palm down (receiving and giving) while the list is read again. We attune to certain jobs as they are read; that is, by meditating on each job, our inner sense tells us what job to go for. Then we raise our hand to volunteer for that job. Often, too many people want the same job, and then someone is asked to relinquish. I attuned to the Publications Studio at Findhorn Caravan Park and worked there in the morning.

This afternoon we played games: releasing games, trust

games, love and togetherness games. In the Planets Game, we closed our eyes and imagined we were planets wandering the heavens alone and then, at the end, hooking up with other planets. This took place in the Ballroom. I enjoyed wandering that great room alone and rarely bumped into anyone. Halfway through we were instructed to touch in greeting if we met another planet and then let go. That also I enjoyed. The final part was to hook up with a group, which would connect with another, and so on, until there was only one large planet made of us all. I was reluctant to do this. I preferred to wander alone.

The Trust Game had one person in the center of a small group, eyes closed, hands over chest, falling either to the back or to the side, while the circle members caught and pushed you upright or to the side. I had no problem with this, although I would have had ten or fifteen years ago. Obviously, my trust in others had grown, and perhaps it comes from my involvement in the women's movement.

Tuesday, February 23. This evening we saw an A.V. (audio-visual) on Roc, a scientist, his connection to nature and to the creatures who are guardians of nature, and his meeting a small faun in a park in Edinburgh and then Pan himself (from whom we get the image of the devil).

While sharing this evening Marie brought up the point that if a Martian saw that slide show, it would never realize that there were anything but men populating the earth. All the creatures that Roc met and mentioned were male: fauns, gnomes, elves, and their king, Pan.

Wednesday, Februrary 24. The young people in the group, particularly the women, are very aware of what people are giving out: their defenses, their openness or lack of it.

Went to Nebold House this afternoon and read from David Spangler's book *Revelation.* Spangler's revelation comes through using the word *man* generically. That made a few ripples. Erica said she couldn't read it the way it was written and substituted people or humankind.

Friday, February 26. We had a sharing of what the Experience Week meant to us. This was to be our last official meeting. It was really very moving. The people in the group, with the exception of Margaret (53) and me (51), are mostly in their twenties or early thirties. For them, the week was an emotional experience. We all ate dinner together that night, our focalizers putting together two large tables in the dining room to accommodate us all. I had a glass of wine which sold for 50 pence.

On the Saturday the Experience Week ended the Essence Program started. Seven of us from the Experience Week went into the program. Five more arrived that Saturday and joined us. Our focalizers, Ian and Jillian, brought the group to fourteen. We would be together for nine weeks.

The Essence Program was created to give the participants a taste of what membership in the community is like. Work is a big part of a member's life. Work as "bringing spirit into matter" and work as "love in action" are sayings at Findhorn. The word "service" is used a lot too. I asked what that word meant in their context and Jillian defined it as "anything that contributes to the well being of the planet."

Sunday, February 28. We are to write our purposes for being at Findhorn. I went into the sanctuary tonight to ask myself what my purposes are. The answer: your purposes are manifold. Being at Findhorn is but one step in your journey.

Monday, March 1. We read our purposes today and they were all written down on a large piece of white paper and hung on the wall so we could remind ourselves of them during the ensuing weeks.

Tuesday, March 2. This morning Nora and two others came to speak to the group. She focalizes Cluny and also runs a Group Consciousness Workshop. She said something that struck me as important: keep our purposes for being here in the forefront of our minds, or else we can fly off in all directions.

In the afternoon we worked at Drumduan, that lovely house through the woods, hauling felled trees; very hard physical work, for me anyway. We broke for tea at 3:30. At 4:00 people started back to work but Nann, Denise and I knew we had enough. We told Ian we wanted to go back to Cluny and not work any more. He suggested we remember the work schedule was from 1:30 to 5:00. Everyone was hard at work when we left. Surprisingly, no nasty little epithets were called out. Walking through Drumduan woods back to Cluny, we kept justifying our decision and rationalizing our position. Part of me felt like a shirker. But I was able to take an hour's nap, which I desperately needed. Findhorn, for me today at least, is like a spiritual Marxist axiom: from each according to her/his ability, to each according to her/his need.

Wednesday, March 3. This morning Marte and I talked about work. I told her what had happened yesterday at Drumduan. Marte supported my decision and emphasized that our bodies know when we've had enough and how important it is to go with our feelings. She also suggested I bring it up with my group.

So after Attunement, I did bring it up. Well, that opened the entire group. Everyone talked about their feelings yesterday, many expressing how they had taken on more than they could handle. It was decided that we not work till 5:00 but until 4:30 so that we would have time for baths and sanctuary at 6:00. Jillian was very supportive of individual needs, in this case for stopping work if necessary.

Friday, March 5. Today we attuned for our work assignments for the coming two months. The list was read twice. Maintenance was on the list, in which I planned to work when I was in the States. I wanted to learn to be a handy person. But in Attunement my inner voice boomed "Cluny Kitchen," so I put in for it. Only two people were needed and three wanted it, so I released it. Then I attuned to the Cluny Dining Room. Too many people had also attuned to that. We want into meditation again, and to make it short, I'm in Maintenance.

Monday March 8. We went to a Core meeting over at the Park. The Core group is made up of ten or twelve women and men who make most of the major decisions affecting the community. Decisions are arrived at by consensus reached through meditation. A project may fail, however, if the community at large does not sustain enough interest in it.

Armand seemed to be the big cheese of the group. I hope he is constantly struggling to find a balance between the very dominant male aspect he projects and the softer, receptive spirituality that one is supposed to work on here. But the meeting was very good.

We came in upon a discussion of monetary problems concerning Universal Hall. After a moment of meditation to return to one's own individual center and more discussion on how to keep the community better informed, there was a break for back rubs. Everyone stood up in a circle and massaged the back of the person in front; then the circle reversed and again the back of the person in front was massaged. This technique released tension and provided touching. This was followed by a moment of silence. What a wonderful way to run a meeting.

Tuesday, March 9. Started in Maintenance today. Went around trying to find shut-off points in order to fix leaky sinks. Dirk and Peter, my Maintenance focalizers, are very nice.

Each work department has a day once a week when the participants have an Attunement and then a Sharing. We share our feelings and thoughts of that week's experience.

Had a talk with Mai this afternoon about older women being invisible. She is feeling it very strongly here. I think that, at the base of her feelings, is the sense that she is no longer sexually attractive to most of the males here and that men of our age are still considered desirable.

Wednesday, March 10. Worked on a toilet tank this morning. Very complicated. There are no parts so it's a matter of making substitutes. My first reaction was to throw the tank out and get a new one. But labor is cheap; in fact, it's free, so it doesn't matter if the job takes two days instead of two hours.

This afternoon we started the group consciousness workshop. We are to take personal as well as group problems to the group. The theory is that if we don't get through the personal stuff first, the person who is feeling the problem won't be with the group anyway and will, in effect, drain it.

Went out to dinner tonight, just the four of us "older women," Mai, Nann, Margaret, and me. We talked about being single, middle-aged women here at Findhorn as well as in the world at large. Mai wants to be seen as the young women here are—still sexually desirable. The population at Cluny Hill is primarily young with a scattering of us older ones. The traditional need to "pair" is still with some of us. I feel it here too, surprisingly. All the thinking that I'm happier alone (and I am), that the choice to remain alone has been mine (it has), still leaves me aware that I am not seen as I once was, young.

Thursday, March 11. The Group Consciousness Workshop will be valuable to me. Part of the process of group consciousness is recognizing where you are in terms of power and, indeed, how we think of power. I think power is the ability to affect people's lives. But really it is the ability to do something. Findhorn's definition: all power is god's energy.

Friday, March 12. This morning Group Sharing was pretty strong. Mai was feeling distanced and separate. I objected to all the Sharing I felt pressured to do every day. So I shared with them my growing annoyance with the process. Unless I had something I wanted to share I would pass.

George finally broke down and cried. He spoke about his wife leaving him, said that he still loves her and that he wants to speak from his feelings not his head. We were all touched and happy this happened, happy for him. He asked for hugs from everyone, so we spent the next twenty minutes hugging each other.

Monday, March 15. Am redecorating a room. Steaming off wallpaper, removing old plaster. Very boring.

Tuesday, March 16. Eileen Caddy spoke to our group today. Beautiful woman, her eyes sparkled. She told us a little of her life and the start of Findhorn. She left a marriage and five children to go with Peter from whom she is now separated. I can imagine what that was like.

Thursday, April 1. Heard Armand talk on Governance this morning. I still feel the lack of human relatedness in him. Abstract thinking, abstract talk.

Wednesday, April 7. Felt very irritated today. It started in the afternoon and continued until bedtime. Graham pulled one of his "the group" and "we" speeches this evening. I felt like throttling him. Told him that perhaps he was projecting his own feelings of apathy or whatever onto the group and to look to himself. I also told him to stop saying "we" and say "I."

Friday, April 9. Worked shoveling and dumping manure at the garden school this morning. We had a special meditation for the full moon in Aries at Universal Hall in the afternoon.

Saturday, April 10. Went to the over-sixties' tea at Cullerne with Mai and Margaret. We asked if we could be invited. We are curious about the older members; we see so few of them here at Cluny.

I brought a list of questions. I got particularly good responses from the women on the questions about women in the community. Good god—they are feminists!

My questions were as follows (answers in parentheses):

1. What percentage of the community is over 60? (8%)

2. What percentage of the guests who stay for an extended period—Essence, Departmental Guest, Long Term Guest—are over 60? (No studies done on this, but not many.)

3. Is there any forum for older members outside of the tea? (There used to be. But we came to object to any and all rules and regulations. We have teas now once a month because there is always a birthday and that's our reason for getting together. The tea is focalized by the birthday person and everybody makes cakes or cookies.)

4. Are the older women primarily in traditional work roles? (If you mean cooking and cleaning, no. Everybody cooks and

cleans, not only women. Several women are trustees. They manage, focalize, conduct workshops, run departments.)

5. What proportion of the membership are women? (Over 50%)

6. If the majority are women, is this reflected in the governing branches? (It is, all except the executive branch, and that only because no woman member has the financial background and skills necessary for that job.)

Tuesday, April 15. The men and women here are friendly and loving but not too much seems to go on in the way of relationships, except among the permanent members of the community, the younger members. There's not much pairing with the long-term guest members. My feeling is that the women would like it but the men are reluctant.

Wednesday, April 21. Mai spoke to me about her work in the kitchen and the related problems. She decided today to release the work. The decision feels right to her. Mai feels she has done all she could to awaken Rudi's consciousness about older women not being nonexistent because they were not sexually attractive to him.

Had a talk about relationships at dinner. Dan was pretty interesting on the topic. He said everything is a relationship. He also said that Findhorn was a fishbowl, everybody knowing everything. So there is a lot of care given. And the energy normally given sexually is discharged through a lot of hugging. (One focalizer told her group that a person needs a minimum of fourteen hugs a day.) You find, he said, that you love a lot of people here. Exclusivity is very difficult and not desirable for everyone.

We did not discuss the fact that the sexual energy discharged by hugging is mainly for younger women, since the males here are also young. As Ruby said, "Ageism is sexism in disguise."

Wednesday, April 28. Dirk switched my last Maintenance Attunement to this afternoon so I could take part. His meditation in sanctuary was mostly directed toward me, putting me in the light, metaphorically, and thanking me for bringing love and joy

to the department. I was very moved. He also bought pastries
for my last Sharing.

Thursday, April 29. We, the Essence Group, made ourselves a
wonderful farewell dinner (chicken, vegetables, salad, dessert,
and coffee) and ate in the family room downstairs. We had it all
to ourselves. Singing with guitar later. Such a pleasant evening.

Friday, April 30. Started the morning with a meditation. It
was good, strong, very strong for me. We continued the Appre-
ciations, which is a process of telling each other the beautiful and
special things about ourselves. Then we broke for a silent Circle
Appreciation to music, holding hands, and looking into each
other's eyes. Claire was the second or third for me. I started to
cry. I felt such strong love for her, for all of them.

Saturday, May 1. Said goodbye again to the group. Lots of
hugs all round. It took a long time. Goodbye, Findhorn, for the
time being.

Most of the people who come to Findhorn, either to live or
to participate in the numerous programs offered, are middle-
class, well-educated, and financially solvent—many with well established careers. They come from all over the world.

Like any living organism, Findhorn is ever growing and
changing. As a New Age Light Center, it takes its responsibility
for the planet very seriously. An Ecovillage was planned as well
as a world-wide Wilderness Conference in the spring of 1983.
The Publications Studio at the Park is in the process of reprinting all their material, using the McGraw-Hill guidelines to eradicate sexist language.

The Resource Center at Drumduan is engaged in Network-
ing, keeping the communities' extensive files up to date and continuing their contacts with other Light Centers around the globe.

Communities are springing up all over the world, many
started by ex-Findhornites. And although I often think about
returning to Findhorn, I am curious about other communities
closer to hand. I expect to explore them.

Twin Oaks: A Feminist Looks at Indigenous Socialism in the United States

BATYA WEINBAUM

FOR the past 12 months I have been on a vision quest, a search for alternate economic arrangements created by women on women's lands on the East Coast, West Coast, and in the Midwest region of the United States. I found in my search what many have often told me—that I am too utopian.

Of what did I dream? I wanted to locate a women's farm in the United States which was economically self-sufficient, serving women much as the kibbutzim serve Jews. If I was searching for a unit where women were economically self-sufficient, and ran their own income-producing industries for exchange with the outside world, there isn't any such place in the here and now. Because of the society in which we live, women are not conditioned psychologically to think in money-making ways; and women certainly come with too few skills and resources from the outside world to invest in the farm movement. Instead, we come from diverse class positions—marginal on the outside at best—and prone to misplace disappointment by criticizing each other rather than the patriarchy which created the differences among us in the first place, which means that women who do have these resources and skills often end up hiding them.

The farms and lands which do exist serve an important function, however. They operate as centers for cultural and psychic development, to which women can come to cleanse themselves of male, negative, and city energies; and to be exposed to new thinking and psychic phenomena. But the women who run these lands feel burnt out by the numbers coming through in search of women's space and healing land. The communities which have lasted the longest are those which are closed at one time of the year for privacy of on-going members; at other times, they are open for political purposes; and, at still others, they are open at retreat or work exchange rates for women who can afford to come or to pay. Other than that, the only money-gaining activity I found was among women who made and sold music, clothes, scarves, jewelry and greeting cards on the women's craft market. And there was some growing of herbs for market exchange. These were usually undertaken on an individual basis rather than as an investment in collective gainful activity.

I have no argument with the groups that have taken an alternative spiritual focus because it takes a lot to re-program ourselves in entirely new directions. Furthermore, perhaps my search was misplaced, as the lands are feudally more than capitalistically based, i.e., much of the internal exchange is in the form of trade or barter, since members believe in withdrawal from the money world at-large. Since the religions of the New Age (of which the women's spirituality movement is a part) advocate an agrarian, back-to-the-earth approach, the sense of how survival problems are to be tackled goes back to feudal arrangements which allow more personal control over more limited work. For example, trades are arranged directly between energy givers and receivers. If your back hurts, on the farms, I rub it; in exchange, you might cut me wood or perform other services. The women's spirituality movement, dominant in the farms, steps out of the capitalist patriarchy, but a complete revisioning would take a lot of work.

The farms are also based on the biological point of view that male energies are influenced by destructive hormones. Admittedly, I had my eyes opened by this perspective, but to go back to the material planes, to the socialist feminist point of view, that is, to the view that the differences between men and women are socially constructed: what do we want to look for in the social structure? What would we want an economic reorganization to do?

Assuming a Marxist analysis, we would look for the breakdown of the "double duty" labor of the housewife—working for the capitalist in the workplace and for the family in the home, as designated by Engels in his analysis of the origin of the state. We would also look for a reorganization of "consumption work," which requires the wife to relate to centers of goods and services for her family members.[1] Once these two problems have been solved (currently keeping women at a disadvantage under both socialism and capitalism), we would then want to see a restructuring of the division of labor by sex and age in the workplace itself, which, in the larger economy assumes 1) the pooling of income by family members across sex and age lines—keeping women in low paying jobs—and facilitating the accumulation of capital, and 2) the unseen, unpaid labor of women.

Unable to locate the object of my quest on the women's farms, I will examine in greater depth one particular self-sufficient community where I lived and worked for one month in the South. Although this particular pocket is operated jointly by women and men, it has much that works in terms of breaking down sex and age division of labor and substituting a labor credit system for money exchange.

This smaller social system accounted for the unseen, unpaid labor of women in the labor credit system. Consumption of goods and services was organized for its entire population as an enlarged consumption unit. The reward system was not based on the assumption of pooling income in a smaller family unit. And thus great strides have been made in breaking down traditional sex and age divisions of labor.

Twin Oaks is the smaller economic unit on which I lived and worked. How did I find it? During a week in a land-encampment of six to seven thousand half-naked women at the annual Michigan women's music festival, I had the opportunity to work in a structure that was not alienating but exhilarating. As I volunteered my labor by cooking and working security, I experienced being an active participant in the creation of a positive alternative cooperative structure. I saw evidence everywhere that elements which had made my life unbearable had inspired others to create alternatives. Did I get hassled in the sauna by men when I tried to put in my seventy-two laps a day at the local jock university? Here was a T-shirt from some major city advertising WOMEN'S GYM. Did I get harassed, ridiculed, and ripped off by mechanics? Here was a T-shirt promoting WOMEN'S GARAGE. Was I afraid to walk out at night either in the big city or a small town? A slogan, TAKE BACK THE NIGHT. Did I get depressed? Here was a sticker WILD WOMEN DON'T GET THE BLUES. Had the Jewish religion conditioned me to feel unsuccessful if I was not married and didn't bear children? Here was Z Budapest doing her rituals and making the rain stop amidst spiralling circles of self-blessing women. Piece after piece of the larger picture fell into place; weights lifted. Sitting around a campfire at a security post one night, in awe and fascination I listened to a woman strum a banjo and sing about living on a women's farm, building women's land: an intentionally-created, all-women, income-pooling community. At the Women's Pentagon Action later that fall, a friend gave me a recruitment leaflet from Twin Oaks, which stated that this community of people living in Virginia was economically self-sufficient, and that the community serviced its own cars. The leaflet indicated that within this larger group a women's living space existed; and that the group, a mixture of heterosexual, lesbian, and bisexual sisters, was committed to the creation of women's culture. The leaflet said, "If you have feminist energy, we need you." I wrote to request a visit immediately.

Twin Oaks is but one of many intentional communities that have grown up across the United States. The sociological definition of intentional community is a group in which the primary bond among members is other than blood or legal. (In some of these communities, the members are united through a common religious bond; in others, the unity is provided by a common philosophy or commitment to certain experiences.) Communities that make such bonds pool resources, develop mechanisms for group decisions, often divide labor in ways which break down traditional roles, share child care, and experience some sort of dialectic between individual and group priorities. Throughout America, these communities have been created more in times of hope than despair; they seem to follow on war experiences. The ones that survive the longest seem to be the most conformist. In the 60's and 70's America saw a resurgence of these communities as the family and traditional values lost their hold. Usually, the groups that have lasted have championed a cause: in the last century, anti-slavery and women's rights; now, psychological well-being as opposed to the stress of the larger society.

At Twin Oaks, the community, initially not socialist or feminist in intent, is both, in function and in fact. The labor credit system I will describe below was originally designed in a study of pigeons when founded 16 years ago to enact Skinnerian psychological philosophy, not intentionally as a revolutionary challenge to societal division of labor. However, the system is run to meet people's needs, not for ego enhancement and profit, and so many of the structural requirements for the liberation of women are met. The community operates a hammock industry from which income is derived, and a farm on which some foods are grown, animals raised, and animal products processed. Twin Oaks also organizes consumption for each of its seventy members. Thus, it serves as a collective production and consumption unit, requiring little circulation of money to purchase goods and services for household and individual purposes. Because of the collective living, there is also a reduction in amounts spent on stoves, kitchen equipment, furniture, or decoration.

Every individual of age works the quota hours—forty-seven a week—and, in exchange, can live, eat, and receive an $11 monthly allowance. Forty-seven hours might sound steep, but on the outside, income-producing labor, in addition to commuting and organizing personal services (going to the bank, shopping, cleaning, cultural stimulation, etc.) takes at least sixty hours a week per individual. Eleven dollars a month is low, but necessary outlay is less: for example, yoga classes on the grounds by members are free, and one needn't pay for car upkeep or subways. And you don't need a clothes budget as you can get what you need to wear in the centralized, free thrift store known as Commie Clothes.

All labor for the quota is valued equally, although this wasn't always the case. In the beginning, if the work was desirable, it was given one credit; if it was undesirable, more credits were assigned to give people the incentive to do it. For example, you could get paid more credits for cleaning toilets than construction work, which many wanted to do. This system was dropped as being too complicated to figure, and now an hour of laundry earns credit equal to an hour of auto repair or community planning.

Thus, domestic work disappears for the individual "homemaker" as she joins the community living-situation and no longer carries the double burden of work for the employer and work for the house, which has led some political feminists on the outside to demand that wages be paid for housework. From an analysis of the 1982 labor budget, I found that 30% of the hours are allocated to the otherwise unpaid work of women; 20% of the budget is operation of on-farm service work; 50% of labor hours are directly income-producing. The unseen structure of consumption work for women also disappears—for example, going to service centers to organize input for family members. Less unpaid labor time is required to get children to school, because school happens right on the farm. Family members don't have to be taken to the doctor, because a labor-credited health system operates right on the property. As needed, a labor-credited office person organizes group expeditions to the dentist, and so on. The work is done collectively so that each individual housewife/mother does not have to stay on top of the needs of her family.

Of course, these changes benefit all women, not just women who find their family responsibilities lessened by joining the community. An individual is similarly relieved by not having to calculate what is earned and what is spent. Furthermore this recognition, that women's previous labor was unpaid and now needs to be counted, is subversive, and makes room for other changes. For example, labor credit can be granted for one-way counseling sessions, since nurturing others or listening to expressed feelings is work.

Additionally since work in production does not depend on unseen labor servicing the home, and income-pooling is not facilitating capital accumulation by means of division of labor by sex and age, the basis is laid for breaking down much of the "standard" social divisions. Men can and do work in child care, laundry, and kitchen; women can and do work in auto mechanics, planning, and construction. A woman doesn't have to become a "superwoman," handling the running of a home while she aims for a promotion in the office. Neither male nor female is at a particular disadvantage as both must work forty-seven hours a week and neither has individual or total home responsibility. Also there are no full-time jobs: someone working ten hours a week in the auto shop can also work twenty hours a week as kitchen manager. As a result, doing work out of one's traditional sex role does not have to be threatening and undermining to the society or to the individual.

Of course, affirmative action is still necessary to get women into non-traditional jobs. This does dissipate the energies of the few feminist women there. The economic argument, that it takes more time to train women than to operate with peers, is still heard, yet it is encouraging that those who run the shop make an effort to rectify the situation. They teach auto mechanics to girls and encourage women to sign up for six-week car-maintenance shifts on a rotation basis. All this can occur because there is no structural economic basis supporting psychological prejudice, intimidation, and conditioning. Some feminist women have recognized that and taken advantage of the situation.

The institution of motherhood has been reevaluated and the traditional experience of childhood along with it. This is the third way labor-crediting is subversive. Decisions are made at the community level about how many births can be handled each year. In the history of the community, this began as an economic issue since pregnancy is considered work and the labor-credit system grants pregnancy hours. The pregnant woman is also able to earn labor credits throughout her pregnancy, and her absence from "normal" labor-credit work is not extensive because, if she is not feeling well, she can produce a product in bed, sew for Commie Clothes, or have a planning meeting scheduled in her small-group living situation so that she can attend without much exertion. The separation between work and home being obliterated, a woman doesn't require a long leave-of-absence and she can be reintegrated into work quite easily.

Given the decision which must be made about how many

hours the community wants to invest each year in this way, the economic basis leads to an overall stance of community responsibility. Because the community must decide to take on the responsibility of another child, the community has a stake in developing a different kind of childhood. This is congruent with its ideology of developing an environment which will alter the status quo; 15% of community resources go into child education programs to make this so. The psychological theories of Freud and Freudian feminists would lose their theoretical basis in this community, as the child does not get the primary home-mother/working-father images impressed upon the brain at the earliest cognitive level. It is not necessary to have a father present, and the community has financed artificial insemination; however, if there is a father around, he has as much contact with the child as the mother. The child has many adults as models, and many sources of affectional contact. Childhood sexuality is recognized and much peer interaction and group support among children exists; there is no isolated or terrorized dependency upon a single source of love, hate, punishment, approval. If, as some theorists (Chodorow, Dinnerstein, etc.[2]) have suggested, the problem with development of interpersonal adult sex roles is that the adult female is socially responsible for early parenting, then the social basis for sex roles might be really broken down.

Besides areas in which there is massive subversive potential, there are important process issues: first, the dominance of female values, or values that have been associated with women rather than with men in the dominant culture. For example, nurturance rather than intimidation is the norm in the learning-experience. On the job in the modern capitalist world, one has to present a macho image of self-confidence rather than express fear of working with machinery or acquiring skills in on-the-job training. At Twin Oaks, fears can be expressed to the trainer or teacher, who will often share his or her experience of the difficulties in mastering procedure. Second, people cooperate with each other rather than compete to show who can do the most or best. Individual work rewards—economic or otherwise—are not preferred. If a production push is needed, a goal is set for the entire community of how many hammocks must be produced that day, rather than giving a speed-up number to each individual worker. Increased productivity is encouraged by group reward or reinforcement—rather than by intimidation. For example, cookies are baked and served in the group work area, readings are organized to entertain the shifts and entice workers to spend more time there.

Another dominant female value is the definition of self as a well-rounded whole person rather than through occupation. Because of the amount of rotation (planners' terms are only eighteen months), you can't ask, "What do you do?" and expect the person's career to define the way the person relates to you. In the larger capitalist world of work, in the patriarchal division of labor, there are four main categories. In my book *Pictures of Patriarchy*,[3] I defined four jobs based on family roles. The *Daughter* moves around a lot, never gets a place to call her own. The *Father* generates the work of others, accumulates skill, and feels as much at home on the job as at home. The *Brother* worker competes to rise to be like the *Father*. The *Wife* works separated and isolated from all the rest performing domestic functions, enforcing *Father's* rules, and socializing *Daughter* and *Brother*. It is encouraging that none of those categories applies at Twin Oaks. Everyone moves around and rotates jobs. The job that would be classified as "Father" on the outside and would demand the greatest economic reward and respect—planner—is the least attractive because it requires more time and responsibility. Everyone feels at home throughout the entire workplace. Everyone can personalize the space at work by dressing however one wants to and by operating the selection of music. *Wife* work is not separated and isolated and it is rotated. *Brothers* do not compete in order to rise. Instead, much community pressure has to be applied to get anyone to take on positions of responsibility. In some respects, the *Daughter's* position is generalized; everyone moves from job to job, making relatively short-term commitments.

Trying to break out of the sex role and acquire non-traditional skills is considered the norm rather than an oddity in the environment. No one—employees, bosses, the culture—expects you to accept the outrageously oppressive conditions of work as

"natural." When I tried to study auto mechanics under traditional circumstances, I had to deal with the reactions of the
instructor, and the people in the shops who sold parts. To them,
that I wanted to learn at all was astonishing. At Twin Oaks, you
can concentrate on learning rather than negotiating how to interact with males who resent your invasion of their dominance
of machinery. And you can benefit from the abundance of cultural inputs which inspire change in a different direction:
women's music over the headphones in the shop; regularly organized spiritual activities; changing of names which act as a
consciousness-raising; rampant discussion of language like the
use of "co" rather than "his" or "her" in bureaucratic edicts, and
so forth.

A final step in the process of challenging patriarchy is what
I want to call the "economic efficiency breakdown." There are
those who think that affirmative action and task rotation are not
economically efficient and that investing labor time in teaching
women construction detracts from reaching other investment
goals. But the counter-argument is also heard: the goal is to
improve the standard of living, which might be different from
improving the material wealth of the community. If it can be
argued that breaking down sex-role socialization improves the
quality of living, that androgyny is better than rigid sex-role
socialization, then gains for women might be made. But to argue
that a less repressive, freer environment leads to greater efficiency in the long run would be an even bolder statement.

In spite of the progress, obstacles to further development
arise. There is the gap between the structure which is so potentially liberating and the low level of feminist consciousness. The
gap originates in the discrepancy between non-sexism, which
implies equal opportunity, and feminism, which implies the cog-
nizance of a different oppressive history and the development of
different norms. So sexist *experiences* still abound for the visitor
or member, even though the objective structure for liberation is
profound. A man prefers that another man help him lift boxes.
In the interviewing process, assumptions are made about lack of
skills of women applicants. There is minimal discussion of issues
from a feminist perspective, and too much open feminism will

cause others, even women, to turn against a visitor for "rocking the boat." The problems could be overcome if there were a political force to push, but the existing women's group does not play an overtly political role, have a unified position on established principles, take concerted action, or get turned to as spokesgroup for the women in the community. Certainly, living at TO is not a step towards female nationalism unless it is seen as a training ground where women can learn skills and gain cooperative experience, nor is it a feminist utopia, in which androgyny would be achieved. It is, however, an attempt to structure a more humane society which inadvertently drops many of the oppressive structures based on the division of labor and the women's "double duty" unseen domestic and consumption work.

In conclusion: I came away from Twin Oaks with a strong feeling for the importance of working out feminist utopias in as much detail as Skinner did in *Walden II*, which inspired the Twin Oaks phenomenon. My vision was to abstract all the essential components of feminist theory and feminist utopian novels, to get together an analysis of these with women who have been trying to create international communities, as Twin Oaks is only one of many.

NOTE

1. See "The Other Side of the Paycheck," by Bridges and Weinbaum, in *Capitalist-Patriarchy: The Case for Socialist Feminism*, edited by Zillah Eisenstein (New York: Monthly Review Press, 1979).

2. Nancy Chodorow, *The Reproduction of Mothering: Psychoanalysis and the Reproduction of Mothering* (Berkeley: University of California Press, 1978); Dorothy Dinnerstein, *The Mermaid and the Minotaur: Sexual Arrangements and the Human Malaise* (New York: Harper & Row, 1976); and some essays in *Politics of Desire* edited by Ann Snitow (New York: Monthly Review Press, 1984).

3. Batya Weinbaum, *Pictures of Patriarchy* (Boston: South End Press, 1983).

Utopia in Question: Programming Women's Needs into the Technology of Tomorrow

JAN ZIMMERMAN

GIVEN the gloomy promise of the present political landscape, it's no surprise that the unconquerable, receding frontier of time unshackles the imagination from the fetters of day-to-day struggle, energizing efforts of social change with the whispered myth of a better tomorrow. In analyzing the technological component of tomorrow, I wish to explore the realities that technology could impose on women's lives. For instance: science fiction, by any but women writers, displays women providing services—all of the traditional ones—to men; advertisements provide images of women of the future using Lestoil "to make the moon a cleaner place to live"; projections of futurists, as in a recent description published by the *Los Angeles Times* of that city in the year 2080, often include no women at all.

In her poem "Autumn Sequence," Adrienne Rich writes that "The future reconnoiters in dirty boots/ along the cranberry-dark horizon." In this article, I propose to take a good hard look at those boots as they trample on women's lives in the office, in the home, and within their bodies.

Before proceeding to an examination of those three environments, it is essential to recall some basic realities about the relationship between technology and the economy. Economic growth in Western capitalism is measured by the development

of new products, and new consumers for them; increased productivity is assumed to derive from capital investment in high-cost, high technology, as a substitute for inefficient labor;[1] and the pre-eminent status of the United States as an economic power is perceived to be challenged by the technologically advanced economies of Japan and West Germany.

Any forecast of an economic future must rest upon the foundations of the economic present, a present which only grudgingly acknowledges that the economy is a woman's issue, in spite of the feminization of poverty—two-thirds of those households below the poverty level are headed by women. In addition, women's jobs are segregated at the low end of the pay scale—a 1978 survey showed that women in the federal government fill 77% of the lowest-paying slots GS-1 thru -4, but only 5% of the highest-paying slots of GS-16 and above.[2] And women continue to provide 80% to 90% of the unpaid labor in the home in spite of the rise in two-career households.[3]

The measurement of technological progress for women must assess whether new technology ultimately alters those economic realities, or if it leaves women in the state of the Red Queen in *Alice in Wonderland,* running faster and faster to stay in the same place.

The office environment is enjoying a surge of attention unmatched since Charles Dickens first exposed bureaucratic exploitation. New computerized office equipment could reduce drudgery, eliminate time wasted in retyping reports, and speed the search for electronically-stored information, thus improving a secretary's workday in qualitative ways. However, many companies, rather than introducing technology in a decentralized, work-integrated manner, have reconstructed the old typing pool, degrading the work of secretaries, 98% of whom are women, to that of data-entry or word-processing operators, placing them in a job situation that has no possible career ladder attached to it. It is hardly a coincidence that the move to office automation is occurring at a time when women are demanding equal pay for work of comparable worth, when office workers are unionizing, when women in the pink-collar ghetto have initiated national media campaigns to raise issues of job equity.

It is far too simplistic, and unfair, to look only at the loss of traditional and often unrewarding women's jobs as a measure of the impact of technology. If women are trained to handle new technologies, and if they receive commensurately high wages for their skills, technology can mean new careers for women in fields with a high demand, a shortage of skilled workers, and challenging opportunities for growth. This will, however, require some long-range planning and more foresight than has yet been evident, particularly for highly-touted computer careers.

In its July 1980 issue, *Computerworld* magazine described tomorrow's programmers as lower-paid clerical workers who will be "more adaptable to factory-style production environments." Eventually, software systems that generate other software "will reduce the need for human programmers to almost nothing." Simultaneously, the magazine headlined a National Science Foundation grant to the University of Texas at Austin to train women in computer science, "primarily to become programmers."

Such events can only prompt worry that women are ordained to receive "hand-me-down" technology. There is no reason—except the maintenance of power—that women must play the role of the "neglected orphans of the technological age," as Alice Embree observed in a germinal essay in *Sisterhood Is Powerful.*

Since most women have two careers, it is critical to consider the effects of technology on their second workplace, the home. Will new household technologies really alter the wry comment that "now, as always, the most automated appliance in a household is the mother"?[4]

Microprocessor chips, basically corn-flake sized computers, will be integrated into numerous appliances and systems to provide continuous energy-monitoring, automatic "on/off" switches for everything from lights to coffee-makers, and computer-managed household inventory and security systems. As home computers become more prevalent and cable/telephone interfaces proliferate, there will be an enormous shift to the electronic mediation of daily activities. Without leaving the house, it will be possible to read the newspaper, order groceries, pay bills and make bank deposits, vote on local issues, check entertainment schedules, book travel arrangements, do research, help the kids with their homework, and select video programs from the local library. Systems like these are now being evaluated to assess their market potential in communities from California to Florida.[5]

While telecommunications may save time and gasoline, living better vicariously will have its costs. First, women, the primary home consumers, will find themselves performing without pay the labor that used to be done by other women who got paid for it: bank tellers, grocery clerks, bookkeepers. For another, women may find their feet bound once again, this time with optical fiber, as electronic technology eliminates reasons to leave the house, making it more difficult to connect with other women, to facilitate political change, or to gather the most important information, the unexpected kind. Third, the gathering of demographic information on the basis of purchases[6] may lead not only to the invasion of market privacy, but to the preselection of news slanted to meet the expectations of a particular socioeconomic group.

The implications of re-privatization or re-isolation of women in the home is not receiving very careful scrutiny. Futurist Alvin Toffler, in his book *The Third Wave,* joyfully predicts the day of the electronic cottage, when it will even be possible to work from home using a computer. With not a shadow of shame, Toffler rejoices in the advent of new systems that will allow "married secretaries caring for small children at home to continue to work." Nary a word is said about the possibility that men working at home would be able to share child care.

All too often, new technologies are designed by men (only 1.6% of the electrical engineers in the United States are women[7]) who hold old values. By continuing to assume the primacy of the nuclear family, by refusing to acknowledge that women's roles have expanded, many male technical designers seek to replicate in the future those conditions that comforted them in the past. As architecture critic Ada Louise Huxtable lamented, albeit in the context of postmodernist architecture, "All over the country, now, the future is being repealed."

Having considered the office and the home, it is now time to consider the most personal of domains, a woman's body. For those few readers who were able to purchase Genetech stock at a low and sell at a high, the impact of biotechnology may be obvious. For the rest of the noninvesting world, however, the rapid growth of biological industries poses unexpected questions. What do stories about test-tube babies, surrogate mothers, and a cow bearing a calf that was conceived in a laboratory imply about a woman's control over her own body?

The history of male desire to control reproduction, the one aspect of nature that has eluded men's hands, is well documented.[8] From control over the development, marketing, and legal availability of contraceptive devices to the usurpation by male obstetricians of female midwives' role in the birth process, history has shown that in spite of the advent of the birth control pill, overall women have lost power in determining their own reproductive futures. It is especially timely to consider new reproductive technologies when women's right to abortion is under fire, for if women lose the right to say "no" to an unwanted pregnancy, they may also lose the right to say "yes." Without active concern by women, decisions about who can bear a child, or whose genes are considered "acceptable" or "preferable" will be left by default to male doctors who are pursuing research down these paths, accountable only to the stock market. A woman's role in biology may be reduced to that of an avatar of male pleasure.

Because of women's lack of knowledge about science and technology, their unfamiliarity with the vocabulary of the ruling technocracy, and their socialized helplessness when confronted with machines, women have been deceived by the myth of technological determinism. It's time to stop blaming Mother Nature and recognize that the fault belongs to Father Time and Uncle Sam.

By the time most technology hits the marketplace, a company has invested hundreds of thousands, perhaps millions of dollars in its development. At what point in development can or should social assessment of technology be made? When is it too late? How can women sensitive to women's concerns work in industry, not just as executives, but as early participants in the design process;

women who will say, "No, boys, that just won't sell," changing a product design at a time when it is still malleable?

The other problem is Uncle Sam. In many cases, the direction of technology is predetermined by the government through a course for research and development set years, even a decade, earlier by military and aerospace defense contracts. In such other direct ways as the "war on cancer," the government defines the allocation of resources and their direction. There are additional indirect ways, such as the deregulation of the cable television and oil industries, by which the government decides what kind of services will reach the public. Last, there are extremely subtle ways, such as the Supreme Court decision allowing new forms of life to be patented,[9] in which the government shapes the future. When the mask of nature is removed, technology is found to wear a familiar, political face.

As an example of this myth of technological determinism at work, consider the experience of the National Women's Agenda in using a NASA satellite in 1977. As the Agenda planned its program, it ran into unexpected "technical" snags: if the words "lesbianism" or "abortion" were mentioned, the satellite would fall from the sky, leaving all the NASA engineers running around like so many Chicken Littles.[10] By the way, no satellite fell to earth when women leased privately-owned transporters for the United Nations Mid-Decade Conference on Women in Copenhagen or for the American Association of University Women's 1981 convention.[11]

But once aware of the fact that new technologies, either in form or content, can reconstruct a patriarchal value system, what can be done about them? How can women reverse the path of what Jacques Ellul described in *The Technological Society* as "a civilization in quest of continually improved means to carelessly examined ends?"

First and foremost, women must open up the questions of technological development to public debate, educating the general population in the language and methods of technology, starting at the elementary school level. Second, women must strive to reduce the gap between technological "haves" and "have nots," a gap which will reproduce inequities in power as surely as those produced by income differential. These lofty goals require the construction of new strategies of which the following are but a few examples:

Public hearings could be held on the impact of technological industries as a prerequisite for local business licenses, zoning variances, and tax write-offs; not only for those industries which present environmental health hazards from toxic and/or radio-active waste disposal, but for those which have implications for social dislocation through telecommunications or information accessibility. The process of public debate over biotechnology or interactive video is crucial to generate the kind of awareness that turns consumer acceptability of a new technology into an issue.

Developing a feedback and response mechanism between consumers and corporations that would be more effective and more accurate than the faulty, manipulated marketplace is essential, but unlikely, unless women can be represented at all levels of technological development. To do this, programs are needed to encourage girls and women to enter technical fields, to overcome math anxiety, sex role stereotyping, and financial barriers to technical training. Supportive learning environments for all women wishing to gain computer and technical literacy must also be provided.

In these days of increasingly job-focused education, one of the most difficult tasks will be to alter engineering education to encompass questions of values, ethics, and social consequences. And new support associations need to be developed for women who are already in technical positions, to help them understand the implications for women of the products now under development and to end their isolation from feminist organizations.

Technology is not a neutral force. It does not spread its benefits equally, regardless of sex, race, or economic class. Of each new technology women must ask: Will the relative economic status of women improve? Will the technology set new limits, such as restricted access to information, on women's drive to achieve equal power? Will it further a woman's control over her own life and enable her to develop her full potential as a human being? If so, how can we ensure that the benefits of new technology are available to all? If not, how do women take hold of technology to create the world they want to live in? Although trapped in the mire of day-to-day survival, women must direct time and attention to the creation of alternative visions of the future, or else they may be left out of it.

NOTES

1. *U.S. News & World Report,* November 12, 1979, p. 89.

2. Philippa Strum, "Women at Work: Is Discrimination Real?" *Perspectives: The Civil Rights Quarterly* (Summer 1980).

3. Janice Mall, "Women's Work Is Still Never Done," *Los Angeles Times,* October 5, 1980, part 7, p. 6.

4. Beverly Jones, "The Dynamics of Marriage and Motherhood," in *Sisterhood Is Powerful,* ed. Robin Morgan (New York: Vintage Books, 1970), p. 56.

5. "Push-button Telephones Link Shoppers to a Computer Base," *San Jose Mercury News,* May 17, 1981; Linda Grant, "Computers for Home Use Put to Test," *Los Angeles Times,* September 28, 1980, part 1, p. 7.

6. Sandra Salmans, "Scanners Monitor Buying," *New York Times,* August 17, 1981, p. D8.

7. *Engineering Manpower Bulletin,* no. 52 (April 1981), Engineering Manpower Commission.

8. Adrienne Rich, *Of Woman Born* (New York: W. W. Norton & Co., 1976).

9. Jim Mann, "Scientists May Patent Life Made in Lab, Justices Rules," *Los Angeles Times,* June 17, 1980.

10. Jan Zimmerman, "Women and Satellites," *Media Report to Women* (July 1978), pp. 4–10.

11. Donna Allen, "First Satellite Teleconference by Women," *Media Report to Women* (July 1980), pp. 1, 3, 4, 10, 11: author participated in teleconference origination, WGBH-TV, Boston, June 24, 1981.

The Craft of Their Hands

FRANCES WHYATT

for Erika and Diane who build geodesic domes and
Egges

I AM afraid of the women here
The house is full of their abilities
It sings with the craft of their hands

Erika the fixer
Goddess of broken stoves
Hot water heaters
Cars that go bump in the night
Fingers switched on by propane
Folding in like greedy spiders on wires
Wrenches, ratchets, hammers, an occasional screw
Driver of turbines, of switched on connections
The slide ruler sits herself down upon her nest

Egge's? Artiface out of womb
Or house seen as polyurethane egg
The womb of the fixer holds a mack truck
Bigger than the senate, than a room full of tools
Than an ocean of juggernauts

The house of her head is calculean
And wired for sound

She carries the weight of multiple equation
The spirit rests on symmetrical planes

    in the sky blesses the fixer
Blesses her blue jeans
Blesses the wires kissed by her teeth
Blesses fiberglass crystals in her hair
Blond curly strands falling into gadgetry
Blesses her eyes as they stare down technology
Blesses her electrons, her telepathic sleep

Diane the builder
Goddess of the handmade bow, she
Who hones the edges to satin
Whittles at the universe, fashions a table
Takes her staple gun and insulates the world
Raphael cherub's hair smelling of elmer's glue
The book cases new and her stamp on the walls
Homemade is the huntress
Who builds the frame

Carving out spice rack
The mind sizes wood, counts centimeters
The hands say hosanna to the hammer
Hosanna to the carver's knife
Small, suresharp, infinitely gentle at its task
Hosanna to the planks as they fit together
Neat and sexual as lovers moving toward a bed

She makes her shelf amidst the chick peas
The cottage cheese and yogurt
Great Neck girl of the revolution
She'll build the hall in which she dances

At home with the women
Under the full sail of their abilities
I count my fingers and wish them buildings
I count my legs and wish them hammers

I count my arms and wish them bulldozers
I look into my eyes and wish them geometry
I look into my head and wish it a compass
I look into my heart and wish it architecture
I look into my womb and wish I had designed it

I bless invention from their fingers
I sing Hosanna to the craft of their hands

Imagining a Different World of Talk

BARRIE THORNE, CHERIS KRAMARAE,
AND NANCY HENLEY

THE recognition that the personal is political—a central feminist insight—has turned attention to daily experiences long taken for granted. Feminists have uncovered a "micropolitical structure" of dominance and submission in the ways men and women talk, gesture, move, touch.[1] We are making connections between the use of speech and nonverbal communication, and larger political and economic inequalities which they reflect and reinforce. And we are reconsidering language use in women's groups as interaction which can be used to empower each other rather than to dominate.

ASYMMETRIES IN THE TALK OF WOMEN AND MEN

When women and men converse, in intimate and more formal settings, men usually talk more, both in amount and time and number of turns at talk.[2] Men exert conversational control not only through sheer quantity of speech, but also through interruptions. In a variety of experimental and naturalistic studies of cross-sex conversations, Candace West and Don Zimmerman have found that men disproportionately interrupt women. When women interrupt, men tend to treat the violation as inconsequential.[3] Women and men also have different address rights in public; when women walk down public streets,

Barrie Thorne, Cheris Kramarae, and Nancy Henley, "Imagining a Different World of Talk," copyright © 1984 by Barrie Thorne, Cheris Kramarae, Nancy Henley.

men may stare openly, remark on women's bodies, call them "honey" or obscenities, and yet often fail to recognize how offensive these remarks are to the women.[4] Women do not claim similar rights toward men; street harassment, like other forms of male control, is asymmetric.

In the give-and-take of daily conversations between women and men, women do more of the invisible labor which keeps talking going. Pamela Fishman analyzed tapes of household conversations of three heterosexual couples.[5] The topics men raised were much more often developed than those women raised, largely because of women's greater "interaction work" (answering and asking questions, providing active conversational support, for example, by inserting *ahuh* and *mhm* while the men talked). When women raised topics, the men often made only minimal responses. Men are also less likely than women to disclose feelings and personal information; such withholding is another means of conversational control.[6]

Micropolitical inequalities structure nonverbal as well as verbal behavior. Men tend to touch women more than *vice versa;* in the ways they move, sit, and gesture, men expand, while women tend to condense, taking up less space.[7]

When women learn of these research findings, they often feel a pang of recognition. Awareness of these forms of daily oppression lends urgency to the question: How can everyday patterns of dominance and submission be changed, so women (and other subordinates) are more fully self-determining, and less cut off from resources of talk, movement, space? How might everyday interaction be different in a feminist utopia?

WHAT IS TO BE DONE?

The most popular strategy for change is epitomized by assertiveness training, an approach which argues that if women want to claim more verbal space, they must change the way they speak. This approach assumes that women's ways of speech and interaction are intrinsically weak and uncertain. Lakoff, for example, describes a number of features which she believes characterize "women's language," claiming that women are disadvantaged relative to men by their socialization to "feminine speech."[8] However, empirical studies of sex differences in these speech features have yielded conflicting results; it is not clear that there is any "women's language," nor is it clear that the features of language associated with women speakers are intrinsically weak. Nevertheless, writers in the assertiveness-training mode urge women to speak up, reciprocate interruptions, take up more space.

Altering their speech and styles of interaction may indeed help women command more presence in competitive, male-dominated situations, but there are serious problems with this strategy. The assertiveness-training approach is highly individualistic and tends to blame the victim for problems which lodge elsewhere: *the problem is taken to be women's speech, not men's control of women's speech.* In general, men take their language more for granted than women can or do; and those who focus on female speech apart from interaction context make the same error, treating male language as normal and female language as problematic.[9]

Instead of asking how individual women can "better" their speech, we need to understand women's language in context. If women speak in ways that sound uncertain or if they take fewer turns at talk in mixed-sex encounters, it may be, at least in part, because women are differentially interrupted and ignored. Attention needs to be paid to ways in which men actively control and restrict women's speech. Perhaps it is men, more than women, who need to change the way they talk.

The assertiveness-training approach does not challenge the fact that women and their talk are largely defined by and in terms of men. Unless these assumptions, which are anchored in patriarchal institutions, are changed, no matter how women speak, their talk will be devalued.

A more deeply feminist approach seeks to change the world on our own, not patriarchal terms. Putting talk among women at the center of vision helps break with the assumption that men's ways of speech are intrinsically more desirable.

TALK AMONG WOMEN

Early in the last decade, largely owing to the revaluing of women and their bonds which was a gift of the feminist movement, researchers came to see how little we know about the talking and nonverbal worlds of women with women. There is far more information about male-male interaction (for example, research on small groups and vernaculars was initially conducted only with men and boys). Recent research on talk among women has begun to undermine the stereotypes ("clucking hens") which have so often been applied to women's groups. There is imaginative new research on women's gossip, humor, and story-telling, which are no longer trivialized but made visible, and revalued as verbal art.[10] And there are more studies of the speech and nonverbal patterns used by groups of women and girls.

When women converse with women, there is more mutality of interaction work. Susan Kalčik describes narrative styles she observed in two consciousness-raising groups of white women.[11] The women paid careful attention to turn-taking, encouraging everyone to speak, and asking for comments from the individuals who were relatively silent. The talk was strongly collaborative rather than competitive. In an experimental study, Elizabeth Aries found more symmetry in the interaction of all-female than in that of all-male and mixed-sex groups. In all-female groups, leadership was more flexible or rotating, while the all-male groups established a rigid dominance order among speakers.[12] Finally, Marjorie Goodwin compared the spontaneous speech of a group of girls with that of a group of boys at play in a Black working-class urban neighborhood. She found the boys continuously negotiated hierarchies through their speech, by issuing direct commands, contradicting the proposals of others, and usurping turn space. In contrast, the girls, although also often argumentative, used more symmetrical language. Their group had a more fluid hierarchy, and through directives like "let's" and "we gotta," they constructed directions as suggestions for future action, lessening distinctions between speakers and hearers.[13]

We have much yet to learn about talk among women, and among girls, and we need far more attention to variations by age, social class, and race. But these scattered findings have already challenged traditional frameworks of analysis, which were originally developed in the context of all-male or mixed-sex talk. Research centering on women's speech has suggested alternative models for understanding the choreographies of conversation. Carole Edelsky found that women participate more actively when the "floor" of talk is more informal and collaborative than the model of discrete turns which is used by conversation analysts.[14] The collaborative forms of story-telling (one person begins a story and others help elaborate) which Kalčik[15] describes in women's consciousness-raising groups depart from the conventional models of narrative which more sharply distinguish speaker from audience.[16]

Talk among women also provides a fresh vantage point on questions of change. The value of speech strategies and styles which women use more frequently than men—especially when women are with one another—needs to be reassessed. The collaborative patterns which are central to talk among women—drawing out other speakers, supportive listening and head nods, mutual sharing of emotions and personal knowledge, respect for one another's conversational space—are "weak" or "power-less" (as the assertiveness-training approach claims) only when contrasted with their opposites. For example, open, sharing behaviors become weak only when another person in an interaction refuses to reciprocate them. Being sensitive to others' needs—inviting them to take turns at talk, drawing out the topics they raise—is heard as ineffectual only when this sensitivity is not reciprocated. Revealing emotions is a disadvantage only when others are being reserved and refusing to share or to show emotion. Women's speech is "powerless" only relative to the power of so-called masculine patterns. When only women are told to change their behavior, and essentially to adopt "male forms," the characteristics of male speech are ignored, and the assumption of power as domination is reproduced.

THE FEMINIST VISION OF EMPOWERMENT

A feminist definition of power—power as energy, effective interaction, and empowerment—contrasts with and challenges the traditional assumption of power as domination or control. The feminist challenge, Nancy Hartsock observes,[17] is to develop forms based on this alternative vision as a way of transforming institutions based on dominance. This perspective suggests an alternative strategy for transforming gender asymmetries in interaction. The patterns of talk associated with women suggest ways of changing the larger world of speech, empowering all participants and challenging the communication patterns used by those in control.

Mischa Adams provides an example of this process in a discussion of telling moments when women and men have transformed stereotyped interactions.[18] She describes a graduate seminar in which the women were rendered silent, while the professor and most of the male students monopolized talk, controlling the floor through eye contact, interruption, and throwing the floor only to one another. Those who were squeezed out analyzed these patterns and set out to change them, not by adopting the dominant discourse, but by empowering one another. They arrived early and sat in a way which diffused eye contact around the group; they built on one another's comments in the discussion, giving the mutual gift of interaction work; they invited the silent to speak. Rather than overvaluing and imitating the dominant style (monopoly of turn-space, interruptions, topic control), they used collaborative patterns to draw in, and empower, more participants.

A second example of feminist transformation of language, again starting from women's experiences, comes from literature: Adrienne Rich's efforts to create a new language which transcends the patriarchal legacy of received forms. As Joanne Fiet Diehl observes, this is a bold, even heroic venture, but Rich does not undertake it in the aggressive ways of patriarchal discourse. She uses a "gentle poetics," speech close to women's experiences and intimate conversation, language which is empowering rather than dominating.[19]

If revalued and examined closely, talk among women suggests that daily life can be structured in more cooperative and mutually empowering ways, enhancing relationships where people "help each other belong to themselves."[20]

We have turned to present experiences to imagine a different future, and in so doing we have neglected several different problems. Most of the research on gender and language focuses on white, middle- and upper-middle-class speakers.[21] Differences, and inequalities, among women and men of varied races, classes, ages, and sexualities make the picture far more complex than we have painted. We have also glossed over tensions and conflicts among women, and the fact that women's talk—even when they are apart from men—has emerged within patriarchal contexts and is shaped by subordination and oppression, as well as by women's resistance and creativity. The feminist struggle involves sorting out the dimensions of experience we want to leave behind, from those we want to retain and build upon. Close attention to talk among women can help us envisage a more desirable future. We need such imagining to know what we're struggling towards.

NOTES

1. Nancy Henley, *Body Politics: Power, Sex, and Nonverbal Communication* (Englewood Cliffs, N.J.: Prentice-Hall, Inc., 1977).

2. For supporting documentation of this and other speech and nonverbal patterns described in the paper, see "Sex Similarities and Differences in Verbal and Nonverbal Communication: An Annotated Bibliography," in Barrie Thorne, Cheris Kramarae, and Nancy Henley, eds., *Language, Gender and Society* (Rowley, Mass.: Newbury House, 1983).

3. Candace West and Don H. Zimmerman, "Small Insults:

A Study of Interruptions in Cross-Sex Conversations between Unacquainted Persons," in Thorne, Kramarae, and Henley, *Language, Gender, and Society.*

4. Carol Brooks Gardner, "Passing By: Street Remarks, Address Rights, and The Urban Female," *Sociological Inquiry,* 50 (1981), pp. 328–356.

5. Pamela Fishman, "Interaction: The Work Women Do," *Social Problems,* 25 (1978), pp. 397–406.

6. Jack W. Sattel, "The Inexpressive Male: Tragedy or Sexual Politics?" *Social Problems,* 23 (1976), pp. 469–477.

7. Henley, *Body Politics.*

8. Robin Lakoff, *Language and Women's Place* (New York: Harper & Row, 1975).

9. Cheris Kramarae, *Women and Men Speaking* (Rowley, Mass.: Newbury House, 1981).

10. Marta Weigle, "Women as Verbal Artists: Reclaiming the Sisters of Enheduanna," *Frontiers,* 3, No. 3 (1978), pp. 1–9; Deborah Jones, "Gossip: Notes on Women's Oral Culture," in Cheris Kramarae, ed., *The Voices and Words of Women and Men* (Oxford: Pergamon Press, 1980), pp. 193–198: Ruth Borker, "Anthropology: Social and Cultural Perspectives," in Sally McConnell-Ginet, Ruth Borker, and Nelly Furman, eds., *Women and Language in Literature and Society* (New York: Praeger Publishers, 1980), pp. 26–44.

11. Susan Kalčik, " '. . . like Ann's gynecologist or the time I was almost raped': Personal Narratives in Women's Rap Groups," *Journal of American Folklore,* 88 (1975), pp. 3–11.

12. Elizabeth Aries, "Interaction Patterns and Themes of Male, Female, and Mixed Groups," *Small Group Behaviour,* 7 (1976), pp. 7–18.

13. Marjorie Harness Goodwin, "Directive-response speech sequences in girls' and boys' task activities," in McConnell-Ginet, *et al., Women and Language,* pp. 157–173.

14. Carole Edelsky, "Who's Got the Floor?" *Language in Society,* 10 (1981), pp. 383–421.

15. Kalčik, " '. . . like Ann's gynecologist,' " pp. 3–11.

16. Mercilee M. Jenkins, "Stories Women Tell: An Ethnographic Study of Personal Experience Narratives in a Women's Rap Group" (Paper given at the Tenth World Congress of Sociology, Mexico City, 1982).

17. Nancy Hartsock, "Political Change: Two Perspectives

On Power," in Quest Staff and Book Committee, eds., *Building Feminist Theory* (New York: Longman, 1981), pp. 3–19.

18. Mischa B. Adams, "Communication and Gender Stereotype" (Ph.D. diss., University of California, Santa Cruz, 1980).

19. Joanne Feit Diehl, "Cartographies of Silence: Rich's *Common Language* and the Woman Poet," *Feminist Studies*, 6 (1980). Lee Gershuny, in Part Three of this volume, describes other ways in which women are combing through and redefining language to fit their needs. In *Native Tongue*, a science fiction novel about linguistics (in press), Suzette Elgin creates a new language (Láadan) to express the perceptions of women. In the novel (which contains a grammar and dictionary of Láadan) women are able to carry out their dangerous project of creating a language adequate to their perceptions, because men don't take them seriously—first, because it is *known* people can't really create new languages (as opposed to revising existing ones); second, because if anyone *were* going to do language-making, it would not be women; and, third, because whatever women did create would be silly. However improbable it may seem to men, women *are* language-making, an activity which will help us redefine ourselves and our conversations.

20. In *Among Women* (New York: Harper & Row, 1980), Louise Bernikow uses this phrase to refer to experiences of close friendship with women.

21. The speech of Black women in literature defines some patterns for study. For example, in her novel *Their Eyes Were Watching God* (New York: Negro University Press, 1969), Zora Neale Hurston provides illustrations of the richness of Black female storytelling and mythmaking, reflected in conversations.

The Linguistic Transformation of Womanhood

H. LEE GERSHUNY

IN criticizing patriarchal institutions, feminist writers have generated a *parole feministe*[1] both to transform and transcend patriarchal paradigms. To perceive herself as subject in present or future worlds first requires what Mary Daly calls an "exorcism" of masculinist language and, secondly, a means of expression that reveals and unravels feminist consciousness. Starting from different perspectives, feminist writers are developing that language in forms as varied as philosophical treatises and utopian literature. The result is that feminist metaphors, models, myths, and methods not only reflect a unified sensibility, but an integration of three phases of feminist consciousness: analysis and criticism, transformation, and transcendence.

PHASE I—ANALYSIS AND CRITICISM

In the first phase, feminist researchers demonstrated how language structures and perpetuates the perceptions and values of an androcentric world. The language of various media—television, film, texts, and social institutions, i.e., language in everyday use—is analyzed, and patterns of linguistic sexism de-

Part of this article originally appeared in H. Lee Gershuny's paper, "Metaphors and Metamorphoses. Language and the Transformation of Womanhood," presented at the International Conference on General Semantics, Toronto, Ontario, Canada, August 12, 1980.

scribed. Studies that have already become classics in the field identified the following patterns of linguistic sexism: (a) *stereotyping*, (b) *derogation* of female associated language, (c) *syntactic and semantic subordination* of feminine terms, (d) *syntactic and semantic invisibility* of the feminine, and (e) *trivialization* of female concerns, issues, and achievements.[2] These patterns polarize the qualities of each sex stereotype into hierarchies dominated by masculine traits. I and thou, mind and body, objectivity and subjectivity, heaven and earth, female and male, are ranked and divided. In general, active "masculinity" dominates and controls passive "femininity." Dualism, opposition, difference, and dominance characterize patriarchal myths and metaphors that echo throughout the Judeo-Christian cosmology and moral order. Such constructs help to institutionalize racism, sexism, and fragmentation of self from environment. In patriarchal perceptions, *man conquers the land, controls nature* and *keeps woman in her place.* Difference is perceived as opposition, outside of and not part of self.

PHASE II—TRANSFORMATION

In response to widespread criticism of linguistic sexism, many professional organizations and publishers devised non-sexist guidelines for writers and editors. During the last fifteen years, nonsexist terms have come to life in both speech and writing. Alternative life-style communities, e.g., Twin Oaks, have used *co,* an alternative to the pseudogeneric *he* and *mankind.*[3] In her novel *Woman on the Edge of Time,* Marge Piercy coined the pronoun *per* for the androgynous beings of the future, along with other morphological and semantic changes reflecting the new consciousness.

In addition to providing nonsexist alternatives, such terms as *herstory, Manglish, Sisterhood of Man, phallustine,* and *testeria* call attention to the inequities embedded in androcentric symbols.[4] Feminist scholars are correcting errors of commission and omission of women's contribution to various disciplines. Women all over the world are reclaiming their own names and their right to name themselves, their perceptions, and experience. Changing language not only helps to change the way we perceive reality, but also provides the methods of exploring and questioning that reality.

PHASE III—TRANSCENDENCE

Androcentric forms are transformed and transcended by means of vehicles compatible with feminist consciousness and values. Metaphors actually change consciousness while simultaneously sparking the dream and generation of a common language. What are the other vehicles of the linguistic transformation of womanhood? To what reality do these vehicles journey? What wondrous womanhood and brave new world does the evolving *parole feministe* construct?

In discarding masculinist maps that polarize female and male into hierarchies, feminist writers have attempted to blend reason and feeling in a unified sensibility. As a result, forms of feminist inquiry merge poetry and philosophy, history and myth, psychology and religion, and the personal and the political. Their voices, trained in the language of traditional disciplines, argue that a reality structured on Cartesian dualities splits mind from body, life from death, and good from evil. Such dualities create the illusion of separation and polarization. They suggest that clear boundaries divide mind and body as distinctly as God separated light from darkness and woman from man. Dualism blinds us to the interaction of mind/body, the changes of mind/body during these interactions, and the wholeness of mind/body. In Western cultures, the body-flesh is not only linked with the female pole, but subordinate to the superior male pole of mind-spirit.

The hidden dualistic assumptions in patriarchal language, identified by feminists, have also been examined in Korzybski's principles of General Semantics. Feminists, like general semanticists, have used language to bring deep structure to the surface and background to foreground. In general semantics, *etc.* acknowledges the non-allness of language. For a feminist, however, *etc.* doesn't go far enough since the omitted secondary details of "and others," and "and so forth," have often referred to unheard and invisible female experience. Initial formulations of feminist consciousness expanded the semantic space of *etc.* Herstory was revealed in published diaries, art retrospectives, literature, film, theology, women's history and psychology, and general criticism of language and society. Expanding the semantics of *etc.* does not mean simply adding token female representation to specific fields of inquiry or changing a god to a goddess. Feminist transformations of gender-linked taxonomies and models are nonadditive; their formulations and modes of expression go beyond revisionary nonsexist alternatives to revolutionary revelations and rituals.

Once women name and define themselves, they step outside existing androcentric categories and hierarchies into uncharted territory. In transforming patriarchal patterns, we not only re-create ourselves, but also reclaim the power to name and define the world as we see it.[5] Novelists like Ursula LeGuin in *The Left Hand of Darkness* and Marge Piercy in *Woman on the Edge of Time* have constructed and named utopian worlds where they literally plotted the territory of a feminist philosophy and world view.

In her paper, "Toward a New Language, Consciousness and Political Theory," Carol Pearson observes that in feminist utopian fiction in general, women seem to agree about the kind of society they want:

The ideal uniformly is decentralized, cooperative anarchies, in which everyone has power over their own life, and no one controls anyone else's. There are no laws and no taboos, except the cultural consensus against interfering with another's life. The basic unit of social organization is like an extended family, but without a basis in biology. People do not live together because they are related, but because they choose to be together. . . . There is no central government, no big cities, but there are highly developed communication networks between social units, and great opportunities for horizontal mobility. Within the microcosmic social units, people know and cherish each other as in an ideal family; the good of the individual is thus not considered to be in opposition to the good of others because none of us profits from gaining anything at the expense of anyone we love.

The basic values of these societies are the growth and autonomy of each individual; yet, individuals understand that no man or woman is an island, all personal growth occurs in the context of one's relationships with others.[6]

Expressing feminist theory in the language of fantasy literature becomes the *means* and the *method* for unifying language with consciousness and the political with the personal.

In her prose work of feminist theory, *Woman and Nature: The Roaring Inside Her,* Susan Griffin uses poetic expression in what Adrienne Rich called "new perceptions of reality creating their own form." In the "Preface," Griffin describes how her language and forms of expression evolved from feminist feeling and philosophy:

> In the process of writing I found that I could best discover my insights about the logic of civilized man by going underneath logic, that is by writing associatively, and thus enlisting my intuition, or uncivilized self. Thus my prose in this book is like poetry, and like poetry always begins with feeling. One of the loudest complaints which this book makes about patriarchal thought (or the thought of civilized man) is that it claims to be objective, and separated from emotion, and so it is appropriate that the style of this book does not make that separation.[7]

The format and different type style juxtapose Griffin's impassioned, embodied voice, textured by the voices of other women, to man's disembodied objectivity in an implicit dialogue.

Like Griffin's, Dorothy Dinnerstein's perceptions create their own new form. In what sometimes seems like a labyrinthine maze of notes, parenthetical remarks, and boxed commentaries, expanding the textual *etc.,* Dinnerstein's dialogue between reasoned argument and feeling suggests our ambiguous participation in the human/animal world, and gives form to the metaphor and title of her book: *The Mermaid and the Minotaur: Sexual Arrangements and Human Malaise.* She describes her method as:

> . . . a distillation from an inner reservoir in which personal experience has flowed together with varied streams of formal thought:

social-philosophical, social-scientific, literary, and psycho-analytic streams. . . .[8]

Others, writing in more traditional forms, have also embraced symbols of unity and community in evolving new consciousness. In her book, *Behind the Sex of God*, Carol Ochs, for example, proposes a monistic view of divinity that challenges the duality and opposition inherent in patriarchy. As a result, she reconceives the nature of the deity as:

> . . . not apart from, separate from, or other than this reality. We, all together, are part of the whole, the All in All. God is not father, nor mother, nor even parents, because God is not other than, distinct from, or opposed to creation.[9]

To give form to her insight, Ochs suggests that her relationship to God is analogous to the relationship of a cell in her body to herself. Her argument rejects belief in either patriarchy or matriarchy, and as such, represents a major revolution.

A similar revolutionary vision is explored by the feminist/ theologian/psychologist, Naomi Goldenberg, in her book *Changing of the Gods*. Goldenberg criticizes the metaphorical and mythical images of an external male god, the rituals reenacting male supremacy, and the traditional polarization of body/soul, sex/celibacy, and secular/religious experiences. Goldenberg rejects surface text revisions and opts for full-scale theological revolution. In urging women to "cease depending on the metaphor of Jesus *him*self,"[10] she explicitly states that no feminist can save god, the father. In place of Judeo-Christian religious rites and traditions, she suggests the process of Jungian depth psychology to "tie together the diverse strands of feminist work in religion and help advance the healing of the split of mind/body."[11]

Goldenberg holds feminist witchcraft as most promising in providing a medium for the reinvention of womanhood collectively and individually. Feminist witchcraft not only elevates the image of woman in religious symbology, but that of natural life-processes as well. These rituals do not focus on death, martyrdom, and self-denial, but return religion to greater involvement with life-processes of birth, growth, and decay. Witches have changed god's image "from a celibate male above and beyond humanity to an image of a vibrant female who is a part of our physical and psychic life."[12]

The underlying principle in each writer's language—her method and formulation—is not only the unification of heart and head, but of self with human society and the environment. Some feminists have revived and redefined *androgyny* as a metaphor of unity and community, but many scholar/poets who have been critical of androcentric language and instrumental in evolving a *parole feministe* have rejected androgyny as a metaphor rooted in patriarchal myths and meanings.[13] *Androgyny,* they argue, suggests, in form and connotation, the dualism feminists wish to transform and transcend. As Mary Daly reiterates, "*androgyny* is a confusing term . . . conveying something like John Travolta and Farrah Fawcett-Majors scotch-taped together."[14]

The implicit dualism perceived in *androgyny* raises a more subtle issue about feminist metaphors. If feminists are so interested in transforming gender semantics, why do they seem to accept the traditional stereotypes of mind-reason as "masculine" and body-feeling as "feminine"? The feminist language I have described does *not* accept polarization of gender and human behavior. Rather women are re-valuing and redefining human qualities and behavior previously ignored, demeaned, and attacked as weak, womanish evils. In developing a language consonant with our consciousness and experience, feminists are wrenching familiar terms from dualistic contexts and charging them with new meaning. In the process, pejorative [+female] terms are being returned to their source, rejuvenated, and ameliorated. Words, such as *cave, earth, goddess, witch, androgyny, water, chrysalis, crone,* used as metaphors by men, have connoted either negative, ambiguous aspects of "femininity," or "natural" traits. In feminist contexts, however, the metaphors are not only ameliorated, but connected in images of spiralling processes.

This is precisely what Mary Daly does with *Hag, Crone,* and *Spinster* in word play transformations of time and space in her work *Gyn/Ecology: The Metaethics of Radical Feminism.*[15] Daly defines her book and the transformed word of its title, *Gyn/Ecology,* as a "metapatriarchal journey of exorcism and ecstasy." The journey resembles revelatory and utopian literature that unites passion and thought in nonlinear metaphors of space and time.

The metaphor *Gyn/Ecology* not only reflects Daly's image of unity and community, but is representative of the way she uses the print medium as the message. Daly's use of hyphen, slash, capital, and lower-case letters expresses connectedness, process, and continuity of foreground/background and part/whole. Her work is both visual and musical. Her verbs, *wrench, castrate, exorcise,* are powerful and precise in expressing her method of transforming language and thought. Her puns, neologisms, portmanteau words, metaphors, juxtapositions, reversals, derivations, and definitions create what she calls the "method" for evolving spiritual consciousness.[16] She encourages the reader/voyager to hear her own voice, develop her own expressions, discover her own limits, and give birth to herself. Daly provides the vehicle, form, and route toward transformation and transcendence. In her work, language is both the medium and the message.

The evolving *parole feministe* reveals personal, political, and metaphysical concerns as various dimensions of a single unified reality. It implies a nonlinear reality where multi-dimensional labyrinths of experience interact. In rejecting phallic myth and language, which "generate, legitimate, and mask the material pollution that threatens to terminate all sentient life on this planet,"[17] it eschews alienation in favor of ecology—a unity of Self in Community with other organisms/environments.

The idea is not new, nor is it simply expressed in a new form. That its source is woman—a once silenced voice that, when heard, usually "thought like a man"—is both revolutionary and ecological. While the language of patriarchy distorts our response to "Mother Nature," ourselves, and reality. The language of feminism suggests that reality is a "complex web of interrelationships between organisms and their environments."[18]

Feminist ethics, similar to that implied in the principles of General Semantics, assume the "other" is part of Self. Once the "other" is no longer objectified as an "it"/thing or dominated as an inferior, there is less likelihood of enslaving, persecuting, or omitting the "Thou."

Unlike Newspeak 1984, *parole feministe* expands and transforms semantic space. It diversifies the possibilities of human thought and behavior instead of constricting them. Instead of omitting, it includes and elaborates. A liberating language, according to Daly, speaks in many voices and modes: "Spooking, Sparking, Spinning," as each feminist, woman and man, "transmutes the base metals of man-made myth by becoming unmute, calling forth from our Selves and each other the courage to name the unnameable."[19]

NOTES

1. *Parole,* borrowed from Saussure, refers to the features of actual language use and *feministe* identifies the community using the *parole* described in the rest of the paper.

2. Barrie Thorne and Nancy Henley, eds., *Language and Sex: Difference and Dominance* (Rowley, Mass.: Newbury House Publishers, Inc., 1975) and Alleen Pace Nilsen, Haig Bosmajian, H. Lee Gershuny and Julia P. Stanley, *Sexism and Language* (Urbana, Ill.: National Council of Teachers of English, 1977).

3. Casey Miller and Kate Swift, *Words and Women: New Language in New Times* (Garden City, N.Y.: Anchor Books, 1977), p. 116.

4. Varda One, "Manglish," unpublished paper; Emily Culpepper, "Female History/Myth Making," *Second Wave,* 4, no. 1 (1975); Ann Sheldon, Letter, *The Village Voice,* 17 Dec. 1970; Juli Loesch, "Testeria and Penisolence—A Scourge to Humankind," *Aphra: The Feminist Literary Magazine,* 4, no. 1 (1972–73), pp. 43–45; Katy Barasc, Letter, *Matrices,* n.d.; and Mary Daly, *Beyond God the Father* (Boston: Beacon Press, 1973), p. 172.

5. Julia P. Stanley and Susan W. Robbins, "Toward a Feminist Aesthetic," Conference on Language and Style, New York, 16 April 1977.

6. Carol Pearson, "Toward a New Language, Consciousness and Political Theory: The Utopian Novels of Dorothy Bryant, Mary Staton, and Marge Piercy," MLA Convention, San Francisco, December, 1979.

7. Susan Griffin, *Woman and Nature: The Roaring Inside Her* (New York: Harper & Row, Publishers, 1978), p. xv.

8. Dorothy Dinnerstein, *The Mermaid and the Minotaur: Sexual Arrangements and Human Malaise* (New York: Harper Colophon Books, 1977), pp. viii–ix.

9. Carol Ochs, *Behind the Sex of God: Toward a New Consciousness—Transcending Matriarchy and Patriarchy* (Boston: Beacon Press, 1977), p. 135.

10. Naomi Goldenberg, *Changing of the Gods: Feminism and the End of Traditional Religions* (Boston: Beacon Press, 1978), p. 25.

11. *Ibid.*

12. *Ibid.*

13. "The Androgyny Papers," *Women's Studies* 2 (1974), 139–271.

14. Mary Daly, *Gyn/Ecology: The Metaethics of Radical Feminism* (Boston: Beacon Press, 1978), p. x.

15. *Ibid.,* pp. 14–17.

16. *Ibid.,* pp. 22–27.

17. *Ibid.,* p. 9.

18. *Ibid.*

19. *Ibid.,* p. 34.

Part Four

VISIONS OF
UTOPIA

Introduction

ELAINE HOFFMAN BARUCH

IN reading utopias by men, one often gets a sense that women are literally no place—that they have no place in these new places other than their old one. Despite some of the authors' disclaimers to the contrary, the women are shown as prisoners of sex; they have no future, for their anatomy is destiny. Women's utopias, however, are another story. In feminist utopias, women—and men, too—inhabit a different visionary space and time from those of male utopias. Anarchist, antihierarchical, egalitarian, using technology for human ends, deeply involved in personal relationships, in artistic processes, in the fusion of individual development and the cohesion of the group, women's utopias escape the statism and the cold rigidities of traditional male utopias at the same time that they avoid the glorification of the body to the exclusion of reason that marks the more recent Marcusian school.[1]

Most male utopias have done little to improve women's lot (see Baruch, Part Four). In fact, a slight shift in perspective reveals that dystopia for men may be utopia for women and *vice versa,* a point implied by Shulamith Firestone's *Dialectic of Sex.*[2] Firestone views positively what Huxley viewed negatively in *Brave New World:* the destruction of the family and the home and the use of reproductive engineering. Many of the writers in this section examine the theme of reproduction and reproductive control. Though some feminists fear that reproductive technology will be used to dominate women further since men, at least thus far, control it (Zimmerman, Part Three), Lidia Falcón, one of the leaders of the contemporary Spanish feminist movement, argues that we cannot continue giving birth if we want to reach the status of human being.[3] She envisions the day when reproduction *in vitro* will be a reality. Lees, too, notes that some feminist utopias, Piercy's *Woman on the Edge of Time* most strikingly, insist that reproduction *ex utero* is necessary for sexual equality. Yet many feminists strongly contest this view since, for them, hierarchy is never based on biological causes but only on social ones.[4] Sure to arouse further controversy is Lees' analysis, which suggests that it is precisely those fictional utopias that remove reproduction from the body which seek to extend the experiences of mothering to all, women and men alike.

A notable combination of twentieth-century reproductive transformations and the nineteenth-century exaltation of motherhood is Charlotte Perkins Gilman's *Herland*, published in 1915. Its totally female population is able to reproduce itself. Although Gilman seems, in Sheila Delany's terms,[5] to see "Everywoman as the Blessed Virgin Mary," she also connects motherhood with the advancement of culture and society.

Utopias often reveal the times in which they were written more than the future. Therefore, it is not surprising that some nineteenth-century women's utopias seem couched in terms of "the cult of true womanhood." But there were some feminists in the nineteenth century who were able to make high broad-jumps out of that segregated world. Towards the middle of the century, Flora Tristan in *Union Ouvrière* called for a union of female and male workers and brilliantly equated what she called two races, the proletariat and women. Tristan gained hope from the fact that workers, too, had been oppressed throughout written history until their revolution in France which brought a magnificent flowering in all of the arts and sciences. This will happen to women as well when they have their "89," predicted Tristan. The emancipation of women will bring untold riches to society, she claimed. "It is as easy as understanding that two is twice as much as one."[6]

The vision of equality that Tristan painted in 1843 has not materialized. Women have only occasionally received the support of men, whether in the workplace or elsewhere. This has been one of the reasons behind women's formation of their own organizations and collectives. As Farley indicates, twentieth-century women are often turning more to the idea of permanent separatism in their utopian dreams. Sadly, more than a hundred years after Tristan, Christine Delphy, one of the founders of the new French feminist movement feels that the women's revolution will not happen in her lifetime. She sees utopia less as a construct for the future than as a process, a way of thinking—the ability to imagine that things might be otherwise,[7] a point similar to the one made by Pearson in her essay "Of Time and Revolution." ". . . We cannot create a future world," Pearson maintains, "unless we live in it, to the extent that we envision it and it claims our loyalties." Pearson is more positive than Delphy: "We cannot force or control change, but we can take a leap of faith to be citizens of a utopian society—in process—today." For some writers, utopia lives as much in present thought as future action.

Herself a utopian novelist, Sally Gearhart turns her eye—and her passion—to contemporary feminist utopian fiction, and reveals with great openness how even seemingly egalitarian women writers, with the exception of Marge Piercy, find it very difficult to escape from the insularity of racism. Gearhart even subjects herself to the charge: "truth to tell, in comparison to the rage and fervor that I instantly muster over other issues (e.g., homophobia, sexism) I hardly have any passion at all to confront racism." (Could it be that one of the reasons that Black women do not generally write utopias is that utopian fiction is a privileged genre that requires a certain material condition, and that, confronted with the oppression of the moment, these women of color have no passion left to confront the future?) However, Gearhart does notice, too, the attempt to overcome usual separations in the collective process of so many of these utopias which often have group rather than individual heroes, e.g., *Herland*, and *Les Guérillères*.

Despite the group nature of the heroes, as Khanna points out, characters in women's utopias are far more individualized than are the protagonists of traditional utopias, partly as a result of the feminist emphasis on individual fulfillment.[8] Women writers have the ability to unite the individual and the community in ways that men seldom achieve, perhaps because men's definition of power usually involves power over others rather than power over self or the empowerment of others, as Thorne, Kramarae, and Henley put it (Part Three).

Khanna writes of the great emphasis on art in feminist utopias, particularly those of Lessing, in contrast to the anti-art position of most male utopias. Plato would banish poets altogether because they lie; that is, they don't always say what the state wants to hear. More doesn't speak of poetry at all. Even William Morris, so often lauded for the pastoral beauty of his *News From Nowhere,* is primarily concerned with handicraft to the exclusion of other art forms. And, though Skinner says he wants art and music in his utopia, one wonders how such a static society as Walden II could ever achieve anything beyond mere technique.

Adams' "Therrillium," excerpted from a science fiction novel-in-progress, displays women's use of technology for the creation of art instead of the exercise of exploitative power. The therrillium is a solar-powered instrument that responds like a living creature to the movement of the artist and to the play of light in the environment. It reveals a unity between performer and instrument, nature, technology, and art, not only the art of music but that of design and ornament as well.

The theme of unity also pervades Harris's vision of a women's art museum. In contrast to existing museums, all of which "celebrate and preserve male culture, which is presented as the universal culture, in which women are sometimes admitted to have had a small share," her museum would encourage the mixture of different categories from painting to furniture design, fashion, jewelry, pottery, textiles, and crafts. In place of sanitized, compartmentalized, and hierarchical displays that are the norm in men's museums, Harris's would have a variety of women's art forms in comfortable and inviting settings, with glass walls revealing parks with sculpture. Harris's museum is less a museum in the traditional sense than a whole utopian world, where there is no artificial separation between art and the social context.

Perhaps the reason for the antithetical attitudes towards art in women's and men's utopias lies in the fact that most male utopias want stasis whereas feminist utopias accept change, indeed see it as inevitable. This difference seems to hold true in social reality as well. Rohrlich points out that the shift from a pre-state society that gave women great importance to a state patriarchy in Sumer brought about a decline in art and a rise in propaganda. Art became stereotyped and static, compelled to glorify the warring kings. This is the antithesis of the utopian vision, at least of women.

As Khanna puts it, utopia "is not finally, any one place or time, but the capacity to see afresh—an enlarged, even transformed vision." For Lessing, it is the artist who enables us to change perspective, to achieve the transformation of consciousness which, for Delphy, is the dynamic thrust in all thinking. "Imagination . . . is a precondition, is a prerequisite, of analysis, and imagination is also the thrust of utopia."

What Pladott notes of Broner's *Weave of Women*, which treats a community of women in Jerusalem, who transform patriarchal ritual, is true of other feminist utopias as well. The fixed divisions between ideal and real, reason and madness, before and after, inside and outside, dissolve. Definitions become fluid. Either/or polarities disappear. Beginnings and endings alike are rejected. Utopia is process. It is found in neither past arcadias nor future Elysiums.

The destruction of the masculine logos which is being carried on in feminist fiction, poetry, linguistics, and theory is leading to the creation of new concepts of space and time. Or are they so new? As our first section shows, the Hopis reveal a nonlinear view of reality, and matriarchal societies, particularly Minoan Crete, gave great importance to art. Part of feminist utopian vision entails recovering the realities of the past, the realities of other cultures. To recognize that utopias *have* existed in some place, at some time, is to give us hope for our future, and—perhaps what is more important—hope for our present.

NOTES

1. See, for example, Herbert Marcuse, *Eros and Civilization: A Philosophical Inquiry into Freud* (New York: Vintage Books, 1961) and also Norman O. Brown, *Life Against Death* (New York: Vintage Books, 1959).

2. Shulamith Firestone, *The Dialectic of Sex* (New York: William Morrow, 1970).

3. See Lidia Falcón, "Spain: Women are the Conscience of our Country," trans. Gloria Feiman Waldman, in *Sisterhood is Global: The International Women's Movement Anthology,* compiled and edited by Robin Morgan (New York: Doubleday/Anchor, 1984).

4. This is the position of the important French journal *Nouvelles Questions Feministes* under the general editorship of Simone de Beauvoir.

5. Sheila Delany, "Ambivalence in Utopia: The American Feminist Utopias of Charlotte P. Gilman and Marge Piercy," in *Writing Woman* (New York: Schocken Books, 1983).

6. Flora Tristan, *Union Ouvrière* (Paris: Prévot Libraire 61, 1843), p. 49.

7. Elaine Hoffman Baruch, unpublished interview with Christine Delphy.

8. Lee Cullen Khanna, "Women's Worlds: New Directions in Utopian Fiction," *Alternative Futures: The Journal of Utopian Studies,* 4 (Spring/Summer, 1981), 47–60.

Women in Men's Utopias

ELAINE HOFFMAN BARUCH

AS a recent visitor to men's utopias, it is somewhat dismaying to have to report that with few exceptions, women are no better off there than they are any place else. The most extraordinary exception is perhaps the earliest, Plato's *Republic*, but almost to a man, the others remain problematic. Even Plato has a few blemishes.

The defeat of Athens by its supposedly less civilized neighbor, Sparta (known for its liberated treatment of women), in the Peloponnesian War led to debates on women's "nature" that are still going on. It was in this atmosphere of upheaval that Plato wrote his *Republic*.[1] Plato was one of the first and, ironically, also one of the last thinkers, until well into this century, to suggest that biology was not a sufficient basis for role differentiation. One of the few writers in the Western tradition to use animal imagery in a positive way, he recommends in *The Republic*, Book V, that human beings might profitably follow the examples of dogs, among whom the females do not simply bear and suckle puppies but rather hunt and guard as well. Pushing his argument to its logical conclusion, Plato states that if the difference between the sexes consists only in women bearing and men begetting children, then both sexes should receive an equal education, designed to train them for the same roles. Plato argues for the total political and sexual equality of women, advocating that they be members of his highest class, the guardians, those who rule and fight, activities that are still considered the most mascu-

Some of this material has appeared under the title " 'A Natural and Necessary Monster': Women in Utopia" in *Alternative Futures: The Journal of Utopian Studies*, Winter 1979, pp. 29–48, copyright © Merritt Abrash and Alexandra Aldridge.

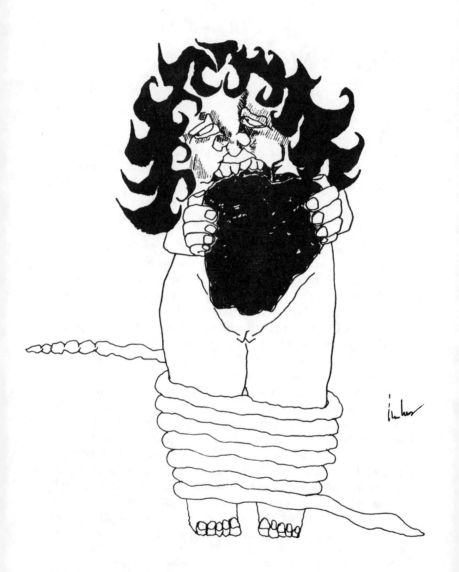

line of preserves. And he is willing to implement his theory with a system of child care that alone is able to free women to be philosophers and soldiers.

Thus far, it might seem hard for any feminist to fault Plato. Yet his plan has nothing to do with the individual and everything to do with the state; it is predicated on a communalization of wives, children, and property, to say nothing of a controlled system of eugenics which turns out to be characteristic of twentieth-century dystopias. And, at least at one point, Plato suggests that while women are capable of doing everything, they will always be surpassed in excellence by the best of men.

Though influenced by Plato, More's *Utopia* (1516) is much more conservative. Despite sharing of work and equality of opportunity—for men, hierarchy remains firmly rooted in a place so taken for granted that readers took little notice of it until recently: the patriarchal family. As a microcosm of the hierarchical structure of Renaissance political life, More's family is under the authority of the oldest male. Wives are subordinated to their husbands as children are subordinated to their fathers. When a woman gets married, she joins her husband's household. Pre-marital intercourse is severely punished on the assumption that if intercourse were unregulated, no one would ever get married. The prospective bride and bridegroom are shown naked to each other in order to prevent unpleasant surprises after marriage, although it is the man's surprises that are stressed. A little more emancipated is the idea that divorce be allowed by mutual consent on the grounds of incompatibility. No man is allowed to divorce his wife simply because she has grown old.

Although slaves do the more laborious work of the kitchen, it is women who prepare the meals in the communal dining halls. Wives sit on the outside of tables so that they may retire quickly to nurseries where they breast-feed their own babies. No communal nursing here as in Plato.

More gives women no opportunity to be rulers; however, he does allow them to become priests. Since only elderly widows are eligible for this office, no doubt they would be few in number; nonetheless, the suggestion must have been something of a shock to More's clerical contemporaries. Protestants later were to be more receptive to the idea, but interestingly enough, More then wasn't.[2] Unlike Plato in *The Republic* and unlike More's treatment of his own daughters, More does not seem willing to liberate his women in utopia, where, despite their outside labor, they remain rooted in the most traditional of roles, bearing and caring for children, feeding children and men.

The Christian literary utopia (and I think that More's ultimately qualifies as such) professes to eliminate original sin, which male theologians see as the cause of male dominance. But unlike the early Gnostic Christians, some of whom were truly egalitarian (see General Introduction, Part 2), More allows such sin to get through the city gates without so much as a passport, for, within the walls, women are decidedly subordinate, an indication that in utopia, as in reality, equality is usually an issue that pertains only to men.[3]

Most utopias posit the possession of goods in common as a condition of the earthly paradise. Bacon's *New Atlantis*[4] (1627) does not. Instead, it suggests that proper method would be sufficient to restore the prelapsarian state, *in which men had mastery over nature*. Bacon's community of scientists is exclusively male, and when he speaks of science benefiting man's estate, one wonders if he is thinking of woman at all. Indeed, as if to make up for men's loss of dominion over nature, men's domination of women in *The New Atlantis* is very strong.

Bacon's family structure, like More's in the *Utopia*, is intensely patriarchal. In his Feast of the Family, the Tirsan (a father with multiple descendants) has a feast paid for by the state. Obedience is owed to him as "to the order of nature." If there is a mother from whom the entire lineage is descended, she is placed at the right hand of the father's thronelike chair but behind a door where she cannot be seen.

The question of sexual equality is never treated by Bacon. As if foreshadowing Freud's later theory of the need to repress instincts to advance civilization, *The New Atlantis*, a scientific utopia, is sexually austere. No doubt Bacon felt that the pursuit of progress was a male endeavor that women would impede.

Yet there is a scientific utopia, written a few years earlier than Bacon's which, influenced by Plato, does provide a near equality of education for women: Tommaso Campanella's *City of the Sun*.[5] There women have many of the same occupations as men, are trained in arms and exercise, and, as a result, are tall and strong of limb. Wearing makeup or high heels here is punishable by death, for they smack of deceit. To be sure, Campanella implies that there would be no need for these ruses; nonetheless, the punishment for the crime seems extraordinary and prophetic of the great dystopias like Zamyatin's *We* and Orwell's *1984*[6] where wearing cosmetics and high heels signals acts of extreme rebellion against the state.

It is an irony of utopias that they often reveal less about the future they sometimes profess to deal with than about their authors' own time. While Plato doesn't speak at all of love between the sexes and More does so only indirectly, it is in the area of love and sex that Victorian utopias deal with equality of the future, not an equality of identity with the masculine norm, as in Plato, but rather one of complementary differences, the assumption being that what is missing in one sex will be supplied by the other. Though in some ways they try to surmount it, these utopias are never far removed from a strong sexual polarization involving subordination.

In Bellamy's *Looking Backward*[7] (1888), a Victorian projection into the twenty-first century, the heroine is far franker about her amorous predilections than were the ladies of the author's own time, but she reveals her Victorian origin in her propensity for blushing, shopping, and retiring early while the menfolk discuss politics and economics.

Yet the women of *Looking Backward* are free from the burden of housework, which has been communalized. They are never dependent on their husbands for support, since the society gives equal economic credits to all of its members, including children. But though women are free to pursue careers, Bellamy retains a division of labor according to sex. In order to minimize competition with men, which he terms "an unusual rivalry," he grants women a giant but separate industrial army. Only women who have been wives and mothers may hold the highest positions. All women are under the leadership of a woman general-in-chief who has a veto in the president's cabinet but only in regard to "women's work." Unlike the Shakers, who had parallel leadership in all ranks, in Bellamy's world men restrict both female occupations and hours in order to preserve the "beauty and grace" of women. Biological difference is interpreted as feminine weakness in Bellamy, and this provides the justification for male domination, disguised as chivalry.

Another way of seemingly effecting equality is by eliminating the predominantly male world of industrialization altogether. This was William Morris's arcadian answer to Bellamy, *News from Nowhere*[8] (1891). Women's status is high in this world, an anti-intellectual paradise where handicraft has displaced technology and pleasure has replaced competition.

In the future, Morris says, women will be clothed like women, not upholstered like armchairs. Their skin will bear a lively tan and their beauty will be suffused with energy for they won't be afraid of using their muscles. What is more, they will appreciate the male body—all of which was not the case among Victorian ladies. Furthermore, Morris's women of the future are free to leave men they don't care for; his utopia recognizes that a court cannot enforce a contract of passion or sentiment. There is no divorce since private property, its major cause, is obsolete in this communistic society.

But although there is increased sexual freedom for women in Nowhere, there is no freedom from housework. While we might be tempted to agree with Morris that housework is undervalued in our world, we are brought up short by the author's assumption that it comes more naturally to women than to men.

As we might expect, maternity is highly valued in Morris's utopia (as it was in Bellamy's), and the nineteenth-century plan to emancipate superior women from the bearing of children is dismissed as a "strange piece of baseless folly," an expression of class tyranny. So too perhaps is the desire to eliminate pain in childbirth:

> Surely it is a matter of course that the natural and necessary pains which the mother must go through form a bond of union between man and woman, an extra stimulus to love and affection between them, and that this is universally recognized.[9]

Morris places his romance in a future arcadia, but as far as biology is concerned, his women are still fallen Eves.

If utopias for men are often dystopias for women, might it be that dystopias for men are utopias for women? It was with this question in mind that I returned to the famous anti-utopias of this century. It would seem that Huxley was writing with bitterness of the disappearance of home, marriage, and motherhood in his future society, and their replacement by community, sexual permissiveness, and artificial reproduction. And yet, reading him today, it is the author rather than the inhabitants of his brave new world who seems naive. Shulamith Firestone, in *The Dialectic of Sex,*[10] surely one of the most radical books to come out of the women's movement, reads like a transvaluation of Huxley some thirty-five years later. Both write of reproduction *in vitro,* but while Huxley wanted to point up the absurdity of rejecting our biology, Firestone wants to show the necessity for doing so in order to gain true equality.

Despite their ostensible attempt to equalize the sexes, Zamyatin, Huxley, and Orwell use women in highly conventional ways—as symbols of men's sexuality. For these authors, modern reality itself begins to sound like utopia. They see sex, when aligned with fantasy, as that which makes us human and keeps us from being machines. But a question we have to ask is whether the sexual act (along with the institutions of marriage and family) bears the same meaning for women in relation to the culture that it does for men. What is liberation for men may be enslavement for women. In *1984,* the fact that the heroine embodies "the animal instinct," and that she has no last name—she is simply Julia, woman, earth mother—may be a delight to the hero but does not endear Orwell to contemporary women readers. Nor does his characterization of her as someone who only understands issues as they relate to her own sexuality. It may well be that Julia was simply exchanging one enslavement for another when she threw off her red sash of chastity, the Party emblem, to fall into bed with Winston, a man who had fantasies of killing her when he thought he could not have her. It may also be that women are better off in Huxley's brave new world than they are on his reservation or its fringes, which Huxley sees as the domain of freedom.[11]

Although Skinner's *Walden II*[12] was written as a utopia, it strikes many readers as a dystopia with its behavioral engineering and its impoverishing restrictions on its inhabitants' space and movement. Ostensibly, Skinner wrote it because he empathized with his wife's wincing over the appellation of housewife; therefore, it is surprising to find the theoretical discussions in his book taking place solely among men—as they do in Huxley and Orwell, but not Zamyatin, we must add, who makes one of his heroines the prime intellectual as well as sexual rebel. It is she who fights against the One State, not the hero, who is politically naive. Great as Zamyatin's influence was on Orwell, it did not extend to Orwell's treatment of his heroine, Julia, whose mind is decidedly inferior to Winston Smith's.[13]

A good deal of *Walden II* centers on marriage and child-rearing, which is not surprising considering that it was written shortly after World War II. No more than in *Looking Backward* is there the possibility here of not getting married. The eccentric Frazier, mastermind of this utopian society, seems to be the only loner in the community, and he, of course, was not subject to its behavioral engineering. The average age of the Walden II mother at the birth of her first child is eighteen, the rationale being to get childbearing over with as quickly as possible so that, by the time she is twenty-three or so, the mother "has made the special contribution which is either the duty or the privilege of woman, and can take her place without distinction of sex." Children are raised communally because "home is not the place to raise children." This in itself would appear to free women for the larger world. Whether such is the case, however, is debatable, particularly since there seems to be no larger world to go to.

In some ways, Skinner's utopia sounds like what an Israeli kibbutz would be if it applied brave-new-world principles of behavioral modification and control, this time through psychology rather than drugs. The author believes that we are all controlled by society, the only question being what kind of control we want to have. What is perhaps most disturbing in Skinner is that, despite his professions of sexual equality, in his society, we only see women in traditional female roles, teaching and nurturing.

We are left with this question: why, for the most part, have women fared poorly in men's utopias? Even when an author decides to give them full rights as in *Walden II,* he fails, perhaps because of his own conditioning. Perhaps, too, it is because men's utopia is primarily the land of repressive civilization rather than that of erotic bliss, and women have traditionally been placed outside the boundaries of the greatest advances of culture. In those utopian thinkers who seek to derepress instinct, from Fourier down to Marcuse and Norman O. Brown, women have fared much better. A kind of reverse Freud, Fourier wanted to give free reign to the passions as the very means of attaining social harmony. Variety, rivalry, intrigue, freedom of choice, luxury, the pleasures of the palate and the body— these will all be allowed in Harmony. While other male utopias smack of the army, Fourier's sounds like a cruise. There will be five meals and four snacks a day in Harmony, and love-making will be a major activity.[14]

Fourier wants to transcend traditional body/mind dualisms. Like twentieth-century feminists, he wishes to liberate language from the tyrannies of conventional hierarchies. As Roland Barthes notes,[15] he seeks unity rather than simplism, associative rather than reductive thinking, the fusion of the real and the marvellous.

As a general proposition Fourier claims, although some feminists find this sadly untrue, that, "Social advances and changes of periods are brought about by virtue of the progress of women towards liberty, and the decadences of the social order are brought about by virtue of the decrease of liberty of women."[16] But his is not a literary utopia. In the mainstream of male utopian fantasy, the female body has provided a natural prison, a self-contained concentration camp in society. One wonders whether biology has much to do with this or rather men's appropriation of that biology for their own symbolic and exploitative purposes. It is this question that is explored in the contemporary feminist utopia.

NOTES

1. Plato, *The Republic,* trans. Francis MacDonald Cornford (New York: Oxford University Press, 1973).

2. Sir Thomas More, *Utopia*, trans. Robert M. Adams (New York: W. W. Norton & Co., Inc., 1975). My colleague Rainer Pineas has pointed out to me that as soon as Protestants did advance claims for women in the priesthood, More rejected them, e.g., in his Letter to Bugenhagen, c. 1526.

3. See Martin N. Raitière, "More's *Utopia* and *The City of God*," *Studies in the Renaissance* 20 (1973), 144–168.

4. Francis Bacon, *The Advancement of Learning and The New Atlantis* (London: Oxford University Press, 1956).

5. Tommaso Campanella, *The City of the Sun: A Poetical Dialogue*, ed. Daniel Donno, Biblioteca Italiana Series (Berkeley: University of California Press, 1981).

6. George Orwell, *Nineteen Eighty-four: Text, Sources, Criticism*, ed. Irving Howe, 2nd ed. (New York: Harcourt Brace Jovanovich, 1982). Yevgeny Zamyatin, *We*, trans. Bernard Guerney (London: Jonathan Cape, 1970).

7. Edward Bellamy, *Looking Backward 2000–1887*, ed. John L. Thomas (Cambridge, Mass.: Harvard University Press, 1967).

8. William Morris, "News from Nowhere," *The Collected Works of William Morris*, Vol. XVI (New York: Russell and Russell, 1966).

9. Morris, p. 61.

10. Shulamith Firestone, *The Dialectic of Sex* (New York: William Morrow, 1970).

11. See Elaine Baruch, "Dystopia Now" in *Alternative Futures: The Journal of Utopian Studies* (Summer 1979), pp. 55–67.

12. B. F. Skinner, *Walden II* (New York: Macmillan, 1962).

13. Elaine Hoffman Baruch, " 'The Golden Country': Sex and Love in *1984*," in *1984 Revisited: Totalitarianism in our Century*, ed. Irving Howe (New York: Harper and Row, 1983).

14. Charles Fourier, *Design for Utopia: Selected Writings of Charles Fourier*, trans. Julia Franklin (New York: Schocken Books, 1971); *Harmonian Man: Selected Writings of Charles Fourier*, ed. Mark Poster (Garden City, N.Y.: Anchor Books, 1971); *The Utopian Vision of Charles Fourier: Selected Texts on Work, Love, and Passionate Attraction*, trans. Jonathan Beecher and Richard Bienvenu (Boston: Beacon Press, 1971).

15. Roland Barthes, *Sade Fourier Loyola*, trans. Richard Miller (New York: Hill and Wang, 1976), pp. 93–98.

16. *Design for Utopia*, p. 77.

Motherhood in Feminist Utopias

SUSAN H. LEES

A SURVEY of feminist utopian literature reveals two fundamentally opposed views of motherhood. One emphasizes the tasks and responsibilities associated with caring for children, and seeks to relieve women of the unjust burden they bear in this regard. The other emphasizes a mother's personal gratification in the love relationship she enjoys with her child or children, and seeks to universalize the social benefits of maternal experience. While the latter approach generally also liberates mothers from sole responsibility for child-rearing, the purpose of this liberation is freedom to enjoy loving children, as much as to do other things. The former approach, in contrast, plays down the love relationship, seeing it as a distraction from "higher" feelings.

Carol Pearson has suggested some common features in the treatment of motherhood in feminist utopias: short duration of childhood; communal responsibility for child-rearing; and reduced emphasis on the biological aspects of mother-child linkages.[1] The last point, I shall argue, is critical, when we consider the question of *how* liberation for mothers, whether from love or to love, is to be achieved in utopia. In the utopias which employ separation in the mother-child link, there is no intervention in the biological process of reproduction. By contrast, utopias which emphasize maternal fulfillment and pleasure depict the intimate mother-child relationship as an essential source of human happiness and virtue which should be universally shared but cannot be, because of *biological* differences in reproductive

roles. The solution to social inequality and injustice, then, involves altering the biological process of reproduction to reduce or eliminate the negative effects of sexual differences.

Radical interventions in the traditional intimacy of mother-child relationships are not limited to the female imagination, as witness Plato's Republic. A number of "intentional" communities, guided by male utopian ideals, treat motherhood, theoretically, as a chore, distraction, and source of oppression which should be eliminated. We will look at two, Oneida and the Israeli kibbutz.[2] While this approach envisions "social" solutions to social ills, the alternative approach which sees motherhood as a source of gratification and a model of human virtue, often employs a "technical fix" to disparities in women's and men's reproduction. Herland, Whileaway, and the Wanderground have no men, and reproduce by means of parthenogenesis or egg-merging. Mattapoisett and Thoacdien use machines for some part of the reproductive process, particularly for eliminating birth. Gethen eliminates sexual difference with an androgynous race: an individual can be a biological mother and a father at different times.[3]

Men's utopian dreams are often unsympathetic to what many people, women and men, see as the benefits (particularly to women) of motherhood. Some women feminists share this position. Other women, both utopian writers and actual participants in male-designed utopian communities, believe that social ills can only be eradicated if the experience of motherhood is not denied to anyone merely on the basis of sex. To achieve utopia, one must eliminate men or alter the biology of reproduction in order to grant men the benefits of assuming maternal roles. While the former group of utopias suggest that women are not "defective men" but "men" who are limited by a defective social system, the latter group suggest that men are indeed "defective women," and many seek to correct their defects by allowing them to be mothers.

LIBERATING WOMEN FROM MOTHERHOOD

Plato's *Republic*,[4] the prototype of "anti-family" utopias, liberated female guardians from child care and other domestic duties, so that they could join male guardians in the job of governing the state. Their children were reared separately, under the supervision of special officers, male or female. Lactating guardian women were brought to the central nursery to breast-feed infants at random, not knowing which of the infants were their own. This system would eliminate family attachments which, in Plato's view, only result in selfishness and unseemly competition, attitudes which the guardians of the Republic could not be allowed to possess.

Plato's elite-governed utopia contrasts sharply with Ursula LeGuin's anarchic Annares,[5] and yet, LeGuin's treatment of motherhood bears some similarities to Plato's. In Annares, everyone has a job, and all domestic work, including cooking, laundry, and child care, is communalized, professionalized, and locally centralized. However, as could be expected in an anarchy, unlike a rigidly governed state, parents have a variety of options. The mother of the protagonist in *The Dispossessed* did not choose to rear him, and he rarely saw his father during childhood. He and his wife, on the other hand, are very attached to their daughter, and spend as much time with their child as possible. There is no place in an anarchy for the conventional patriarchal father, ruler, and lawgiver. Thus, in LeGuin's utopia, relieving women of the "chores" of motherhood does not require sacrificing its rewards; indeed, an anarchy encourages the extension of the rewards of motherhood to fathers.

The types of social interventions imagined by Plato and LeGuin are extreme, but possible to experiment with in the world we know. Analogues to Plato's and LeGuin's treatment of motherhood can be found in a number of experimental communities. An interesting case is Oneida (1849–79), a nineteenth-century religious utopian community, led by John Humphrey Noyes. The Oneidans practiced "complex marriage," in which each member of the community was formally married to every other member of the other sex. Sexual relations were monitored by a committee of elders to prevent the formation of "exclusive attachments" between couples. Close attachments between parents and children were thought to distract parents, particularly mothers, from concentrating on God, Christ, and the commu-

nity. Noyes preached separation between sexuality and reproduction. For the first twenty years of Oneida's existence, sexual
intercourse for reproductive purposes was prohibited. This was
followed by a ten-year eugenics experiment, controlled by a committee which selected couples to mate and bear offspring. More
women than men volunteered for the experiment. Some fifty-
eight children were born during the experimental period (1869–
1879). They were raised separately from their parents by a group
of specialists, comprised of 3 men and 15 women. While mothers
were permitted to visit their offspring at certain intervals, they
were not to form exclusive attachments with them any more than
with other community members. Nevertheless, some of the
mothers did form exclusive attachments and were unhappy
about being deprived of easier access to their children. Would a
more liberal policy regarding mother-child association have had
consequences detrimental to community life?

A somewhat more impressive experiment, the Israeli kibbutz, which has involved thousands of individuals in scores of
communities for three generations, does seem to bear this out.
Today, there are some 240 kibbutzim, with a total of about
100,000 members. The kibbutz is highly egalitarian, operates
by consensus, and is communalistic. Originally, it was against
the nuclear family, which was regarded as oppressive, and antithetical to socialist collectivity. While couples might form exclusive sexual attachments, they might not have an exclusive
family life. Adults ate in communal dining halls, domestic tasks
were communalized, and child care was a community right and
responsibility. Children were removed from their mothers
shortly after birth, to be raised separately in nurseries and children's houses among their peers. While children knew their
own parents, they did not normally "live" with them. Parents
only spent a few after-work hours and the Sabbath with their
own children.

Gradually, however, there were adjustments in child-care
arrangements which resulted in the reconstitution of the nuclear
family in some kibbutzim.[6] First, women demanded the right to
visit their children during the workday. A growing number of
kibbutzim have begun to allow children to sleep with their par-

ents. On kibbutzim where families have their own kitchen facilities, they eat some meals together. The result has been not only a
strengthening of nuclear family ties, but an increase in the private domestic workload of the women who have children.

Apparently, these shifts arose from mothers' demands to be
with their children, and to participate more in their own children's upbringing. In order to do this, they willingly accepted
work near the children's houses (low-status collectivized service
jobs within the settlement) and more private domestic work at
home. Feminist critics[7] have suggested that underlying causes
for these changes had more to do with sexism in Jewish tradition, and in the larger Israeli society, and with pressures placed
on women to reproduce in the context of perennial war.

But if the tradition and environment had not been sexist, if
external pressures, whether military or economic, had been relieved, would kibbutz women have been any happier with separation from their children? Would the ideal kibbutz be utopia
for mothers?

Mother-child attachments do seem to undermine community commitments in male-designed utopias, and are frequently
the cause of conflict in real communities around the world.[8]
Some female utopian writers also see a strong mother-child tie as
a negative social influence. Dorothy Bryant's *The Kin of Ata Are
Waiting for You*[9] illustrates this view. Pregnancy is burdensome
because it must be borne alone; childbirth, while an achievement, is seen as painful. Breastfeeding is the only apparent
gratification the mother enjoys. Others tend the baby—though
what pleasure, or pain they derive from this is unclear.

Children are also portrayed in a negative light in Bryant's
book. Everyone in Ata seeks freedom to dream well. Dependent
children are a source of distraction and affect the ability of
adults to pursue good dreams. In the past, children led to grief
and destruction, as a result of their freedom to act on poor
judgment. This view of what children are and the threat they
pose is diametrically opposite to the views of Charlotte Perkins
Gilman and Marge Piercy, who see children in a positive light
rather than a source of unwanted distraction.

ELIMINATING FATHERHOOD: ELEVATING MOTHERHOOD

Most feminist utopians see motherhood as something to be venerated. But few regard fatherhood in the same light. How can fatherhood be eliminated and motherhood retained? Charlotte Perkins Gilman's *Herland* resolves the problem simply by eliminating men altogether: women reproduce by parthenogenesis. The right to bear a child is an immense privilege, permitted to a woman only once in a lifetime under controlled conditions. All women are mothers, nurturers: their skills are used in nurturing not only children but all growing things. The conventional ideal mother becomes, in Herland, the ideal human being: giving, strong, controlled, gentle, wise, fruitful. Freed from male dominance and oppression, the citizen of Herland is able to direct her maternal virtues to the development of the arts, science, agriculture, and other forms of creativity.

When children are born, they spend their first year close to their mothers, but are gradually shifted to special attendants, though never completely separated from the mothers. Child-rearing was assigned to specialists not to free mothers to "work" but because of the specialists' expertise.

In Joanna Russ's Whileaway, motherhood is of relatively little significance for adults. Mothers in Whileaway resemble indulgent patriarchal fathers of daughters, with none of the responsibility or pain commonly associated with motherhood. Whileaway, like Herland, is a world of women with no men. Reproduction is achieved by mechanical means: the ova of two women are brought together to form a gamete which is gestated in the body of one of the two. Women bear either a single child or twins, depending on demographic necessity, once in their lives. During the five-year period of her life which she spends with her child, which generally begins when she is about thirty, the mother gives herself over to the educational and emotional care of her daughter, though physical care is not her responsibility. The maternal period is depicted as a pleasurable vacation for the mother, who is not obliged to work, and bliss for the child.

While the manner of child-rearing is seen as important in the formation of Whileawayan personality structure, and as not entirely a good thing for the child, it is by no means seen as difficult for mothers. Maternal passions are considered weaknesses, which do not contribute anything to Whileawayan ethics or social structure.

Sally Gearhart's *Wanderground* also depicts a society with no men. The mechanics of motherhood are unclear here, but there is mention of an "implantment" and an "egg-merging." A group of seven women together serve as mothers to a child. Birth is highly ritualized and endowed with immense spiritual importance for the group. Motherhood is a voluntary experience here, to be widely shared and valued.

MAKING MEN MOTHERS: PSYCHOSOCIAL ANDROGYNY

While Gilman, Russ and Gearhart improve the lot of humanity by eliminating men, Marge Piercy simply modifies the reproductive roles of women and men. In her utopian Mattapoisett, conception and gestation take place in tanks monitored by technicians. Every child is assigned three co-mothers who apply for this privilege and share the maternal role until the child reaches puberty, whereupon this role is ritually terminated. Men may also be co-mothers, and are able to share the pleasure and responsibility of nursing their infants by means of hormone injections to stimulate lactation. At least two of the three co-mothers share nursing. There is no father-role in Mattapoisett.

Like conception and gestation, childrearing is a communal enterprise. While co-mothers maintain a special relationship with their child, the children are raised apart, in nurseries, by specialists. As in Herland, this does not preclude free and easy contact between co-mothers and children. The "test-tube" solution to the unequal roles of women and men in reproduction is seen in Mattapoisett as a sacrifice of a power that women have over men, one worth making in order to achieve sharing and mutuality of experience.

Psychosocial androgyny is achieved in a similar manner in *The Legend of Biel* by Mary Staton. In her Thoacdien, embryos are formed and nurtured by machines, and the newborn are tended by them. The baby-tenders, or "Gladdins," are "ideal" nurses, programmed to respond to all the infants' physical needs. Children are not brought into contact with other human beings until they reach a certain level of intellectual and emotional maturity—at which point they ask for their "mentors."

Mentors, who can be either male or female, are responsible for the health and development of their charges until they are grown. The mentor-charge relationship is one of strong emotional attachment, of mutual love, and is not authoritarian. It has all the intimacy of a mother-child relationship but is more exclusive and intimate because the mentor is the only parent, and communication between mentor and charge is not only physical and verbal but also mental. Psychosocial maternity in *The Legend of Biel* thus has an elevated role, while biological maternity is absent. The removal of reproduction from human bodies makes "motherhood" compatible with a gender-free and egalitarian society.

MAKING MEN MOTHERS: BIOLOGICAL ANDROGYNY

While sexual equality is achieved in Mattapoisett and Thoacdien by means of psychosocial androgyny, and in Herland by elimination of fatherhood and universalization of motherhood, other utopias have it both ways—fatherhood and motherhood are universalized by means of biological androgyny.

Consider Ursula LeGuin's Gethen in *The Left Hand of Darkness*. LeGuin's invention of an androgynous people results in equality of opportunity and constraint due to childbearing, elimination of psychosexual relationship between parent and child, and preclusion of gender inequality. Any Gethenian may

become a mother or a father at different times of their lives.
Descent is matrilineal and family ties between parents and children are recognized, though marriage is neither a state nor a
community concern. LeGuin does not elaborate on the subject
of child-rearing on Gethen.

Her earliest precursor was probably the Enlightenment
writer Gabriel de Foigny.[10] His utopia, described in *A New Discovery of Terra Incognita Australis* (1676) is inhabited by an androgynous race he calls "australians." De Foigny goes further
than LeGuin in idealizing motherhood. Birth is painless and
pleasant; breast milk is so perfect that infants need no other
food until they are two years old; babies do not defecate. Children mature rapidly and are left by their parents early in life to
begin their formal education by specialists.

A HETEROSEXUAL SOLUTION: CHANGING FATHERHOOD

Some versions of utopia incorporate "natural" motherhood
and gender equality together, and still retain close mother-child
links. A case in point is Doris Lessing's Zone Three,[11] which does
not eliminate fatherhood, but extends it. There are two kinds of
fathers: gene-fathers and mind-fathers, both selected by the
child's mother. Gene-fathers are simply biological genitors.
Mind-fathers are more significant in that they nurture the fetus
and the growing child. Each child has several mind-fathers.
Their nurturing role is different from the mothers' and is seen
as essential for the child's well-being.

Motherhood is not restricted for the good of society or for
the good of the mother; it is a continual and rewarding state of
being for women. A decline in fertility is seen as a deprivation,
and a sign that something has gone wrong. Conception takes
place only by a woman's intention. Childbirth occurs in a fairly
informal way, with little difficulty. Nursing is pleasurable, but
nurturing with milk is not more important than mental nurturing by both mother and fathers. Children are welcomed and
enjoyed by both. Motherhood and fatherhood are responsibili-

ties, but they are not shown as hampering the individual in any way. They are entirely compatible with Lessing's utopian dream, and need not be accompanied by selfishness, authoritarianism, sexism, or any other evil; these arise apparently only in the context of war.

CONCLUSIONS: CHANGING SOCIETY

With the exception perhaps of biological androgynes, the people depicted in the imaginary societies discussed here are sufficiently like us that we can read them as didactic.[12] The lesson we learn is that social justice, creativity, and fulfillment are impossible when the qualities of motherhood are denied to humanity as a whole. Women are denied enjoyment and expression of maternal virtues because they are dominated by male interests in warfare, competition, and profiteering. Men are denied expression of maternal virtues because their biological nature excludes them from the experience of motherhood: they are biologically deficient. Gilman, Russ, and Gearhart resolve this problem by eliminating men; Piercy and Staton resolve it by making men mothers; Lessing and Bryant provide compensation for men in their mental nurturing powers.

In none of these cases is the resolution possible strictly through social reform; biological intervention is necessary either to permit women to reproduce without being dominated by men or to allow everyone to be mothers. This suggests that these authors believe that social injustice resulting from sexism derives from the manner in which we reproduce. Many other social problems are resolvable through social reforms; sexism apparently is not.

In this sense, these authors appear to take a position not so far removed from such writers as Tiger and Shepher[13] and Alice Rossi,[14] who claim that women's close attachment to their children is biologically derived. Unlike misogynist thinkers, these utopian writers see in mothers' bio-psychological qualities a source of strength. If gender segregation and differentiation derive from a biological difference, they cannot be eradicated by social reform alone. The attempt will inevitably and continually result in dissatisfaction for women and men: this is not the way to utopia. One can only conclude, then, that in order to eradicate sexist differentiation, one must intervene in the process of reproduction.

This sort of intervention is probably better known as a device in dystopias. The most famous of the "test-tube baby" fantasies is in Huxley's *Brave New World.* Women have also employed such intervention in their negative fantasies. A recent example is Zoe Fairbairn's[15] Great Britain of the near future. Here, a government bureaucracy seeking to control women's reproduction arranges first to pay maternity benefits to all women, then to place contraceptive devices in some, then in all women's bodies, and to select only a preferred few to reproduce. A final measure is to introduce long-lasting contraceptives into the general water supply, making an antidote available only to those women selected by the government for their docility, and their dedication to stereotypic maternal virtues. Needless to say, the result is disaster. The lesson is that maternity is a privilege best controlled by individual women. Taking away motherhood will not make women happy, nor will it make society better. Quite the contrary.

The experience of motherhood is usually something feminist utopian writers think women should want to retain and enjoy. Social change should be built by spreading the virtues of motherhood and allowing them to flourish, principally by changing men's roles, such as eliminating fatherhood or making it more like motherhood. The values of motherhood appear to arise not from social constructs but from the experience of motherhood itself, which, apparently, makes women nurturers, encourages environmental awareness and appreciation for conservation, and develops altruism, creativity, and a host of other human virtues.

Perhaps because of its emphasis on liberalization of abortion laws and on opportunities for women to work and succeed outside the home, the women's movement of the past decade has been seen by many critics as hostile to motherhood. This criticism is not supported by feminist utopian fantasies. Given the freedom to imagine the ideal society, feminist writers have not rejected motherhood, but often magnified and elaborated its importance.

NOTES

1. Carol Pearson, "Women's Fantasies and Feminist Utopias," *Frontiers*, 2, No. 3 (1977), pp. 50–61.
2. There is a very extensive literature on Oneida. Information for this essay was taken from the following sources: Pierrepont Noyes, "Growing Up in Oneida," in *Communes: Creating and Managing the Collective Life*, ed. Rosabeth Moss Kanter (New York: Harper & Row, 1973); Raymond Lee Muncy, *Sex and Marriage in Utopian Communities* (Bloomington: Indiana University Press, 1973). On the kibbutz see: Yonina Talmon, "Family Life in the Kibbutz: From Revolutionary Days to Stabilization," in Kanter, *Communes*, pp. 318–333; Lesley Hazelton, *Israeli Women: The Reality Behind the Myths* (New York: Simon & Schuster, 1977); Sheila Kitzinger, *Women as Mothers: How They See Themselves in Different Cultures* (New York: Vintage Books, 1981); Geraldine Stern, *Israeli Women Speak Out* (Philadelphia: Lippincott, 1979); Lionel Tiger and Joseph Shepher, *Women in the Kibbutz* (New York: Harcourt Brace Jovanovich, 1975); Seymour Parker and Hilda Parker, "Women and the Emerging Family on the Israeli Kibbutz," *American Ethnologist*, 8, No. 4 (1981), pp. 758–773.
3. Charlotte Perkins Gilman, *Herland* (New York: Pantheon Books, 1979); Joanna Russ, *The Female Man* (New York: Bantam Books, 1975); Sally Gearhart, *The Wanderground: Stories of the Hill Women* (Watertown, Mass.: Persephone Press, 1979); Marge Piercy, *Woman on the Edge of Time* (New York: Alfred A. Knopf, Inc., 1976); Mary Staton, *From the Legend of Biel* (New York: Ace Books, 1975); Ursula LeGuin, *The Left Hand of Darkness* (New York: Ace Books, 1969).
4. Plato, *The Republic*, trans. Francis MacDonald Cornford (Oxford: Oxford University Press, 1945).
5. Ursula LeGuin, *The Dispossessed* (New York: Harper & Row, 1974).
6. Kitzinger, among others, sees the kibbutz as an arrangement that enhances family life. Relieving family members

of distracting domestic chores and economic pressures, the kibbutz allows families to enjoy and indulge one another as no other social system does.

7. Hazelton, *Israeli Women*.

8. Jessie Bernard, *The Future of Motherhood* (New York: Dial Press, 1975); Kanter, *Communes*.

9. Dorothy Bryant, *The Kin of Ata Are Waiting for You* (New York: Moon Books/Random House, 1971).

10. Frank E. Manuel and Fritzie P. Manuel, *French Utopias* (New York: The Free Press, 1966).

11. Doris Lessing, *The Marriages between Zones Three, Four, and Five* (New York: Alfred A. Knopf, Inc., 1980).

12. Rachel Blau Du Plessis, "The Feminist Apologues of Lessing, Piercy, and Russ," *Frontiers*, 2, No. 1 (1979), pp. 1–8.

13. Tiger and Shepher, *Women in the Kibbutz*.

14. Alice S. Rossi, "A Biosocial Perspective on Parenting," *Daedalus*, 106, No. 2 (1977), pp. 1–31.

15. Zoe Fairbairns, *Benefits* (London: Virago, Ltd., 1973).

Realities and Fictions: Lesbian Visions of Utopia

TUCKER FARLEY

> Bringing my fantasies into the real world frightened me very much. It's not that they were bad in themselves, but they were Unreal and therefore culpable; to try to make Real what was Unreal was to mistake the very nature of things; it was a sin not against conscience (which remained genuinely indifferent during the whole affair) but against Reality, and of the two, the latter is far more blasphemous. It's the crime of creating one's own Reality, of "preferring oneself" as a good friend of mine says. I knew it was an impossible project.[1]

As author-character of *The Female Man,* Joanna Russ is here speaking not of creating a utopian vision of the future, but of becoming a lesbian. Both involved breaking out of "History" and "Reality" as they have been defined.[2] The problem being dramatized is what is possible for a young, white girl brought up in the fifties? What is realistic? And what is reality? On the surface, the tension of the novel lies in the conflict between men and women. But underneath we glimpse the effort to break through to an alternative paradigm, another set of possibilities.

This novel depicts the aspects of Everywoman as conceived in 1975 by its author. Each aspect, represented by a character whose name begins with J, dramatizes an apparently different woman whose ground of being and perceptions about what is real and what is possible differ from those of the others. Author/character Joanna veers back and forth between Jeannine's past-

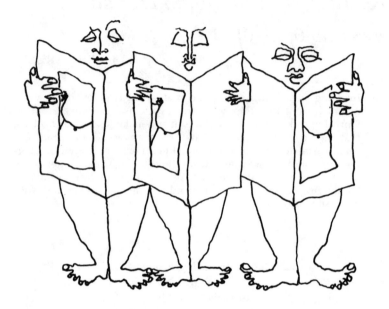

in-the-present, Jael's present-in-a-future, and the secret hope of
Whileawayan Janet who is also unbelievable to her. For Janet is
woman-identified, tied to men by neither love nor hate. Is it
possible, especially for one conceiving of herself as Everywoman, to shift lesbianism from "unreality" or fantasy to "reality"? The novel documents a moment of that struggle.

Before coming out, Joanna had turned herself into a man, a
metaphoric transformation in the quasi-utopian realm of science
fiction whose precedents exist historically among the women
who have passed as men.[3] This "solution" had been the logical
extension of operating within a system of male supremacy ostensibly to subvert it. But was it possible to redefine reality? Simply
to love women and build a just society, rather than to hate men
and fight them? As the novel closes, Joanna kisses Laur while
she reads, expecting the rebuke that will demonstrate the reas-
sertion of the eternal order "(as it had to, of course)":

> *But she let me do it.* She blushed and pretended not to notice. I can't
> describe to you how reality tore itself wide open at that moment.
> It's like falling off a cliff, standing astonished in mid-air as the
> horizon rushes away from you. If this is possible, anything is possi-
> ble . . . nothing that happened afterward was as important to
> me . . . as that first, awful wrench of the mind (p. 208).

After this, the world which she had seen as peopled primarily by men begins to appear flooded by women. She worries how
her changing consciousness will be classified in the minds of
others. "Does it count if it's your best friend? Does it count if you
love men's bodies but hate men's minds?" (p. 209). And whose
definition is right? Joanna moves in mid-sentence from the defensive denial to claiming a presumably ideal "tall, blonde, blue-
eyed lesbian" identity (p. 209).

Part of the difficulty of making a paradigmatic shift away
from male domination was the dearth of models in the culture,
as well as the widespread belief that male and female difference
was biological rather than socially constructed behavior. "I can't
imagine a two-sexed equalitarian society and I don't believe anyone else can, either," Russ commented in 1975. "Where else
(than science fiction) could one even try out such visions? Yet in

the end we will have to have models for the real thing and I can find none yet, and that is why Whileaway is single-sexed."[4]

In the latter part of the nineteenth century, the Freethinker Elmina Drake Slenker, who had been inspired by the "discovery" of contraceptives to advocate free love, shifted her views to seeing heterosexual intercourse as necessary only for reproduction. Finally, believing women's interest would best be served by abstinence, she envisioned a utopian female society perpetuated by parthenogenesis.[5] In 1915, Charlotte Perkins Gilman created the story of Herland, a rational and nurturant society, built on female sex sameness and equality.[6] The question of sexuality among the women is seemingly evaded; or perhaps the author simply relied upon nineteenth-century understandings.

The concept of sexual relations was defined at that time phallocentrically. Women were not expected to be sexual beings or to be sexually aroused by intercourse with males; they were permitted covert affectional and love relations and "lovemaking" with women. Without the phallus, the lovemaking was not defined as sexual.[7] Gilman could expect among her female readers little challenge to the almost invisible love relations among the women, and little regret for the "loss" of the largely unsatisfying duty of heterosexual intercourse. In the nineteenth century, a broad range of romantic relationships among women was common;[8] they were not seen as dangerous if they were conducted in forms that did not tread upon masculine prerogative. It may have been that very implicit solidarity among women—a solidarity fostered both by the conditions that separated the average nineteenth-century white woman from the male world, and by the organized feminist response to those conditions—which enabled Gilman to create and publish her feminist utopia. *Herland* is a fictionalization of Gilman's feminist theories and criticisms of patriarchal capitalism, just as her novella *The Yellow Wallpaper* dramatized the connection between "madness" and the white gentlewoman's imprisonment in genteel marriage.

After the turn of the century, when the medical profession operated as a control system for heterosexuality, loving intimacy was appropriated by male liberals as a new heterosexual standard in order to save the institution of marriage. Lesbian relations had by the twentieth century become possible alternatives to heterosexual relations, and the entrance of women not only into the industrial work force, but increasingly into higher education, the professions, and political life, caused a male reaction which made love relations between women appear perverted, criminal, and insane. Even liberal critics of Victorian society, such as the predominantly gay male Bloomsburyians in England, could espouse homosexual rights and socialism but could not believe women should be "independent of men" and found Sapphism "disgusting." They sent Virginia Woolf to doctors practicing "conversion of the Sodomites," "racial purity," anti-female eugenics, and rest cures[9] such as those Gilman depicted in *The Yellow Wallpaper.*

It was these forces to which Virginia Stephen Woolf, who had been incarcerated by them, referred in her 1936 feminist treatise *Three Guineas,*[10] where she advocates the Outsiders Society. Because her criticism of male civilization was taken as symptomatic of madness—and her lesbianism was viewed as neurosis which developed in women who pursued the unfeminine work of a professional writer—Virginia Woolf veiled the lesbian basis of her vision. The Outsiders Society was a strategic and perhaps utopian proposal. Women constitute an already existing group whose energy, labor, and lives are appropriated by men for their own aggrandizement in a system she saw requiring imperialism and war. During the rise of Hitler, Woolf called upon women to utilize their exclusion to withdraw services and support from the patriarchy. Without explicitly mentioning lesbianism, she tells the reader there are some things even she is afraid to write about because of sanctions occasioned by male fear, insecurity, and power over women.

Very little lesbian utopian vision-making survived in print until, with the advent of the women's liberation movement, journalist Jill Johnston called for "lesbian nation."[11] In 1973, Judy Grahn extended the sexual connotations of "wanting" a lover to the revolutionary—or utopian—dimension of wanting a city safe and healthy for women; "I wanted her as a very few people have wanted me—I wanted her and me to own and control and run the city we lived in. . . ."[12]

In France, Monique Wittig envisioned a global confrontation of men by women, supported by a woman's culture, powered by cultural and material force, and encompassing women of all races, ages, and backgrounds. The diversity of the women in *Les Guérillères*[13] contributes to their strength rather than dividing them, and they battle, sing, and celebrate their way to worldwide feminist victory. A few longhaired men, who are willing to accept a feminist society of primitive communism, are allowed to live. Highly romantic, stylistically disrupted from linear, causal or dramatic/narrative structure, the novel envisions a female culture as a strength for battle and simultaneously denounces it as a fragmented vision inadequate to the new world. The counter-weight to glorification of battle and killing of males is located in a persistently witchlike women's culture.[14]

Here lies a central contribution of the work and one which has had broad appeal in the feminist movement as it evolved from the left, susceptible to believing "Paradise exists in the shadow of the sword" (p. iii). Wittig connects revolution and change not only with guns, but also with language and with the cultural bases for empowering women.

> The women say they have learned to rely on their own strength. They say they are aware of the force of their unity. They say, let those who call for a new language first learn violence. They say, let those who want to change the world first seize all the rifles. They say that they are starting from zero. They say that a new world is beginning (p. 85).

Wittig also assumes the necessity for transforming culture and putting women at the center by using the force of language and culture to crack (male) history. What appear as gaps in male history are women's experiences, and from this, called our weakness, we can build our strength. That message was crucial, particularly for women trapped intimately within white patriarchy.

> They say, we must disregard all the stories relating to those of them who have been betrayed beaten seized seduced carried off violated and exchanged as vile and precious merchandise. They say, we must disregard the statements we have been compelled to deliver contrary to our opinion and in conformity with the codes and conventions of the cultures that have domesticated us. . . .

They say that there is no reality before it has been given shape by words rules regulations. They say that in what concerns them everything has to be remade starting from basic principles. They say that in the first place the vocabulary of every language is to be examined, modified, turned upside down, that every word must be screened (p. 134).

For white women whose culture was that of white male imperialism, the act of separating from male myth, language, tradition, mores, by using the intimate forms of self-expression available to them, especially to the more "educated," has been imperative for liberation of any sort. To express ourselves in forms that deny us is self-destructive.

What are the sources for a definition and naming of what it is we do want? Where do we turn to find ways to talk about the wisdom, love, peace, equality, and freedom we want to make manifest in the world? This is not only a linguistic and philosophical, but also a cultural, and spiritual, question. As Audre Lorde said in 1977:

> The woman's place of power within each of us is neither white nor surface; it is dark, it is ancient, and it is deep. . . .
> For women, then, poetry is not a luxury. It is a vital necessity of our existence. It forms the quality of the light within which we predicate our hopes and dreams toward survival and change, first made into language, then into idea, then into more tangible action. Poetry is the way we help give names to the nameless so it can be thought.[15]

The writers discussed here understand the importance of culture to the creation of radical consciousness; each seeks to empower women to act in her own interests, a process which cannot be postponed "until after a revolution" but which takes place every minute in creating a sense of alternatives to oppression, impotence and silence. But as we recover from powerlessness by turning our "weakness" through anger into our strength, have we kept the categories of victimization? Because biological difference has been used as a vehicle for power differentials, it is easy to assume that the powers of one group and those of the other are inherently different.[16] While there seem to be advantages under conditions of struggle in being able easily to define "the adversary," the danger of using biological difference as a liberatory strategy is that the struggle for liberation also becomes biologically bound—and murderous.

Sally Gearhart in *The Wanderground*[17] begins with a vision of woman and nature as the victims of men, and natural allies in the last great struggle to save life on earth. The ritual connection of woman and earth as daughter-mother lovers is a powerful lesbian mythos. The rape of earth and the revolt of the mother provide the context for female solidarity and a definition of female energy as life-giving and male energy as violent; but Gearhart does not simply accept this dualism. Although she introduces virgin birth, retains her mistrust of "maleness," and does not envision the possibility of humane heterosexual society, Gearhart not only does not write men off, she even allows them to challenge the moral superiority and righteousness of women-as-victim. Claiming they are a special breed, different from other men, "the gentles" have learned to become autonomous and no longer feel they need the women; they are developing their own type of non-violent psychic powers. Evona distrusts them:

> "Non violent? Never. You know what will happen. You'll use your new power all right. You'll use it, perfect it, manufacture it, package it, sell it, and tell the world that it's clean and new because it comes from a different breed of men. But it's just another fancy prick to invade the world with. And you'll use it because you can't really communicate, you can't really love! . . .
> Andros did not flinch. But her words had reached him. He spoke quietly. "You still want it all, don't you? Just like every-woman since the dawn of time. You demand your holy isolation from men so you can develop your unique female powers, but you are threatened to the core by the suggestion that we might have equally unique powers—don't even whisper that they might be equally valuable" (pp. 170–80).

The underlying drama of the work is here revealed as the threat of the (male) "gentles" to female superiority. The radical feminist stance and the utopian vision of women's empowerment have been created on the moral notion that the victims of

male oppression were better than the victimizers. When an ideology assumes that social behavior is inherent, it is locked into an
assumption that the oppressor cannot change. This is generally
reinforced when he will not. But what if some do? Gearhart has
been correct in utilizing the assumption, hidden so well in patriarchal culture, that men are dependent upon women for survival. And women know this, too, fearing they would indeed be
murderers if they stopped holding up men. This self-protective
tie is different from standing beside them. For if women really
believed men did not need them to survive, women would not
feel guilty for freeing men to support themselves. This truth has
been so buried that to reveal and use it is a service.

Gearhart is careful, however, to describe the "gentles' " evolution as the product of practice, discipline, and painful growth
to mutual dependency, not—like the women's—a "gift of nature." The maintenance of this distinction allows her to retain
the possibility of biological superiority for females, a kind of
moral ranking system for humans (women on the top, gay men
next, and then men), while fudging questions about distinctions
among women. Apparently, lesbians aren't biologically different, although the novel displays, while denying, a high level of
disgust for city women—the distinction of geography replacing
that of sexuality for women. Thus, there is no intermediary,
organizable group of women, no space that is not either hill
country or city space, either the women's community or female
slavery. Women must either submit, or pass as men, in the city,
or they can be part of building the new, all-female, utopian
society. Utopian writing serves the function of highlighting present tendencies by solidifying and distancing them in a dramatic
context that reveals their characteristics and contradictions; yet,
by changing their context, it makes them inaccessible, remote,
and apparently immutable.

Amid debate about whether women have ever lived free of
male supremacy, in fiction as in anthropology, some women
have looked to the pre-patriarchal past for evidence of the possibility of freedom for women.[18] In *Retreat: As It Was!*[19] Donna
Young created a fantasy past, a vision of an advanced yet healthy
civilization on the eve of its destruction by invading forces caus-

ing the genetic mutation that created males. The pacific women decided to reverse their millennial stance of nonviolence; they retool for war, and the novel ends with the town in ruins, a few survivors setting forth with the new male child to begin again, presumably to build the patriarchal society we have inherited.

The patriarchal city in several novels so radically disempowers women as to render them victims outside the realm of feminist action. In Charnas' *Motherlines*,[20] where procreation for an all-female society is achieved through intercourse with women's "more natural" allies, horses, the focus is entirely on divisions among women. The interest in the novel lies in the tension between the femmes, who have escaped from their servitude under patriarchal rule, and the Amazonian race of horsewomen, descendants of women who had programmed their own survival in the laboratories of the patriarchy before escaping to the land. The novel closes before we discover if the battle between the newly organized femmes and the men freed those enslaved in the city—or destroyed all the women.

Rochelle Singer's *Demeter Flower*[21] takes us into a fictional future after the holocaust when patriarchal fiefdoms have been established, except for an enclave of women who live secretly in northern California hills. The women fight among themselves, the younger women determined to leave and start another women's community elsewhere. Will their venture bring detection and pursuit? Will the divisions weaken the groups? Divisions also rock the community when a male invades and strategy must be determined; should they keep this enemy among them, kill him, or evict him and risk betraying their existence and location? There is no answer; the novel focuses more on the dangers to the women's unity than on working out an alternative social order, or addressing the plight of patriarchal city women.

By 1980, fears concerning divisions among women and the need for security against men, maleness, and capitalist patriarchy appear primal, obvious consequences of identifying women as a class and men as adversaries victimizing them. But racism, perhaps the most serious immediate division among women, has not been adequately addressed. *Wanderground* begins. But having two frightened women of color rescued by a group of (all-white?) nonchalantly powerful women does not change the conditions they faced in the group to begin with. Rather, it is a white fantasy about earning unity. It is just these intermediate steps, dealing with the differences among us, that we need to envision and address. As the Combahee River Collective stated in 1977, "If black women were free"—and today they might include other women of color—"it would mean that everyone else would have to be free, since our freedom would necessitate the destruction of *all* systems of oppression."[22] White feminists must ask themselves what prevents women from acting on this knowledge, for that constitutes participation in oppression and destructive divisions among women. And women of color will continue on their own.

Today, the most dynamic and strategically empowering vision comes from women, primarily lesbians of color. Gloria Anzaldúa creates a powerful synthesis between the healing spirituality of her grandmother and the materialist analysis of the left, establishing a vital basis for unity. "I build my own universe, *El Mundo Zurdo*," she writes in *This Bridge Called My Back: Writings by Radical Women of Color*[23]—a brilliant and moving feminist work, calling for an international feminism based on the recognition of the right of the colonized, including third world women in the United States, to form independent movements:

> But ultimately, we must struggle together. *Together* we form a vision which spans from the self-love of our colored skins, to the respect of our foremothers who kept the embers of revolution burning, to our reverence for the trees—the final reminder of our rightful place on this planet.
> The change evoked on these pages is material as well as psychic. Change requires a lot of heat. It requires both the alchemist and the welder, the magician and the laborer, the witch and the warrior, the myth-smasher and the myth-maker.
> Hand in hand, we brew and forge a revolution.[24]

NOTES

1. Joanna Russ, *The Female Man* (New York: Bantam Books, 1975), p. 208.

2. See my article, "Lesbianism and the Social Function of Taboo," in *The Future of Difference*, Eisenstein and Jardine, eds. (New York: G. K. Hall, 1980).

3. See, for example, "Passing Women," in *Gay American History*, Jonathan Katz, ed. (New York: Crowell, 1975).

4. Joanna Russ, "Interview," *Quest* 2, No. 1 (Summer, 1975), pp. 45, 47.

5. Elmina Drake Slenker wrote *The Darwins: A Domestic Radical Romance* (1879), *John's Way: A Domestic Radical Story* (1877, 1884); *The Handsomest Woman* (1885).

6. Charlotte Perkins Gilman, *Herland* (New York: Pantheon Books, 1979). First published serially in *The Forerunner*, 1915.

7. See my paper, "Sex, Sexuality and Love Among Women Around the Turn of the Century." Forthcoming.

8. See, for example, Lillian Faderman, *Surpassing the Love of Men: Romantic Friendships and Love Between Women from the Renaissance to the Present* (New York: William Morrow, 1981).

9. E. M. Forster to Virginia Woolf in 1928, during the trial of Radclyffe Hall's *Well of Loneliness*. See my paper, "Azalea Bushes and Asparagus Beds: Virginia Stephen Woolf and the Medical Backlash." Forthcoming.

10. Virginia Stephen Woolf, *Three Guineas* (New York: Harcourt Brace Jovanovich, 1936).

11. Jill Johnston, *Lesbian Nation* (New York: Simon & Schuster, 1973), reprint of her articles from *The Village Voice*.

12. Judy Grahn, *A Woman Is Talking to Death* (Oakland: Diana Press, 1974).

13. Monique Wittig, *Les Guérillères*, trans. LeVay (New York: The Viking Press, 1971).

14. "They speak together of the threat they have constituted towards authority, they tell how they were burned on pyres to prevent them from assembling in the future. . . . Then they chant the famous song that begins, Despite all the evils they wished to crush me with/I remain as steady as the three legged cauldron" (pp. 89–90).

15. Audre Lorde, "Poems Are Not Luxuries," *Chrysalis* 3 (1977), p. 8.

16. A science fiction writer who raises some fundamental questions in terms of gender and race (while staying outside explicit feminist and lesbian thought) is Octavia Butler. Her ulti-

mate male power figure survives by a murderous dependence on the lives of others; neither his human and genetic experimentation nor the exercise of his authority is bound by "human values." Her ultimate female power is a healer. Can she either convert or defeat him? Without jeopardy to her offspring? The two characters are pitted against and bound to each other through centuries of genetic development, accounting for vast differences among humans. Arising from realities of living in a dark skin, Butler's fictions are compelling, though her vision of patterning raises doubts about non-biological social change.

17. Sally Miller Gearhart, *The Wanderground: Stories of the Hill Women* (Watertown, Mass.: Persephone Press, 1978). The history of this alliance is brilliantly treated in Susan Griffin's *Woman and Nature: The Roaring Inside Her* (New York: Harper & Row, 1978).

18. Elizabeth Lynn's *Northern Girl* (New York: Berkley, 1980), third novel in a trilogy, while not exactly a utopian novel, also creates a past peopled with strong women, who can do anything that the men can do (except impregnate and rape). Although showing some fluidity among the characters of different classes, this is the only work discussed here not abolishing antagonistic class relations as a matter of course. Structured around the power of the old Tarot, the novel exhibits ambivalence about the use of violence. The spiritual and material are combined as forces, and while good city governance might require a ban on swords, the old dance-defense included them, and the ban exiled people of wisdom and spiritual strength. How to reconnect and achieve a balance of forces?

19. Donna J. Young, *Retreat: As It Was! A Fantasy* (Weatherby Lake, Mo.: Naiad Press, 1978).

20. Suzy McKee Charnas, *Motherlines* (New York: Berkley, 1978). Another non-lesbian writer, Marge Piercy, depicted a technological form of reproduction in *Woman on the Edge of Time*, adding a biological equalization of birthing and nurturing childcare work between males and females, without which, presumably, sex equality in Mattapoisett could not have been envisioned as a possible future. It is one, moreover, founded upon a continuing military war.

21. Rochelle Singer, *Demeter Flower* (New York: St. Martin's, 1980).

22. Combahee River Collective, "A Black Feminist State-

ment," in *Power, Oppression and the Politics of Culture*, eds. Farley, Jensen, Goodman, Lorde, Smith (New York: Goodman, 1978). Reprinted in *This Bridge Called My Back*, Cherrie Moraga and Gloria Anzaldúa, eds. (Watertown, Mass.: Persephone Press, 1981), p. 172.

23. Gloria Anzaldúa, from "Toward a Construction of El Mundo Zurdo," *This Bridge*, p. 209.

24. Anzaldúa, "El Mundo Zurdo: The Vision," *This Bridge*, p. 196.

Neither Arcadia nor Elysium: E. M. Broner's A Weave of Women

DINNAH PLADOTT

THE term "utopia" plays on the double meaning of the Greek *ou topos,* no place, and *eu topos,* good place.[1] In her book, *A Weave of Women,* E. M. Broner plays a far more complicated word game. She portrays a universe which combines the ideal and the real, but evades both the fantasies of a perfect utopia and the nightmare of anti-utopias.

The stage for the action is neither a mythic locale of past grandeur, nor an imaginary place, but a land which is grounded in both past and present—contemporary Israel. It is the birth-place of the Bible, the native land of the historic Jews who dreamt about it in exile, and the magnetic pole to the Zionists who have returned in modern times to rebuild it in the shape of a perfect Jewish state. The Zionist dream of a Jewish utopia has been overlaid with the dream of creating a socialist and human-ist utopia, in which democracy and equality would flourish. The kibbutz is only one expression of this utopian desire. As Broner's book opens, however, the Zionist and socialist utopian dreams have already been eroded.

Against this backdrop of contemporary Israeli reality, where idealistic dreams and sobering events constantly clash, Broner portrays a group of women who slowly work their way toward another type of community. The group is heterogeneous and international. It includes Israeli-born Sabras and Anglo-

E. M. Broner, *A Weave of Women* (New York: Bantam 1982 reprint of Holt, Rinehart and Winston edition, 1978).

Dinnah Pladott, "Neither Arcadia nor Elysium: Broner's *A Weave of Women,*" copyright © 1984 Dinnah Pladott.

Saxons, high-brow intellectuals and blue-collar workers, young and old, prostitutes and virgins. As these women gradually form "the holiest of families" (p. 111), they are also engaged in what Carolyn Heilbrun has termed "reinventing womanhood."[2] Gravitating toward Jerusalem and one another, forging ties of mutual caring and support, this "family of women" represents solidarity with suffering and victimized women; it also demonstrates that "being a woman" covers a rich spectrum of behavior and thinking.

Broner plunges us into this close communal kinship as she opens the book with the experience of Simha's childbirth. Simha is giving birth out of wedlock, away from institutionalized medical care; but she is surrounded with care, in all senses of the word:

> Gradually the experts gather. They surround Simha, crouched on her stool. They have books of instructions in several languages.
>   Antoinette is in the room, a Shakespearean from London. Joan is there, a playwright, a Britisher, but from Manchester. A scientist arrives, originally from Germany. Dahlia is there, a singer from Beer Sheva. Tova has been there all along, the curly-haired actress from New York. Hepzibah jitneys from Haifa wearing her padded scarf against the wrath of the FatherLord. Mickey arrives in the midst of her divorce. Gloria, the red-head, has been there for the fun. She came from California for the fun. Another social worker arrives from Tel Aviv, serious Polish Vered (p. 3).

The supporting love these women share is refracted through the consciousness of Deedee, the Catholic woman. "The Jews are something else!" she thinks with amusement, and reflects: "She is Irish and prefers her own, and the Greeks, and then the Jews. But Israel is warm and she has women friends who will neither let her starve nor weep" (p. 3). It is typical of Broner's method that Deedee's commentary, mixing condescension and serious respect, is fully illuminated only in Chapter 18. Having digressed through time and place, we finally enter into the musings of Deedee's antagonist, an orthodox youth, which unravel a violent story. First, he lets out the fragments detailing his participation in the stoning of a noted pathologist, who has raised the ire of the fanatic "keepers of the gate" by performing autopsies. Then the youth recapitulates how he followed, befriended, made love to, and finally stoned, the uncomprehending Deedee. In the next chapter, we learn that she is saved from death only through the intervention of the "family of women," who abduct her from the "care" of the hospital. This is a real rebirth. In the women's house Deedee learns Hebrew, a language which distinguishes "male" and "female" adjectives. It so happens that "the pairs of the body are female and the single members male," her sisters explain (p. 231). But Deedee is defiant for the first time in her life. "My head is female," she insists, "my nose is female, my mouth is female, my heart is female" (p. 232). Broner links the birth of Simha's daughter, Hava (Hebrew for Eve), with the near-death and rebirth of Deedee. In the safety of the women's haven, Tova says to Deedee, "You're home." "Home?" "With women," says Terry. "You're safe." "Safe?" "From men," says Mickey bitterly, "the damned stone-throwers. Every look a dart, every action a war" (p. 229).

A Weave of Women is neither polemical nor abstract. Broner weaves a tapestry in which fact and fiction, fantasy and surrealistic horror, tall tales and comic incidents, are juxtaposed and interpolated. She blithely explodes rigid generic definitions, such as Frye's neat separation of the fantastic "romance" from the realistic "novel," and both of these from the intellectual, discursive "anatomy."[3] At times, her characters are the stylized figures of "anatomy" who are just "mouthpieces of the ideas they represent," as Frye puts it. But at other times they oscillate between the insubstantial dreaminess of "romance" and the visceral realism of the "novel."

Consider, for example, the realistic stories, which convey the strong suppportive core of this female community.[4] The term "novel" is fully justified, for example, by the realistic depiction of the women's attempt to protect the shelter for juvenile girl delinquents, "The Home for Jewish Wayward Girls." Equally novelistic is the depiction of Terry's visit to Hepzibah's house, and her discovery that Hepzibah's daughter, Rahel, is suffering from incest delusions. Rahel's fear that she has been impregnated by her tyrannical father is palpable; yet Broner mixes the realistic and the mythic. The strongest antidote the women have to the ravages of terror, pain, and destruction, is the power of ritual. Faced with the crises of life, they support one another by forging links of new communal rites which reinforce energy and encourage growth. Confronted with Rahel's hysteria, Terry "has a sharp longing for her family in Jerusalem, Simha and Hava. It is a sensible family, no incestuous dreams, no shouting and soothing. Terry's is an ideal home" (p. 77). The longing does not, however, obscure Rahel's pressing need. Hence Terry fashions a ritual which delivers the girl from her obsession (p. 77).

This rite is a micro-reflection of the more elaborate ritual the "family of women" creates in order to release Mickey from the Dybbuk that has bloated her beyond recognition (pp. 105–112). Whereas Rahel is freed by a single ritual blessing of the chicken and the wine (p. 77), Mickey's "divorce" from the invading "Magda" is a long, gradual process. The "selected" participants in this rite alternately scold, cajole, entertain, feed, entreat, and threaten the spirit of "Magda," while emphasizing the experience of sharing. When it is finally clear that Magda is one of the miserable women fruitlessly seeking the release of divorce, the "fair tribunal" undertakes to divorce the possessor and the possessed:

> "Magda and Mihal," says Simha, "we are declaring you divorced in the tradition of our nomadic people, the way of our Bedouin ancestors. Magda/Mihal, repeat after me three times, 'I divorce you'" (p. 112).

The "family of women" tap the life-encouraging force of ritual in the defence of all those shattered or threatened by existential pressures, male as well as female. When Vered's brother stops eating and begins a passive suicide in a reaction to her love affair, the women visit him in turn. By stirring his senses, his zest for living, they also reaffirm the bonds of affection, compassion and sisterhood (pp. 86–88). "A brother must, at all costs, be brought back to life" (p. 84). A different coloring marks the Tall Tale of Dahlia's experience in the Sinai desert. As a true folk heroine, she survives in the waterless and lonely wasteland without any preparation or training. But Dahlia also undertakes two symbolic acts. She saves a stork whose leg is broken, sustaining in the process the ancient symbol of the human thirst for freedom in the shape of airy flight. And she initiates the son of a Bedouin chief into the mysteries of sex. "The boy will never forget this rite" (p. 99).

These life-giving rituals which nourish male figures stand in stark contrast to the rapacity of males toward women. Shula, a juvenile delinquent—reformed due to the women's caring and love—becomes the victim of male sexual omnivorousness on a European train. At the end of a surrealistic account which blurs the border between fact and fantasy, the bare bones testify to the horrendous reality:

> From every orifice her seat mates had drunk her, biting the flesh of her nose, opening her mouth, eating the tongue, the ears. Her face is leprous, sections missing from their hunger. She was the communal lunch, the licked bones (p. 275).

A similar male predatory attitude drives the girl Robin to a mythic metamorphosis into a real bird (p. 169). The irrational violence which threatens is also exemplified in the senseless killing of baby Hava by the Bedouin nomad. Crystallized here is the truth implicit in various other episodes, namely, that the relations of Arab and Jew, of man and woman, adult and child, parents and offspring, in the towns as well as in the country, are marked by similar alienation and incomprehension, which carry the seeds of violence and destruction.

In their struggle against this ugly reality, "the family of women" invoke the power of love and the magic effects of ritual. Thomas More's *Utopia* elicits from Raymond Chambers the classic emphasis on the redemptive power of reason: "The underlying thought of *Utopia* is, With nothing save Reason to guide them, the Utopians do this."[5] But in the opening to her thirteenth chapter, Broner indicates that absolute justice and reason exist only in books: "In this Chapter the thirteenth all will come to right. Allotments will be fair, time apportioned and justice preside" (p. 145). Her women warriors consequently fight with a different weapon. "Always at war" as they are, according to Dahlia, "in our land and in our lives" (p. 26), they fight, yet with love and nurturing rites. "The women in the stone house have performed their good deed," we are told after the resuscitation of Vered's brother. "They are temple priestesses, renewing themselves and saving lives" (p. 88).

Broner avoids both the aesthetic and the philosophical pitfalls which await the utopian literary visionary. First, by playing hopscotch among diverse types of fictional representation, she proves an exception to Leavis's "elementary distinction" between "the *discussion* of problems and ideas, and what we find in the great novelists."[6] By creating a patchwork composition she juxtaposes the various narrative modes, creating a new generic type which encompasses all the others.

Philosophically, as well, Broner questions the moral absolutism on which many utopian works have been wrecked. The male utopian imagination which posits an unbridgeable chasm between the Ideal and the Real, between Reason and Madness, can visualize the Good Place—*eu topos*—only in the nonexistent Dreamland—*ou topos*. Broner, in this book, discredits such absolute distinctions. In one of the most humorous scenes in the book, Broner demonstrates that she is supremely aware of the arbitrary and malleable nature of seemingly "absolute" verbal entities. The much maligned Home for Jewish Wayward Girls, long a target of criticism by the Ministry of Welfare and the Ministry of Religion, finally faces dismantling. This venomous animosity toward the Home has a deep-rooted significance, since such a shelter is an emblem of the cancerous rot lying in the very core of the national Jewish utopian dream. Terry, however, understands that a dynamic relation exists between words and the reality they describe. She intuits that the sanctimonious officials object not merely to the Home, but its function as a symbolic blot on the dream of utopian perfection. Hence, she undertakes to change the objectionable name, and, in so doing, to remove the stain:

> Let them dismantle Wayward House. She has bigger plans. Girls Town of Haifa.[. . .] The House will be located in a religious

neighborhood and be supervised by a *tsadika,* a saint [. . .]. The Ministry of Religion is somewhat interested. Funds will pour in from all over the world, says Terry. Maybe they'll make a movie: *Girls Town* [. . .]. The Ministry of Religion is more interested" (p. 206).

The incident, which may appear merely lighthearted, gains coherence and gravity when we examine it in the light of the insights of Foucault.[7] In his analysis of discourse in psychiatry, medicine, and the human sciences, Foucault repeatedly exposes the power of discourse to *create* the reality it purports to *describe* by pointing to the arbitrariness of every rule of exclusion and every norm of hierarchic ordering.[8]

Foucault traces in the realm of general discourse what feminist critics have long noted about the insidious "description" and "classification" of women's writing by male critical discourse.[9] Like Foucault, Broner emphasizes the potential of discourse to reshape the entity it attempts to outline. Yet as we have seen, one of the most potent instruments wielded by the women warriors is the ritual act, which draws upon the capacity of words to transform reality. The treacherous nature of discourse is thus turned to beneficial use.

Consider, for example, the previously quoted example of the ritual of Dybbuk exorcism. The women appropriate here one of the most anti-female ceremonies: the Moslem rite in which a husband can posthaste divorce his wife by saying three times "I divorce you," and against which the woman has neither recourse nor appeal. Once the exclusion of women from the privilege of using this oppressive tool is perceived in its full arbitrariness, the "family of women" is free to use it in order to deliver Mickey from the stifling embrace of the Dybbuk. As this productive potential of language becomes progressively clearer to the women, they harness it with greater skill, creating ceremonies that dissolve the harsh reality. This "family of women" goes down to the Dead Sea, literally as well as metaphorically, only to rise again rejuvenated and refreshed (pp. 133–144).

The form as well as the content of the novel-romance-anatomy seems now not only natural but inevitable. If no absolutes exist, then the "logocentric"[10] concept of perfect utopian justice and rationality collapses. Hence Broner creates a universe where opposites coexist. The Jerusalem of *A Weave of Women* is neither the dream of ideal perfection envisioned by Father Surtz as the real goal of *Utopia*,[11] nor the "Golden Jerusalem" of Zionist yearnings and Jewish prayers. It is the locus of the slowly forming community of secular Israelis, who clash with the rabid orthodoxy of fanatic zealots, and rub elbows, not always smoothly, with the Arab citizens of the Old City and their old ways. There is no way, Broner implies, in which one may simply and naively escape the ravages of historical time by a regression into a mythic Golden Age, a perfect Arcadia, which has existed *in illo tempore*.[12] Equally implausible is Schiller's suggestion that utopian poetry should direct man not backward, to Arcadia, but forward, to Elysium.[13] Broner eschews such linear teleology just as she dispenses with the novel's traditional linear form.

Form and content converge as Broner's work demonstrates the limits of any simplistic belief in utopian progress toward some possible Elysium. As the fragmented configuration confounds all notions of "before" and "after," so the almost exclusive use of the present tense precludes any causal interpretation of the action. Everything is presented as equal in value, as concurrent in time. Moreover, with the rejection of "logocentrism" comes a rejection of all definitive beginnings and all final endings. Broner's opening as well as her closing paragraphs gaily play with mythic materials so that beginning merges into ending, like a snake biting its own tail.

The novel opens in a birth scene—the birth of Hava—which is the legendary emblem of all beginnings. It terminates with dusk, the traditional poetic signal for closure. However, placed side by side, the paragraphs reveal that the action has taken us a full circle. The time of day, the place, and the *dramatis personae* are identical:

> They embrace and face Jordan. They are turned golden in the evening light, like the stone. There are several of them [. . .]. The women breathe with Simha. Heavy labor has not begun yet. They sit in the doorway of their stone house in the Old City (p. 1). Night. The women bed down. There is no heat and it is chilly. The candles turn to stubs and the bonfire to embers (p. 294).

In the second paragraph, the burning down of fires and candles reinforces the sense of denouement, completion and annihilation signified by nightfall. Broner, however, links birth, in the opening paragraph, with the conclusiveness of "evening."[14] In the last lines of the novel a blurring takes place, so that past, present and future are held in suspension. The male tradition is invoked in female form, moreover, so that the words of the Old Testament are transformed into a female vernacular. The repossession of the past male tradition by the present female heroines constitutes an unequivocal victory. But such victories, like the triumph of the rituals, must be reenacted periodically. They do not hold any definite teleological promise; the women are able, at this moment, to reclaim "the ruins," but in Broner's open-form utopian work, the future is always shrouded in doubt:

> What will happen to them, this caravan of women that encircles the city, that peoples the desert?
>
> How goodly are thy tents, thy reclaimed ruins, O Sara, O our mother of the desert (p. 294).

NOTES

1. See Robert G. Elliott, *The Shape of Utopia: Studies in a Literary Genre* (Chicago: University of Chicago Press, 1970), p. 85.

2. Carolyn Heilbrun, *Reinventing Womanhood* (New York: Norton, 1979, 1981). In a previous study, Prof. Heilbrun has noted the limited scope of action accorded to female "heroines" in male novels. "She is the woman the hero pursues, or loves, or both, the woman he marries or doesn't marry." *Toward a Recognition of Androgyny* (New York: Norton, 1974, 1982), p. 51.

3. Northrop Frye, *Anatomy of Criticism* (New York: Atheneum Publishers, 1970), pp. 308–309.

4. See Nina Auerbach, *Communities of Women: An Idea in Fiction* (Harvard University Press, 1978).

5. Raymond Chambers, *Thomas More* (London: Jonathan Cape, 1935), p. 128.

6. F. R. Leavis, *The Great Tradition* (London: Chatto and Windus, 1948), p. 7.

7. Michel Foucault, *Madness and Civilization: A History of Insanity in the Age of Reason,* trans. Richard Howard (New York: Random House, 1973); *The Birth of the Clinic: An Archaeology of Medical Perception,* trans. A. M. Sheridan Smith (New York: Pantheon, 1973); *The Order of Things: An Archaeology of the Human Sciences* (New York: Pantheon, 1970).

8. "The Discourse on Language," an Appendix to *The Archaeology of Knowledge,* trans. A. M. Sheridan Smith (New York: Pantheon, 1972), p. 233, terms this phenomenon the "instance of discursive control." In other terms, this is "the power of affirmation," by which, Foucault explains, "I do not mean a power opposed to that of negation, but the power of constituting domains of all possible objects" (*Ibid.,* p. 234).

9. See, as only a few representative examples, Ellen Moers, *Literary Women* (Garden City, N.Y.: Doubleday Anchor, 1977); Elaine Showalter, *A Literature of Their Own* (Princeton: Princeton University Press, 1977); Patricia Meyer Spacks, *The Female Imagination* (New York: Alfred A. Knopf, Inc., 1972); and the pioneering Virginia Woolf, *A Room of One's Own* (New York: Harcourt Brace Jovanovich, 1981).

10. Like all other concepts and categories, Foucault insists, "logos" is not an absolute term but a mutable language construct: "in truth, logos is only another discourse." "Discourse on Language," p. 228.

11. Father Surtz asserts that for More, the real ideal of perfection would be not the secular model commonwealth he depicts in his fiction, but "the Holy City, New Jerusalem, coming down from Heaven from God" (*Rev.* 21:2). See Father Surtz's reading of Utopia in *Utopia: The Praise of Pleasure* (Cambridge, Mass.: Harvard University Press, 1957); and *Utopia: The Shape of Wisdom* (Chicago: Loyola University Press, 1957).

12. See Elliott, p. 9.

13. See *Naive and Sentimental Poetry* and *On the Sublime,* trans. and ed., Julius A. Elias (New York: Ungar, 1966), pp. 145–54.

14. See Barbara Herrnstein Smith, *Poetic Closure* (Chicago: University of Chicago Press, 1972).

The Land of Ordinary People

For John Lennon

ELEANOR ARNASON

I.

Welcome to the land of ordinary people.
Our buildings are low.
Our roads are made
for bicycles not limousines.
As for our public monuments, they celebrate
achievements of day-to-day life.

Here, in the main square,
the cube of bronze
ten meters tall is for
the Unknown Inventor of Bean Curd.

And here, above the boulevard,
this line of wash
made of heavy plastic
and hung on steel—
this celebrates
the housewives and laundry maids
throughout all history.

Oh women with muscular arms
beating sheets on rocks by the river,
we honor you!

We shall not forget
your labor in the cause of cleanliness!

II.

Our streets are named for flowers and for trades.
At the moment, we stand
at the corner of Magnolia Lane
and Keypunch Avenue.
Further down
is the fountain at the start
of Plumbers' Promenade.

Notice the shape: a giant bidet
shooting jets of water
that glisten in the sunlight.

III.

Politicians?
We have none, holding—as we do—
the very name accursed.

No soldiers
nor theologians,
not even one philosopher.

But a multitude of gardeners
and potters,
mechanics
and extruders of plastic.

IV.

In the center of every town, we build
a hall—

large and lined with mirrors.
We bring our children there
on days off when it's rainy.

"Look around," we say.
"This is the source of power.
Here are the heroes.
Here are the leaders.
The ones who sing,
the ones who are sung about—
all are here.

"Look and see
how they return your gaze."

Of Time and Revolution: Theories of Social Change in Contemporary Feminist Science Fiction

CAROL S. PEARSON

To the extent that feminist theory has been based upon nineteenth-century notions about time and the nature of history, it has locked feminists into patterns of analysis which cannot be adequate to the great changes occurring in the last quarter of the twentieth century. There is emerging, however, in recent feminist science fiction—such as Marge Piercy's *Woman on the Edge of Time*, Dorothy Bryant's *The Kin of Ata Are Waiting for You*, Mary Staton's *From the Legend of Biel*—and in certain poetic works of feminist theory—for instance, Susan Griffin's *Woman and Nature* or Robin Morgan's "Metaphysical Feminism" (in *Going Too Far*)—a political theory based on hypotheses radically different from those which have dominated political discourse in recent centuries.[1] Based upon modern scientific ideas about time, these theories are beginning to move us out of a politics based solely upon notions of linear progress, causality, and struggle. They begin, in fact, to promote a radical disbelief in the traditional concerns of politics—power, ownership, and control.

The three major principles which emerge from this new politics are all paradoxical:

1. Time is linear; *and* it is relative. To the degree that we live only in linear time, we are locked into a world governed by laws

of causality, dualism, linearity, and struggle. But we also have available to us a reality based upon relativity. In this dimension, time and space are not separate, and time/space is curved. It then becomes possible to understand that we can change not only the future but the past. Such analyses focus on concepts like paradox, synchronicity, responsibility, commitment, and transformation.

2. Although past, present and future co-exist and are equally real in the present, the only point of action in which anything can be changed is in the present. Paradoxically, widespread social change occurs only as a result of the solitary decisions of individuals to step outside linear time into the "eternal now." Yet, at the same time, no one moves fully into the new world alone. No one is fully there, until we all are.

3. The move into a new, utopian future occurs when we simultaneously take responsibility for our own lives and relinquish all illusions that we can control anything—others, the flow of history, or the effects of our own actions.

Explaining the bases for these theories, Mary Staton in *From the Legend of Biel* writes,

> If we can apply to time the same principle we apply to matter—i.e., that it cannot be destroyed, only transformed—then it follows that all time, which contains all events, exists right now, in one form or another. Times past, present, and future are simultaneous (p. 321).

In the novels of Bryant, Piercy, and Staton, the utopian "future" worlds (and in Piercy's novel also a dystopian one) coexist with the present. As Barbarossa, a citizen of Piercy's utopian Mattapoisett explains, "all things interlock. We are only one possible future. . . . Yours is a crux-time. Alternative universes coexist." He continues: "at certain cruxes of history forces are in conflict. . . . Alternative futures are equally or almost equally probable . . . and that affects the shape of time" (p. 189).

Actually, time is paradoxical: it is linear, *and* it is relative. Described in linear terms, the existence of Piercy's Mattapoisett is the result of all the accumulated choices of ordinary people who begin living differently and also of a thirty-year war culminating in a revolution. Described in terms of relativity, we learn that the war is continuing and the "past is a disputed area." The existence of Mattapoisett is dependent upon the "present" actions of people of the "past." In particular, Connie—a Chicana, former welfare mother, present inmate of a mental hospital, and protagonist of the novel—is the key to the survival of the utopian future. Connie is part of an experiment in genetic engineering designed to make people who are perceived as deviant and destructive become conformist and obedient. This experiment is part of the distopian "future" and will help insure its continuity. Connie affects the existence of the "future world" (which coexists with the present one) when she kills the doctors conducting the experiment. What is important for a consideration of time and revolutionary change is that she would not have done this if she had not, in fact, interacted with a future world.

This interaction makes no sense when time is viewed linearly unless the plot is interpreted metaphorically: we cannot create a future world unless we live in it, to the extent that we envision it and it claims our loyalties. This metaphorical interpretation certainly makes sense in Piercy's novel, but the plot of Staton's seems to call for a more literal belief in our capacity to change the past. In this work the psychic interaction between Biel—a pioneer in the utopian, future Thoacdien world—and Howard Scott—an astronaut from a time just a bit more advanced than our own—changes the course of Thoacdien history. It is not Scott's culture which is changed, but himself: he dies and is reborn a Thoacdien. The interaction, however, changes the future (Biel's present). Scott dies from information overload when he listens to tapes left by the Thoacdien culture, tapes which recount the "legend of Biel." Now, this legend is the story of Biel's interaction with Scott, an interaction which changes Thoacdien civilization, but one which when seen in terms of linear time is impossible: it hasn't happened until Scott listens to those tapes!

When past, present, and future are not imaged as simultaneous, they are circular or spiral, and the terms used to describe historical change are more typical of mystic or philosophical writing than of political analysis. Indeed, ideas in feminist science fiction are reminiscent of those in T. S. Eliot's *The Four Quartets:* the "new world" is also "the old made explicit, understood," and the journey of discovery is circular:

> *We shall not cease from exploration*
> *And the end of all our exploring*
> *Will be to arrive where we started*
> *And know the place for the first time.*[2]

Accordingly, Piercy's and Bryant's heroes are confused when they first encounter the future world because it seems as much like the past as the future. Connie complains, "You sure we were sent into the right direction? into the future?" (p. 62). Joanna Russ, in another utopian novel, *The Female Man,* describes Whileaway as "so pastoral that at times one wonders whether the ultimate sophistication may not take us all back to a kind of Paleolithic dawn age, a garden without any artifacts except for what we would call miracles."[3]

A major change in the Thoacdien civilization occurs when in a moment of trauma Biel's genes get mixed up with Scott's. It is out of the stress of this confusion, the massive effort required to grasp the resulting internal turmoil, that Biel is able to understand new realities that move the Thoacdien society forward. Such processes—as described in the novels of Bryant and Piercy, where a protagonist changes drastically as a result of contact with either a "past" or a "future" society—are analogous to those of effective therapy when something new emerges out of the creative interaction of past with present experiences and insight.

In therapy, we essentially change the past by changing our responses to similar situations in the present. The past is "caused" by a complex of actions and responses, including our own. We free ourselves from the determinism of the past, when our present understanding frees us to act in ways we have never done before. "The way it has always been" only determines "the way things are" as long as we believe it has to.

Individually and collectively, we are limited in our actions by events and attitudes which actually prevail in the present, but we typically feel much less free than we are because we tend to be weighted down by the power of history. Actually, history does not have an existence of its own. "History" is merely an abstraction for the accumulated decisions and actions of individuals through time. History does not exist; there are only people, and people can always choose to change. Staton suggests that we move into a utopian future by stepping outside standard concepts of time and causality which limit our imaginations. The Thoacdien dome, Staton tells us, carried a message like "a hand extended through centuries of brutality which said, 'None of that was necessary. Come and forget. Come, Begin Again.' " (p. 35)

When we break the causality chain and "begin again," the resulting freedom feels like a miracle—indeed, miracles may be just that, a release from linear time. Susan Griffin, in *Woman and Nature*, moves from her understanding that time and space are elliptical and curve back upon themselves to explain that "miracles" occur, "Not at the end," for there is no end to an ellipse, but in the center. "Time in space," she explains, is "the half note pushing the air, the quarter note transversing the earth. The bud, the egg, the risen bread, the right time for things." This is time as process, not controlled, linear partriarchal time. Process time holds the secret to miracles. The new world is not at the end of a linear progression, but in the core, and its space in time is the "right time," "now" (p. 174). We each have the potential to "step off the edge" and fall into ourselves and into an alternative utopian world by moving outside of concepts of linear time and causality into the elliptical present of infinite potentiality. Similarly Robin Morgan writes in "Metaphysical Feminism,"

> *How to make you realize the imperative of this moment?*
> *How to stretch out a hand and whisper, yes, here, step*
> *out over the edge, the drop is only magnetized toward*
> *your density's grave center.*
> *May your insurrection and your resurrection be the same (p. 294).*

Dorothy Bryant's *The Kin of Ata Are Waiting for You* dramatically illustrates this principle. The protagonist is a successful man of his time. Like the hero of Norman Mailer's *The American Dream*, he is a wealthy, famous writer, a chauvinist, and a murderer. Bryant's protagonist has an automobile wreck and, after having killed his girlfriend, escapes and awakens in Ata, where he lives a long full life and learns to live as an Atan; that is, he becomes whole, gentle and feminist. Then one day he awakens in a hospital bed to discover that only two weeks have elapsed since the car wreck. All evidence and logic indicate that his "long life" in Ata was only a dream, a hallucination. His lawyer advises him that he is about to stand trial for murder, but if he merely lies, he will be acquitted and can go back to his "normal life."

He does not know what to do until the moment he must make his plea: then he understands that the only way to find out if Ata is real is "to believe . . . even if it meant throwing away my life" (p. 217). He laughs, recognizing that now that he knows what it meant to be an Atan, his old "successful" life would be "no less vicious a prison," "no less a death," than life imprisonment or execution. Acting like an Atan, he tells the truth and the courtroom is filled with "warm, glowing light," and he knows that Ata exists; indeed, he created it there in the courtroom: "I was part of the light and all the other things that shone in and with the light. All were one. And whole" (p. 218). Instead of waiting for the safety of a cultural consensus that Ata exists, he steps off the edge of his own time into the core of his own integrity, and lives as an Atan.

As here, it is at the intersection of linear time and eternity that the miracle of creation occurs, for while stepping outside linear time frees us to know infinite possibilities, its restraints require choice. The need to choose in a world of limitless opportunity made suddenly finite creates commitment, which itself necessitates trust.

Because the key is a leap of faith, revolutionary change in these novels is imaged in mystic or spiritual terms: rebirth. Augustine in Bryant's *The Kin of Ata* explains that "No one can bring you here [Ata]. You must want it with your whole soul." (p. 72) Staton describes Howard Scott standing before the Thoacdien dome, "before an invisible but tangible barrier—his time on one side, an entire new civilization on the other. Willingness to change was the key to passage through." (p. 68) He literally dies and is reborn an infant in the Thoacdien culture and this rebirth is a metaphorical enactment of his total relinquishment of control. He knows nothing about this future world except what he surmises from the dome; he just wants to live there.

The "revolution" which created the Thoacdien civilization was "bloodless and thorough," involving no struggle, no coercion, no attempt to convert people or force change. It involves only the accumulated transformations of numerous curious individuals who choose to go through the Hall of a Thousand Chambers and to move thereby from simplistic to complex modes of understanding reality and of communication. Before this, "human beings were sick" in ways "encouraged by . . . the language."

> Hidden deep in the sounds of their words was despair and fear. Repeated use of the words and phrases only reinforced those feelings. The essential thrust of their language was control and ownership [of land, animals, mates, progeny, emotions, ideas] where control and ownership are not possible (p. 176).

Howard Scott breaks the chain of despair and fear which results in repression and oppression by taking responsibility for his life while relinquishing control over it or over other people. He refuses to leave the dome and return to his spaceship as he is ordered to do, saying, "You have lost control. . . . I am awake" (p. 61).

The concept of taking responsibility for one's life while relinquishing control over it is beyond the dualistic debate about individual freedom versus determinism. Paradoxically, we are both free and oppressed, and it is only in both fully recognizing the extent of our oppression and choosing to act fully on the freedom and power we do possess that we and our culture are transformed. Both Piercy and Bryant emphasize the need to exercise fully the freedom we do have by placing their characters in desperate situations—one is an inmate in a mental hospital about to undergo an operation against her will, the other a prisoner on trial for his life—in which freedom is much more severely limited than for most of us. Yet even these people have the power to withdraw their personal allegiances from an oppressive system and live their lives with full loyalty to the world of their dreams.

Furthermore, these cases demonstrate the paradox of independence and interdependence. We move into the new world only individually, but we will never fully inhabit that world alone. As Bryant explains, people wake up one by one in Ata and truly experience a utopian society beginning with their individual awakening. But it is also true that Atans are part of the human race, and that "we are all kin . . . we must draw them all back again if any of us is to go . . . to what we are for. One cannot go alone; it must be all or none" (p. 14). The power Atans have as revolutionaries is through living their lives as Atans. Ata and Thoacdien both essentially work as magnets. No violence draws people to them, only curiosity and in Howard Scott's words, "the formless reach of his desire" (p. 35).

The implications of these ideas about time, causality, and the nature of social change for our political theory are immense. Most discussions of feminist theory focus on a cause-and-effect analysis. In this historically deterministic view, we are essentially all individually stuck with our oppression until we collectively redress its root cause.

There is despair inherent in the causal analysis, whether we identify the root of patriarchy as (1) oppressive sex role conditioning (liberal feminist), (2) class oppression (socialist feminist), or (3) biology or motherhood as an institution (radical feminist). Virtually all these divergent viewpoints converge on this one shared hypothesis: we must have a critical mass of people who agree with our hypothesis to redress the root cause of our cultural and individual oppression. When such consensus fails to emerge and when oppression continues apparently unabated, we feel powerless and turn our anger on each other.

The works discussed in this essay suggest political practice that is at once very difficult and very simple. It is difficult because it calls for great faith, integrity, and humility, but it is far simpler than much of current feminist practice. When we stop wasting time on futile attempts to control the movement or to force social change and focus on fully claiming our own lives and integrity (which may well include taking strong political stands and working hard for social change), we will have all the time we need. We cannot force or control change, but we can take a leap of faith to be citizens of a utopian society—in progress—today. The paradox is that as we take the risk to move into the new world alone, we find to our surprise—as Staton's and Bryant's heroes do—that we awaken into a new community which has co-existed with the old all along. Only our lack of belief kept it from view.

NOTES

1. Marge Piercy, *Woman on the Edge of Time* (New York: Alfred A. Knopf, Inc., 1976); Dorothy Bryant, *The Kin of Ata Are Waiting for You* (New York: Random House, 1976); Mary Staton, *From the Legend of Biel* (New York: Ace Books, 1975); Susan Griffin, *Women and Nature* (New York: Harper and Row, 1978); Robin Morgan, "Metaphysical Feminism," *Going too Far: The Personal Chronicle of a Feminist* (New York: Random House, 1977), pp. 290–295.

2. T. S. Eliot. *The Four Quartets,* in *The Complete Poems and Plays, 1909–1950* (New York: Harcourt, Brace & World, Inc., 1952), p. 145.

3. Joanna Russ, *The Female Man* (New York: Avon Books, 1974), p. 14.

Change and Art in Women's Worlds: Doris Lessing's Canopus in Argos: Archives

LEE CULLEN KHANNA

> It is because it is so hard to think ourselves into the possibilities of the ancient dream of free man that the nightmare is so strong. . . . And the artists have been so busy with the nightmare that they have had no time to rewrite the old utopias. . . . Yet we are all of us, directly or indirectly, caught up in a great whirlwind of change; and I believe that if an artist has once felt this . . . has once made the effort of imagination necessary to comprehend it, it is an end of despair . . . the beginning of something else.
>
> DORIS LESSING, "The Small Personal Voice," in *A Small Personal Voice: Essays, Reviews, Interviews,* ed. PAUL SCHLUETER (New York: Alfred A. Knopf, Inc., 1974), pp. 9, 11, 20.

Historians and critics have tended to regard the twentieth century as a dystopian age, both in fact and in fiction. Despite the obvious justification for such a view, recent utopian novels by women qualify this pessimistic outlook by generating positive and persuasive social alternatives. This substantial body of recent fiction represents the first fully conscious articulation of female ideas about the "good society."[1] Despite its importance, however, this fiction has been too little studied, both in assessments of the utopian tradition and in predictions of the future. For example, in their thorough and thoughtful survey, *Utopian Thought in the Western World,* Frank and Fritzie Manuel bemoan the current lack of utopian inspiration. In our time, they say, "we witness the multiplication of ways to get to space colonies, to manipulate the genetic bank of species man, and simultaneously the weakness of thought, fantasy, wish, utopia. Scientists tell us that they can now outline with a fair degree of accuracy the procedures necessary to establish a space colony in a hollowed comet or an asteroid. But when it comes to describing what people will do there, the men most active in this field merely reconstruct suburbia—garden clubs and all—in a new weightless environment."[2] It is, of course, the "men" most active in this field the Manuels do consider, for a close reading of recent utopian novels by women produces a much more original picture.[3]

Instead of the proliferation of technologies of production, consumerism, and warfare, the societies depicted by women use science as a tool of the community to enhance the quality of life for each citizen. In Marge Piercy's utopian world, for example, menial and boring tasks are done by machine; every child plays with sophisticated tiny computers as educational devices; computers aid communication and memory, and medical technology and genetic engineering are dramatically advanced. Yet the people build no bombs, no giant industrial complexes, no shopping centers.[4] Their social priorities are, rather, education, individual development, genuine equality for all, institutions that foster both individual distinctiveness and communal involvement. Interpersonal relations are a primary value and are characterized by openness and experimentation. In fact, the only significant social taboo is actually injuring someone else. The utopian style of life, devised by women, is varied but consistently reflects a respect for nature, and many citizens remain "close to the soil" both literally and figuratively.

The primacy of the natural cycle in ordering social customs and institutions is, in fact, typical of these utopias. The basic events of human experience: birth, growing up, sexual and creative drives, aging, and death are all fully explored. Inherent in this recognition of the cyclic nature of life is a respect for process rather than product. Therefore, the theoretical basis of utopian speculation is transformed. No longer is the good society to be seen as a static ideal—a perfect organization achieved through rational inquiry, then strictly ruled by law. Plato's *Republic* is the archetype of that static ideal, and Socrates would banish poets lest their powers subvert the laws of the achieved ideal. Similarly, in Plutarch's description of a utopian Sparta, the society's founder, Lycurgus, left the state forever with the parting precept that nothing be changed until his return.

For women, however, the "best social order" is dynamic. The inevitable changes of life are not denied or downgraded in the rush to produce and accumulate. Rather, each stage of life is respected, attended by communal concern and ritual, even celebrated. In addition, the recognition that change is necessary allows for tolerance in human development and a more relaxed sense of human interaction, certainly a more fluid political structure. The good society is thus viable only so long as it is constantly re-evaluated, revised, responsive to individual and communal growth. In most of these worlds designed by women, art—whether dance, music, storytelling, or multi-media events—accompanies moments of significant change. In fact, women's utopias differ markedly from the male utopian tradition in the importance attached to both change and creativity.[5]

This distinctiveness permeates Doris Lessing's contribution to the genre: *Canopus in Argos: Archives*. The specific social priorities associated with feminist utopias, the importance of art, and the underlying theory of mutability mark all of the novels in the series written to date. Most striking, though, is Lessing's study of the process of individual and social change in the context of utopian/dystopian speculation. An investigation of the nature of such transformations informs both the content and the style of the first novel in the series, *Shikasta*. At the very beginning of the book, its principle narrator, Johor, admits his relative ignorance despite his advantage of great age and years of service in the most advanced society in the universe. In fact he doubts the certainty of any truth and says, "Things change; that is all we may be sure of."[6] Throughout the book change is often reflected in the shifting balance of opposing forces.

These conflicting forces are both mythical and realistic. Although the focus of the narrative is the planet, Shikasta, other powerful alien galaxies battle around it. Canopus, the beneficent galactic empire, and Puttiora, the evil galaxy, seesaw in their control over Shikasta and its people. Within that archetypal struggle between good and evil, multiple minor battles are waged. As the narrative unfolds, the reader sees that Shikasta is our own earth and that Lessing is doing no less than recounting our history from totally new perspectives. The archetypal struggle is repeated dozens of times in increasingly realistic human conflicts.

Yet Lessing's insights depend not only upon the wisdom of the dialectic that pervades her philosophy, but on the way she presents the dialectic—her style. *Shikasta* is a radically experimental book, presented in a series of totally different narrative perspectives. Johor's narrative is often interrupted, first by the staccato reports of the Canopean archivists, and then by the journals, letters, recollections of various "individuals" living on Shikasta. The reader is thus confronted with such disparate points of view as the vast, compassionate perspective of Johor, the impersonal reports and orders of Canopean chroniclers, and the moving diary of a young girl, Rachel Sherban, speaking in a particular human voice. One is barely used to one stance before being suddenly accosted by an entirely different tone and point of view. The narrative method is thus discontinuous, forcing the reader to adjust her mode of apprehension, her emotional state, again and again. Of course, discontinuity is characteristic of our culture; collage styles of writing are fashionable. In *Shikasta,* however, Lessing shapes the modes of twentieth-century thought and style to new ends. The ends are no less than the expansion of human consciousness, and the means are the reordering of time and perspective by disorienting the reader.

Actually much of Shikasta revolves about the corrupted human—in other words, the political, social, environmental problems of our own day. The sojourn in Rohanda—the name of Shikasta before its degeneration—is as brief as it is beautiful. The progress through time, which, in fact, returns us to ourselves—our present world—dawns slowly, like a blurred picture coming into focus. Gradually, we recognize that Johor describes World War II—or our exact environmental plight in the 1980's.

The details of slaughter, famine, and political mismanagement become horrifyingly realistic.

Rohanda is left behind; yet, startlingly, utopia remains. It remains, not as the focus of the story, but, in a remarkable reversal of traditional utopian fiction, as the perspective provided by narrative voices. The Canopean perspective, seen most consistently in Johor, conditions the reader's perception of history. Further, the Canopean perspective, as presented in archival reports, transcends linear Shikastan time, collapsing past, present, and future. The effect on the reader is as if each of us approached our planet through limitless Saturnalian rings, each ring providing a new temporal or spatial lens on its Shikastan center. As we hear the voices of Canopean chroniclers, Johor's reports and others, we must see ourselves and our society in new ways, must subtly and continuously revise. In the process, we come to understand something about the nature of utopia itself. It is not, finally, any one place or time, but the capacity to see afresh—an enlarged, even transformed vision.

Since seeing in a new way is crucial to Lessing's utopian vision, the artist can be expected to be important as well. In *Shikasta* art often takes the form of "song" and songs are a crucial link between past and future utopian visions. But although "song" is important in the entire Canopus series, the second novel, *The Marriages between Zones Three, Four, and Five,* can deal more fully with the issue of art, because its narrator is, in fact, a "singer."

Ostensibly the focus of the narrator, Lusik, is the story of Al.Ith, the beautiful queen of Zone Three—a delightful feminist utopia. But the telling gradually becomes as important as the facts of Al.Ith's adventure. Those facts can, indeed, be summarized quite simply. At the beginning of the book, Al.Ith is ordered, the narrator tells us, to marry Ben Ata, king of the militaristic and despised lower world, Zone Four. These orders come from "the Providers" who remain mysterious superior figures whose authority is never questioned. In the course of the novel, Al.Ith learns to love Ben Ata and teaches him much about the nature of women and, indeed, responsibility for a kingdom. She herself, however, suffers from this love by experiencing a possessiveness and jealousy she had never known in Zone Three, and, at last, by losing the husband and son she has come to care about so terribly. Her ultimate fate seems to be alienation from both worlds, with only the suggestion of some mysterious ascent to Zone Two to compensate for her very real pain. But the novel is paradoxical in more ways than one: the once-happy Al.Ith must lose her autonomy in order to grow; the peaceful and pleasure-loving utopian world of Zone Three must experience discontent and preparation for war in order to stay vital, and, finally, the reader's attachment to Al.Ith and Ben Ata must yield to the realization that it is the song itself, the tale of Al.Ith that matters most.

Lusik sings of Al.Ith's wedding in terms that recall other somber marriages. He paints scenes of mourning—the Queen in dark blue, her hair loose about her, grieving. The funereal quality of this wedding reminds us of Persephone's marriage to the god of the underworld. Echoes of that myth, the descent of Inanna and, indeed, Christ's descent to earth are evoked by the symbolic rendering of Al.Ith's tale. Al.Ith does die to her former self, losing her gaiety and ease. Yet, as her identity is painfully transformed and she becomes an exile in all the known zones, she frees her people to grow. Like Inanna, Persephone, and Christ before her, Al.Ith's death and resurrection (descent and return) insure the fertility of the land, the salvation of her people.

The insights granted by this tale of descent and rebirth are finally more complex than most interpretations of the Christian myth, however. Christ descends, suffers, dies, is reborn to save mankind—but not, presumably, heaven itself. Lusik's tale of Al.Ith's similar descent and suffering redeems not only the clearly inferior and perverted lower worlds from their corruption but also redeems utopia from its perfection. For the disease at the heart of the lovely Zone Three, as the singer comes to see and share with his audience, is its static self-satisfaction. That world had lost its knowledge of lower zones and so forgotten Zone Two as well. The people of Zone Three no longer suffered or aspired. But, when Al.Ith returns from Zone Four, she redeems the insularity of utopia. She realizes again "the knowledge, which was the base of all knowledges, that everything was entwined and mixed and mingled, all was one."[7] And by the end of the novel Lusik's tale has made his audience realize that a vital utopia requires change and interaction with alien forces; otherwise, it becomes a barren and useless idea.

In the course of telling the tale, the artist himself is changed, for he experiences the transforming power of imagination. He becomes his own story. Lusik meditates on this phenomenon in the following way:

> I am not only a Chronicler of Zone Three, or only partially, for I also share in Al.Ith's condition of being ruler insofar as I can write of her, describe her . . . and so I record here only that when Al.Ith sat and dreamed of Zone Two, she was Zone Two, even if in the most faint and distant way, and her imaginings of its immaculate fire-born beings brought her near them, and when she thought of us, the Chroniclers, she was us . . . and so now, in this footnote to Al.Ith's thoughts on that occasion, I simply make my cause and rest it: Al.Ith am I, and I Al.Ith, and everyone of us anywhere is what we think and imagine (*Marriages*, p. 199).

The recognition that teller and tale are one and that art can even, in some sense, create life must result in a keen awareness of the dangers as well as the positive potential of imagination. For just as art can devise the marvelous images of a better world, so too can it summon the nightmares of human experience and make them real. This is the fact that so disturbed Plato. But, whereas that first utopian would banish the artist if he dared sing of anything but the rational, good, and beautiful, Lessing's singer comes to celebrate the total power of art. Lusik says:

> We Chroniclers do well to be afraid when we approach those parts of our histories (our natures) that deal with evil, the depraved, the benighted. Describing, we become. We even—and I've seen it and have shuddered—summon. The most innocent of poets can write of ugliness and forces he has done no more than speculate about— and bring them into his life . . . Yet there is a mystery here and it is not one that I understand: without this sting of otherness, of— even —the vicious, without the terrible energies of the underside of health, sanity, sense, then nothing works or can work . . . the very high must be matched by the very low . . . and even fed by it (p. 198).

Thus Lessing's artist finally affirms a dialectic, the dramatic flux of life, the necessary descent and consequent ascent symbolized by Al.Ith's marriage and ultimate movement into Zone Two. But the reader comes to see that only art can envision and give significance to such dislocating transformations. Without the song, there is only suffering. Mutability in human experience is inescapable, but art can enable us to hear hard truth and turn it to good. Certainly, in Lessing's dynamic utopian vision, it is art that facilitates and gives meaning to change.

Lessing's third novel, *The Sirian Experiments,* centers on the theme of change in the education of the narrator, a Sirian official, Ambien II. Although the Sirian galaxy is superior to Puttiora and Shikasta, the officials of Sirius are also bound by rigid thinking as Ambien slowly and painfully comes to understand. Words are shown to be inadequate for either individual or social change; instead one learns through harsh experience and through the power of art. Towards the end of the novel, Ambien has such an aesthetic experience, one that symbolizes the central theme of necessary transformation. The artistic medium is visual—images of Shikastan society and of a Canopean spaceship. It is, in fact, the Canopean "Crystal" that directs Ambien's attention to the revelatory image of Shikasta:

> I hovered there near the monitoring Crystal and saw again how the edges of the continent were squeezed up into its mountain folds, how the deserts lay and spread, how the great forests of other times had gone, and realized that I was seeing something extraordinary. A grid had been stamped over the whole continent. It was a mesh of absolutely regular rectangles. I was seeing a map or chart of a certain way of thinking . . . this was a way of thought, a set of mind, made visible. It was the mind of the Northwest fringes, the mind of the white conquerors. Over the variety and change and differentiation of the continent, over the flows and movement and changes of the earth—as vigorous as that of the air above, though in a different dimension of time—was this stamp of rigidity . . . I had not noticed it before . . . I had seen how the growth and unfolding of the material of the continent displayed itself in surface contours, and in the disposition of its waters and vegetation. But now between me and the language of growth and change was this imperious stamp. This pattern. This grid.[8]

What Ambien learns here is what every reader of feminist utopias must come to understand. There can be no better society without allowance for growth, variety, and change. Indeed, if there is any larger whole to which all life belongs, as most women's worlds insist there is, then its only law seems to be—as Johor first told us—the law of inevitable change.

Ambien's vision of a gridlike, rigidified Shikasta contrasts with another image—the flexible and beautiful symbol of Canopean society, the spaceship or "crystal." Ambien studies this image as well:

> The Canopean Crystal floated down and lay in the air in front of me. It was in its most usual shape, a cone . . . it moved off, slowly, and I followed. I did not understand this lesson, which I assumed it was, but only watched . . . the Crystal became a tetrahedron . . . then a globe . . . it elongated and became like a drop of liquid at the moment when it falls from a point . . . this exquisite drop of crystalline glitter was thus because of the pressures of the atmosphere, it was adjusting itself to the flow of the jet stream . . . my guide was changing again, was showing how it had to change, and flow, and adapt, for all the movements or alterations of the atmosphere we were submerged in like liquid molded this Globe, or Rod, or Streak, or Fringe . . . how many shapes it assumed, this enchanting guide of mind, as we followed the flowing streams of the upper air of Rohanda . . . how it evolved and adapted and shone! (*The Sirian Experiments,* p. 276.)

Doris Lessing's marvelously varied new series of novels, like the Canopean Crystal, dazzles us with changing images of multiple worlds. The power of her art allows us to glimpse many forms of utopia; her insight into human nature and recognition of the inevitability of change guarantee that we will remain in none.

NOTES

1. I have discussed the phenomenon of this new and positive utopian fiction by women in a recent article, "Women's Worlds: New Directions in Utopian Fiction," in *Alternative Futures: The Journal of Utopian Studies,* 4 (Spring/Summer, 1981),

pp. 47–60. In that article I referred to more than a dozen novels written in the last ten years. Since then, my own reading and the research of colleagues in the field, most notably that of Carol Kessler and Lyman Tower Sargent, have identified at least fifteen more recent feminist utopias. Therefore, approximately thirty utopian novels by women, written in the 1970's and 80's, have been currently identified. Among this stylistically varied yet highly comparable group of novels, I think the following books are especially important: E. M. Broner, *A Weave of Women* (New York: Holt, Rinehart and Winston, 1978); Dorothy Bryant, *The Kin of Ata Are Waiting for You* (New York: Random House, 1976); S. M. Charnas, *Motherlines* (New York: Berkley Publications, 1979); S. M. Gearhart, *The Wanderground* (Watertown, Mass.: 1979); Cecelia Holland, *Homeground* (New York: Knopf, 1981); Ursula LeGuin, *The Dispossessed* (New York: Harper & Row, 1974); Doris Lessing, *Canopus in Argos: Archives* (New York: Knopf, 1979–1982); Marge Piercy, *Woman on the Edge of Time* (New York: Knopf, 1976); Joanna Russ, *The Female Man* (New York: Gregg Publishing, 1975); Monique Wittig, *Les Guérillères* (New York: 1971).

2. Frank E. Manuel and Fritzie P. Manuel, *Utopian Thought in the Western World* (Cambridge, Mass.: Harvard University Press, 1979), p. 811.

3. Our traditional notions about the best social order, whether in the theories of Plato, More, Marx, Skinner, or in the actual practice of democracy, capitalism, socialism, or communism have been largely shaped by men. It is especially interesting, then, that these utopian novels by women offer remarkably different values and political and cultural systems.

4. The absence of technologies of warfare seems to have misled some readers into dismissing feminist utopias as "primitive" and a step backward from twentieth-century advances (see Krishan Kumar, "Primitivism in Feminist Utopias," *Alternative Futures: The Journal of Utopian Studies,* 4 (Spring/Summer, 1981), pp. 61–66. Kumar's claim ignores the extensive technologies of reproduction, communication, and aesthetic experiences that form the focus of feminist science in these books.

5. When men have speculated about the nature of the good society, they have rarely shown much affection for the arts. Plato certainly considers artists in his classical utopian work, *The Republic,* but approves only of artists who are subservient to the

philosophic precepts of the state. Since art, in Plato's view, appeals simply to the emotions, it is far removed from truth. Thus the rational guardians must control artists so that they imitate only those actions which the state deems beautiful and good. Of course, Plato recognizes the power of art and pays more attention to it than most subsequent utopists. In the sixteenth century Thomas More's utopian citizens might enjoy some music and incense while dining, but no painting, writing poetry, singing, sculpting. And most "modern" utopists, despite the Romantic revolution which made individualism and self-expression more respectable, have followed in More's footsteps. In the hundreds of utopian novels of the nineteenth century, almost no serious attention is given to the major forms of art. Although William Morris's *News from Nowhere* is a significant exception, Edward Bellamy's *Looking Backward* is far more typical. And in that enormously influential utopia, technology fascinates the characters far more than the aesthetic. Although Julian West listens to symphonies, he does so via the new technological wonder—the radio—which, Dr. Leete assures him, provides much more pleasure than live concerts. Interestingly then, it is only in recent feminist utopian fiction that serious attention to art and a celebration of its function have become part of the genre.

6. Doris Lessing, *Re: Colonised Planet 5, Shikasta* (New York: Alfred A. Knopf, Inc., 1979), p. 3. All subsequent references to the novel will be cited from this edition and documented in the text.

7. Doris Lessing, *The Marriages between Zones Three, Four, and Five* (New York: Alfred A. Knopf, Inc., 1980), p. 77. All subsequent references to the novel will be cited from this edition and documented in the text.

8. Doris Lessing, *The Sirian Experiments* (New York: Alfred A. Knopf, Inc., 1981), p. 277–8. All subsequent references to the novel will be cited from this edition and documented in the text.

Therrillium

MISCHA ADAMS

SUMMARY

"THERRILLIUM" is excerpted from a science fiction novel-in-progress entitled *A Season of Song*. The action takes place on an earthlike world and concerns relations between three distinct cultural groups: the Galhejans, a clan-based culture which practices equality between the sexes; the Kalmythicans, a patriarchal feudal society; and the Hycekinthians, an island culture which is egalitarian like Galheja, but which is ruled by two moieties, the Iron and Grain Priesthoods.

The novel's two protagonists, Evanthea and Coren, have been chosen, along with several other Kalmythican artists to join the first delegation of mainlanders to visit the island of Hycekinth in over one hundred years. Evanthea is actually from Galheja, but is married to a Kalmythican nobleman. In her husband's absence, she has abandoned her post as Baroness of Jaredskeep in order to travel with Coren, a young musician whom she has pursuaded to be her partner in a singing act. Fearful about the risk involved, yet intrigued by their potential to perform great music, Coren has agreed to keep Evanthea's true identity a secret.

During their stay on the island, the singers are drawn into a

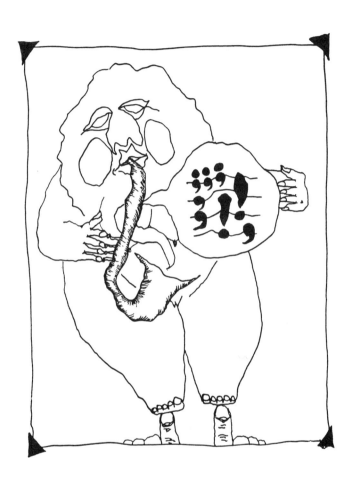

power struggle between the Iron and Grain Priesthoods. In this sequence they witness a performance by Aliki of the Grain moiety, who plays an arcane solar-powered instrument called the therrillium.

As the story progresses, Aliki and Evanthea become lovers, Coren is falsely accused of the murder of a rival Kalmythican artist, and Hycekinth explodes in civil strife. The two singers return to the mainland, where Evanthea must resolve the conflict between her yearning for music and her marriage. She is aided in this task by a famous Galhejan witch.

THERRILLIUM

The brilliant island sun sent its rays slanting into the dome, carpeting the stage with an oblong mosaic of dark colors. A Grain Priest returned to announce the Hycekinthian portion of the concert—the Therrillium. At the very back of the stage stood two massive panels of bronze. A whisper of surprise went up from the front of the hall when these began to rise silently on oiled tumblers to reveal a dark recess covered by a metallic bead-screen. A double file of the military guards emerged from within this shimmering cave carrying on their shoulders two lengths of heavy golden cable.

The detachments of guards always included both sexes, and even for tasks which required physical strength, they did not deploy themselves any differently from military regiments on the mainland. This puzzled Coren greatly, for he reasoned that if they were going to use women guards, they should position them so that they were shored up and covered in the ranks by able-bodied males. Watching them march out with the cables and, at the sound of a gong, begin to strain and haul on the ropes, however, Coren had to concede grudgingly that the women guards were quite as capable as their male counterparts, although they were slightly less muscular.

The corners of a bronze-embossed pedestal emerged through the hanging beadwork. The guards pulled steadily and the Therrillium glided through the curtain, cutting the

beaded strands into decorative slices in its passing. Its movement across the stage made no sound. This was all the stranger
for its heaviness, indicated by the sweating soldiers.

Slowly, ponderously, the instrument crept across the stage
until it came to rest in the exact center of the platform, directly
under the apex of the colored glass dome. The Therrillium was
unlike anything the Kalmythicans had ever seen before. Color-
less, of indeterminate metal, it swept up the bands of jewel-col-
ored light as it passed beneath them. The whole structure stood
nearly two meters high. It was composed of interlocking and
nested dish-shaped concavities of assorted sizes, some of which
were no bigger than wine cups, others the size of barrels and
basins. Its shape was oddly human-like. A central trunk grew up
from the base, nipping in sharply at the waist where two arm-
like appendages projected from the sides.

The "head" was one large shallow dish containing a series of
concentric rings. The edifice contrasted sharply with the base
upon which it stood, which was ornamented with carved Hycekinthian hardwood. Brightly faceted stones were set into the
front-facing bronze inlaid panel in an obscure pattern which
might have represented a star-map of some unfamiliar noctur-
nal sky, picked out in flashing jewels.

The assembled outlanders had only a moment in which to
view the instrument before the Priest Aliki stepped out onto the
stage through the beaded curtain. She was dressed in white and
green as usual, but for this occasion her chiton was sheer and
brief, extending only to mid-thigh. She walked lightly forward
to the edge of the platform and bowed to the assembled throng,
hands clasped to her forehead and then her heart in greeting.
Behind her, the Therrillium loomed, bathed in tiers of colored
light. She removed first one, then another of the golden ropes
from its base and tossed the ends to the waiting guards as if she
were casting off the moorings of a ship. Freed from its bonds,
the great machine seemed to draw breath from the light. Some
of the mainlanders fancied they saw it begin to vibrate.

Aliki retreated to the farthest corner of the stage, far to the
left of the instrument. There she lay down full-length upon the
polished floor and remained completely motionless. Evanthea

recognized a trance induction in progress and shifted forward on her pillow to get a better view. Coren nudged her questioningly, but she ignored him with an impatient shake of her head.

The mute mimes felt it first. Tears started at the corners of their eyes and they searched one another's faces anxiously, using only the language of glances, since their hands had no time to form words. Evanthea felt it next. A vast wave of melancholy seemed to rise up out of the very floor to engulf her. Evanthea shut her eyes, forcing down her fear and allowing the violent feelings to wash over her. Somber colors swirled across the screen of her inner vision. Sequential veils of mauve and violet merged into deepest blue. She put out her hands blindly to steady herself and felt Coren's arm, warm through his shirt.

He turned to look at her in confusion, then quickly returned his attention to the stage where the Priest was still lying face-down, except now her limbs were slightly canted. Her arms and legs were moving so slowly that Coren had to watch closely to see any movement at all. All at once Coren became aware of a sound. He had been hearing it for several moments before he realized it. Gradually it had sorted itself out from the overlay of in- and outdrawn breaths and minute shiftings of position going on all around him. His eardrums throbbed and itched, straining to make sense of a sound so immense, so deep that no previous memory could help him to identify it. It was like the ocean during a violent storm. Or perhaps like the voices of huge seabeasts calling to one another across vast expanses of open water. It made Coren shiver and draw into himself.

"What sort of music is this?" he asked himself angrily, stunned by the intensity of the sound and put off by his own inability to comprehend it. He looked about to see what others were making of it. Evanthea was still in her inexplicable trance with tears running down her cheeks. The mute mimes were linked together, arm-in-arm with their Deaf/Blind leader enfolded into their midst. She seemed to be able to absorb the performance directly through her sisters' skin. Other mainlanders were as swept up in the experience as Evanthea. One small girl to Coren's left was running her fingers softly along the edges of her cushion, pulled into the texture of the fabric by whatever odd spell the Therrillium had woven.

A deep thrumming went on and on as the Priest snaked her way around the foot of the instrument, never rising more than a scant distance from the gleaming floor-slabs. She rolled lazily hip-over-hip and the music lapped itself after her—as a groan, a sigh, a voiced earth tremor drawn by her movements up out of some subterranean cavern.

Her right hand went up and with it a silvery-pure note rose out of the rumble to float above the molten chorus. The hand dipped down and darted, became a bird, an airborne fish, a billowing sea-plant. The music grew from her motion as ripples from a thrown stone, diving back into the audible deep and lancing up again in harmonics of splayed fingers . . . and held . . . and vibrated . . . and ululated, trilled, shrilled, screamed, screeched. Coren clapped his hands over his ears in agony, feeling as if an army of insects was drilling its way into his skull.

Evanthea, eyes squeezed shut and trancing, witnessed the birth of the Hycekinthian Deity in a blaze of brilliance. She felt the earth's vulva pulsating with birth pangs. Drunk on the vision, she used her fingers to pry open her eyes. Opening them on cross-blurred points of light eaten by and reflected from the Therrillium's flat scoops, she searched the stage for the dancer. The Priest danced using only her hands as far as the elbows. Her thighs, knees, lower legs, ankles and toes held the earth's manifold voices steady in rumbling counterpoint, surging up from beneath the more fragile interplay of hands and fingers. She swung her head and instantly a cloud-cover of middle-range tones decorated the spaces between earth and dancing fingertips. Evanthea blinked her eyes rapidly, trying somehow to open her eyes widely enough to take in all of it at once.

Aliki danced in a crouch now, knees bent, hair swinging, elbows tunneling into the sound. As she moved nearer the machine the volume intensified. She wove an intermittent pattern, causing the sound to swell and fall away in cascades. Each time she straightened her posture the entire composition rose in pitch. Every movement of her body brought forth a stunning swath of sound. Often she would reach a hand into the air and pluck down a shrill tone or slowly push another up beyond the range of human hearing. Once she stood elevated on the tips of her toes, her whole powerful body as still as if she had been turned to stone. The sound very nearly ceased. There was only a faint polytonal hum in response to the vibrations of her tensed muscles. Her arms were stretched skyward. She poised herself before the Therrillium, interposing her body between it and the audience. Her face was rigid in trance, eyes rolled back in her head, lids half-lowered over eerie slivers of white. Holding the unlikely posture, she began to move her fingers in dozens of intricate patterns.

Coren could not hear the ultra-sonic cadenzas she was playing, but he heard the rising scales she had played just before. He had marked the position in the air at which the sounds had disappeared. He knew there was music being made just outside his listening range. Again it frustrated him. "Dog-music!" he snorted, "Why don't they just bring all the animals inside since half the fun is meant for them?"

Aliki continued to weave a silent cacophony of needle-sharp tones in the air under the dancing sun colors. She lowered her heels to the stage and flexed her toes carefully in a complementary pattern. No one heard it. But Evanthea lurched backward as if she had been struck in the gut. Clutching her arms protectively around her mid-section, she began to rock herself back and forth on her pillow. All around them in the mainlanders' section, people were reacting in similar ways.

Coren raged, overstimulated by sounds he could not hear. He felt as if some strange and malevolent demon had thrust its way into the space usually occupied by his beloved muse and had then ordered him roughly from the room. He covered his ears again to shut it out, remembering ironically that he could not even hear it. Desperate for distraction, Coren swept the hall with his eyes. There was the little cook who had flirted so outrageously with him yesterday, who had given him spiced fish and wine and had kept offering more and more treats until Coren, realizing what was actually being offered, had suddenly remembered an urgent errand in another part of the palace. The cook was slouched dreamily on his bench drinking air into his lungs, breathing it in as if he could smell and taste every sound. The Therrillium had turned the hall into a savory cook-pot for the delight of his senses.

Turning back to Evanthea, Coren saw that she was just as hopelessly captured as any local. In deep trance, she sat hunched over with her knees drawn up underneath her chin, arms wrapped around herself, an uncommunicative lump. Her eyes were riveted on the stage.

Aliki's body planed and twirled, her elbows and punching fists were holographic batons striking antiphonal music from the air as she went cannoning through the semicircular dancing space. Her composition came from the depths of her trance. She knew the dancing space only as an immense void into which she introduced substance—volume—sound. She filled up the blankness around her with audible objects. Fingers intertwined, she spun her locked arms like a hammer, swerving, veering inward to within inches of the very instrument. Had the sun been at zenith, the power output would have deafened all of the hearing audience. But the edge of the colored elipse had crept nearly to the base of the Therrillium and the instrument was muted by sun-hunger.

She was aware of the sound streaming by her, of its refractions falling away from the angles of her body. Now she was no longer merely a body, but an embodied distinction . . . moving, living connection between movement and sound, between the void and its waxing and waning volume. She *was* the vibrating river of music flowing out of the Therrillium into the Grand Hall, its resonating chamber. Massive crashes and silvery melodies were perceived by her as carved and embellished blocks of space. The whole spontaneous structure of the dance enveloped her. She felt the sound of her upper torso as she twisted and wrenched from side to side, skimming the edges of the darkening patterns of color.

When the voice of the Therrillium had dwindled to a fraction of its initial loudness, the dancer felt the cool, firm bank of silence awaiting her when sound and space should cease their congress. She flirted with the impending silence, swinging more and more slowly along the front edge of the stage, working entirely inside the audible range of the human audience. She tasted infinitesimal sips of silence. These were alternately soft and sharp as she marked them by flowing turns and abrupt jabs of pointed toes. Then she stood still and embraced the silence as a lover. Her tall body was positioned directly in front of the instrument, facing the audience as she had been earlier in the performance. In a convulsive movement so swift that many mainlanders thought she had vanished, the Priest dropped straight backward into a blinding back-bend and lay prone in that position. She lay at the foot of the machine as if dead.

Hycekinthians surged to their feet and roared their adoration, clapping their hands and slapping their feet upon the stone floor of the hall. Two members of the Grain Priesthood came up on the platform and lifted and carried the unconscious dancer from the stage. Soldiers re-attached the ropes and bore them back inside the beaded recess. Silently the giant instrument moved away from its nourishing pool of jewel-light, giving up luster as it re-entered the cavern. The great bronze doors came down.

Outcome of the Matter: The Sun

Androgynous child whose hair curls into flowers,
naked you ride a horse without saddle or bridle
easy between your thighs from the walled garden outward.
Coarse sunflowers of desire whose seeds birds crack open
nod upon your journey, child of the morning whose sun
can only be born from us who strain bleeding to give birth.
Grow into your horse, let there be
no more riders or ridden.

Child, where are you heading with arms spread wide
as a shore, have I been there, have I seen that land shining
like sun spangles on clean water rippling?
I do not know your dances, I cannot translate your tongue
to words I use, your pleasures are strange to me
as the rites of bees: yet you are the yellow flower
of a melon vine growing out of my belly
though it climbs up where I cannot see in the strong light.

My eyes cannot decipher those shapes of children or
    burning clouds
who are not what we are: they go barefoot like savages,
they have computers as household pets; they are seven
    sexes
and only one sex; they do not own or lease or control.

They are of one body and of tribes. They are private as
    shamans
learning each her own magic at the teats of stones and trees.
They are all technicians and peasants.
They do not forget their birthright of self
or their name of animal pride
dancing in and out through the gates of the body standing
    wide.

A bear lumbering, I waddle into the fields of their work
    games.
We are stunted slaves mumbling over the tales
of dragons our masters tell us, but we will be free.
Our children will be free of us uncomprehending
as we of those shufflers in caves who scraped for fire
and banded together at last to hunt the saber-toothed tiger,
the giant cave bear, predators
that had penned them up cowering so long.

The sun is rising, feel it: the air smells fresh.
I cannot look in the sun's face, its brightness blinds me,
but from my own shadow becoming distinct
I know that now at last
it is beginning to grow light.

A Women's Museum of Art

ANN SUTHERLAND HARRIS

M Y particular feminist utopian fantasy is a women's museum of art. No such museum exists. All existing art museums celebrate and preserve male culture, which is presented as the universal culture, in which women are sometimes admitted to have had a small share. What would an art museum be like that took women's contribution as its reason for being? Is it possible to imagine a great art museum devoted solely to women's achievements in the visual arts?

In order to construct the fantasy, you must first define art. Are only paintings, drawings, prints, photographs, and architecture art? Is lace art? Are quilts art? If this museum confined itself to the most prestigious forms of "high art," it would limit itself to art forms in which women have participated to a significant degree only relatively recently. Women, however, have a long history of contributing to and even controlling textile arts such as silk-weaving, embroidery, carpet manufacture and the creation of tapestries and lace, not to mention quilts. A museum of women's art would have to give more prominence to textiles than most non-specialist museums do, even if, in most cases, we will never know the names of the women who created the work. At present, the finest collections of such material tend to be in museums of industry and craft, or they are a minor department of a large, comprehensive museum like the Metropolitan Museum of New York. In neither place are the creations displayed with didactic material that makes the visitor aware of the crucial role played by women in many different cultures in the production of such work. The same argument would apply to all the other so-called minor or decorative arts. For example, the great potter of New Mexico, Maria Martinez, should be well represented but not as an isolated phenomenon, for there have been many other women in the last two centuries, and much earlier, as well, who have made magnificent objects using clay and glaze. In brief, a great women's museum of art is the last place where any snobbery about the relative prestige of different categories of art should be allowed to exist.

This lack of prejudice would be revealed in other ways. I would want this museum to collect not only masterpieces by Mary Cassatt and Berthe Morisot but also masterpieces by women dress and jewelry designers such as Coco Chanel, Nina Ricci, Elsa Peretti and Mary McFadden, not to mention excursions into these areas by painters like Natalia Goncharova and Sonia Delauney. Then I would like to see these clothes displayed near period furniture designed by women like Eileen Grey and Florence Knoll in the same gallery as paintings and sculpture of the same period. I have come to dislike those sanitized museum displays that separate paintings from sculpture, glass from silver, furniture from painting and sculpture (except for minor works used primarily as decoration) because they so totally remove the work of art from any meaningful period context and relate more to the territorial battles of specialist curators than to the true historical significance of the objects themselves. Thus, I wish this fantasy museum to make imaginative use of a mixture of objects of different types but with enough stylistic and formal parallels for their juxtaposition to be aesthetically rewarding as well as intellectually significant.

As I considered the fact that women's contribution to the visual arts has grown exponentially in the last two centuries (and this is true, I think, even if you were, by some great good fortune, able to acquire superb examples of medieval embroideries, eighteenth-century lace and nineteenth-century quilts), I began to imagine a building to house these works that could symbolize women's increasing visibility in the art world as they moved into all areas of the visual arts while continuing to work strongly in the less regarded craft arts. The simplest shape that could represent this growth and the fact that it will certainly continue forever would be a pyramid with the entrance to the museum at one point. As you moved into the museum, the number of galleries would increase, their width and height would grow and the museum would literally expand with women's burgeoning contributions. The end wall would have as much glass as possible, allowing the visitor to look out to a magnificent park (for women have long been great gardeners) where major pieces of sculpture by women would be stunningly located. The visitor would thus be tempted back into the real world but to a place where the artistic genius of women would still be strongly felt.

Museum design is an exceptionally difficult challenge that is rarely met with unqualified success. The main problem is that such a commission invites architects to "make a statement" but such statements must be confined to the exterior. Inside the architect must step back and play the role of the tactful accompanist who lets the soloist shine. Marcel Breuer's design for the new Whitney Museum on Madison Avenue functions well in this respect. Frank Lloyd Wright's Guggenheim Museum on Fifth Avenue is, on the other hand, perhaps the supreme example of the architect's ego going berserk at the expense of the true function of the building. The main circular declining ramp gallery must be one of the most fascinating interior spaces designed in the twentieth century but it cleverly sabotages every work of art placed in it. The uneven floor is psychologically unsettling, reminding the visitor constantly to keep moving, while the fascinating vista above the barrier over the frightening void to the distant galleries overpowers the attractions of the works hung in each alcove. They in turn never seem firmly at home because of the absence of calming flat surfaces, horizontals, and right angles. The East Wing of the National Gallery in Washington is also a stunning piece of architecture with an exterior of almost magic beauty created by the changing light on its angled surfaces of polished pale pink marble but the interior, like the Guggenheim, honors the architect (I. M. Pei) more than the works of art it contains. The main focus is the vast interior atrium, which houses a few cliché examples of twentieth-century art (a Calder mobile, a Miró tapestry) while confining most of the works to windowless cubbyholes along the edges. The women's museum will not make such mistakes. Its architect will understand the harmonizing role that the building must play between its setting and the exterior and between its interior and the works shown there. The problems—conceptual and practical—are formidable but if a woman architect solved them successfully, she would have made a major contribution to our visual culture. The fact that no major (or any?) museum building has yet to be designed by a woman shows how far we have to go. The commission should be awarded after an international competition has been held to find the best design and, in the process, to publicize the existence of many fine women architects who now rarely receive such opportunities.

The museum of art by women would be innovative inside and out. It goes without saying that its shop would be stocked with a fabulous inventory of books, posters, postcards, reproductions, and slides of art by women from the museum's own collections as well as from elsewhere. The restaurant would offer the best of women's cooking at all price levels, restrooms would be plentiful, almost every work would have a chair in front of it and the day-care center would encourage children to make art while their parents visited the museum. The auditorium would have an exciting program of lectures about women's art as well as concerts of women's music, and discussions of all art forms in which women have been active (poetry readings, theatrical performances, happenings . . .). The library would have a fine collection of all the standard works but would concentrate on publications about women's art and collect archival material on women artists (documents, oral interviews, videotapes, and so on). In brief, this would be not simply the ideal women's museum, but a model of what every art museum should be like.

In the galleries, everything would be designed to make the visitor feel comfortable and at ease and so tempted to linger and spend time with a few works instead of rushing round all the galleries and leaving with only superficial memories. Works would be hung lower than usual so that a seated visitor could study them while listening to tapes of recorded information by curators or even, when possible, the artist herself talking about the work, how she made it and what inspired this particular imagery. For all contemporary artists represented, there should be a permanent display of several pieces of different periods, scales and media, mini-retrospectives that would give the visitor a rounded view of their achievements. The constant mixture of categories would be visually refreshing and the constant availability of comfortable seating would keep the visitor from tiring as quickly as they do in normal museums.

It is impossible for us to imagine the impact that such an institution would have on us and on everyone's perception of women's creative ability in the arts. Many people who saw the exhibition, *Women Artists, 1550–1950,* told me how moved they were by it and by the simple discovery that women had made so much wonderful art and, moreover, that what was in the show was clearly only the tip of the iceberg. This fantasy museum should become a reality. Women deserve at least one great museum of their own.

Future Visions: Today's Politics: Feminist Utopias in Review

SALLY MILLER GEARHART

THE last decade's abundance of utopian fiction by women offers some varied feminist futures. Such writing, of course, also reflects the present. I'd like to propose here a working definition of "feminist utopian novel" and then focus on eleven recent works[1] in an attempt to identify and analyze in them five current feminist concerns: 1. collective process, 2. lesbian separatism, 3. the source of violence, 4. technology and nature, and 5. racism.

A feminist utopian novel is one which *a.* contrasts the present with an envisioned idealized society (separated from the present by time or space), *b.* offers a comprehensive critique of present values/conditions, *c.* sees men or male institutions as a major cause of present social ills, and *d.* presents women not only as at least the equals of men but also as the sole arbiters of their reproductive functions.

The following eleven novels fall into the confines of the working definition:

Marion Zimmer Bradley, *The Ruins of Isis* (New York: Pocket Books, 1978) (the planet, Isis)[2]

Marion Zimmer Bradley, *The Shattered Chain* (New York: Daw Books, 1976) (the society of the Free Amazons on Darkover)

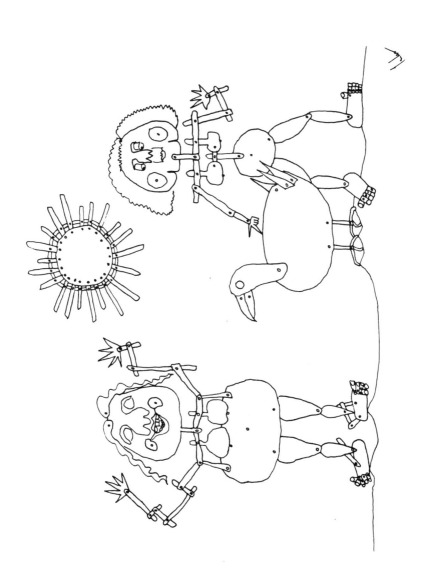

Dorothy Bryant, *The Kin of Ata Are Waiting for You* (New York: Random House, 1976) (the island of the Kin)

Suzy McKee Charnas, *Motherlines* (New York: Berkley Publications, 1979) (the Riding Women of a future earth)

Sally Miller Gearhart, *The Wanderground: Stories of the Hill Women* (Watertown, Mass.: Persephone Press, 1979) (the Hill Women of a future earth)

Charlotte Perkins Gilman, *Herland: A Lost Feminist Utopian Novel* (New York: Pantheon Books, 1979; originally published 1915) (the Herlanders of earth)

Marge Piercy, *Woman on the Edge of Time* (New York: Alfred Knopf, 1976) (Mattapoisett, of a possible future earth)

Joanna Russ, *The Female Man* (Boston: Gregg Publishing, 1975) (Whileaway, a future/parallel earth)

Rochelle Singer, *The Demeter Flower* (New York: St. Martin's Press, 1980) (Demeter, of a future earth)

Monique Wittig, *Les Guérillères* (New York: Avon Books, 1973) (the Guerillas, the fighting women, of a future earth)

Donna Young, *Retreat: As It Was!* (Tallahassee, Fla.: Naiad Press, 1978) (the planet, Retreat)

Among these, the works of Bryant and Piercy might not seem to fit criteria *c* and *d*. The doubt, however, is superficial. Gender equality is a given on both the island of Ata and in Mattapoisett. Reproduction among the Kin depends upon a female's dreams of the man she is "to be woman to"; Mattapoisett's citizens decide in groups of threes to be mothers of "test-tube" children and, since men have taken on the nurturing capacity of women, *i.e.*, developed breasts, that decision is made by females. In fact, though Piercy does not indict her hero's enemies as "men" or "male institutions," Connie's envisioning of a possible future obscures the lines of gender demarcation, so men are acceptable there precisely because they have left behind their "masculine" characteristics. It is significant that women in Piercy's future have also left behind their "feminine" traits in that they do all kinds of work, so that the society emerges as androgynous. Similarly, Bryant's humanism never permits her to name male persons or even male institutions as the enemy.

Yet her whole dream culture is established along the lines of right-brained, intuitive, nonlinear values as opposed to the left-brained, rational, linear values represented by her protagonist. The characteristics of the Kin are associated with the female in western culture, and the author uses the obstinate male hero to demonstrate our present destructive masculinist values, and the change that is possible and necessary from his values to those of the Kin. The remaining novels fit the criteria with far less question than do Piercy's and Bryant's.

COLLECTIVE PROCESS

In rebellion against authoritarian modes, feminists have been concerned to work together in new patterns that will both preserve autonomy and move the group toward collective action. Several feminist utopias reflect a concern for structure and process and for wide participation in decision-making. They presume a commitment to working together in non-hierarchical ways.

One of the strifes in *Demeter Flower* concerns the power of the founders and whether or not they should have the right to meet without the rest of the council. Singer creates women and children committed to frequent meetings, impassioned debate, and the full-community involvement in decisions. The Hill Women of the Wanderground remain all night in "gather-stretch" (channel-linked psychic presence of all the women) struggling for a "clear wish." Young's citizens of Retreat make their most important decisions in circles, holding one another. They rotate tasks—as do the Hill Women and the women of Demeter—and clearly affirm their freedom to act as individuals despite any majority vote. In these three societies, feminists most easily recognize struggles over elitism, party lines, leadership, and criticism. Piercy's future world is a model of a participatory democracy built upon many small units, each of which functions with enthusiastic citizen involvement. Like Singer, Gearhart and Young, Piercy treats us to a community meeting where we see the process at work.

But the remaining novels pay far less attention to questions of process and governance than do these four. The defense of Russ's Whileaway depends upon the fact that there is no real "government," no real centralization of power; and Russ, like most of the other authors, gives few clues to the way the society is run. It's sobering to note that Bradley's reversal of sex roles on Isis has resulted in anything but collective action. There a matriarchate emulates in every important respect the more familiar patriarchal structures. So all is not a picture of collective bliss, even though three or four of the books give ample attention to the issues surrounding collective action and offer some creative ideas on the matter.

But the notion of collectivity is found in the authors' choices of protagonists. In the case of at least five of these novels, the title names a protagonist who is a "group" hero: *The Kin of Ata; Motherlines; The Wanderground: Stories of the Hill Women; Herland; Les Guérillères.* Even if a protagonist is to be identified by some means other than the book's title there is still a tendency toward plural rather than individual heroes. Singer's consciousness shifts occasionally from her hero to her hero's lover; Gilman's first-person narrator describes as much of the action of the other two men as of his own; Charnas' Alldera is sometimes almost forgotten in the episodes of the Riding Women; and Bryant's narrator who is never named (a step in itself toward loss of individualism) is clearly not the character with whom the reader's sympathies lie. Russ presents a multiple protagonist (of four distinct personalities) and both Wittig and Gearhart, though they name their characters, do not name any one of them as central.

Thus there is a strong tendency toward collective process in only four of the novels but the other authors pay some homage to the principle of collectivity in their movement away from single, highly individualized heroes.

LESBIAN SEPARATISM

The conflicts around separatism within the movement have raged for a decade and grow even more intense as women of color—even lesbians of color—make it clear that they do not relate to separatism in the same way that white women do. The question is laden with issues of class and privilege, ideology and strategy, trust and commitment.

The main criticisms of separatist societies are that they are never really separate, that there's always some connection to the male system and that women trying to be separatist are simply fooling themselves. Complete separatism is impossible at present, particularly if women want to continue to reproduce themselves. The utopian authors, however, have answers to the vital question of how reproduction can take place.

Of the eleven novels two presume a predominantly heterosexual world (*The Kin of Ata; Woman on the Edge of Time*) in which the mating is artificial and the foetus developed in brooder tanks; one novel assumes heterosexuality but actually depicts a celibate all-female population (*Herland*); the remaining eight depict lesbian societies of all women with the exception of *Ruins of Isis* which tolerates men for reproductive purposes. Presumably, the lesbian societies of Free Amazons (*Shattered Chain*) and the Guerillas (Wittig), if they do reproduce, do so by heterosexual means, but the Riding Women mate with their stallions and the women of Demeter drink a magic tea to stimulate their parthenogenesis. Three of the lesbian societies reproduce by a form of ovular merging, thus insuring genetic variety (*Whileaway, Retreat,* and the *Wanderground*) and Gilman's celibate culture of Mothers reproduces by desire alone, magically altering the gene pool by the incorporation of the personalities that each woman develops through her life experiences. Thus only five of the eleven cultures need men for reproduction.

While women may have some say in their reproductive life in traditional utopias, few if any are given as much control over it as the women of these eleven novels. And, of course, that impressive picture of reproductive freedom is directly related to the fact that most of these cultures are strictly female, a phenomenon which in itself is new in utopian writing. Another study will have to explore the question of why there are no utopias which are made up entirely of men.

With the thorny question of the method of reproduction out of the way, then, at least in fantasy, the possibility of a true separatism emerges. It is no wonder that some of the recent controversy between separatist and non-separatist women has been in fact stimulated by discussion of some of these very utopian novels.

THE SOURCE OF VIOLENCE

Violence against women (including the violence that women do to themselves and to each other) has become a rallying point for feminist action in the last five years. Feminists seem remarkably unified on the notion that women are the victims of an institutionalized system of violence. Since that system is male-created and male-dominated (even elsewhere beyond its escalated version in Western culture) and since a glance at history shows men to be the primary initiators and perpetuators of violence, at least of the overt physical life-endangering kind, it is easy for many women to locate the seat of violence within the male psyche. In fact, some of the old arguments between socialist-feminists and radical—or cultural—feminists are crystallized in the two positions: 1) male violence is one of many ills which will disappear with the restructuring of economic principles and power; 2) male violence is at the heart of society's ills and its elimination is the essential factor in establishing a revolutionary society.

In the eleven novels, the question of the source of violence becomes intimately bound up with the phenomenon of separatism. Seven out of eleven societies have chosen to live without men and even a cursory reading of each book leaves no doubt that that choice rests on the assumption that the male of the human species is too violent to be lived with. Actually, *Herland* should be added to this list, for even though at the outset the women there express eagerness to begin communication with the wonderful "whole" (*i.e.*, two-sexed) culture outside their country, Gilman's tongue-in-cheek gives way finally to an expression of the Herlanders' honest attitude: they are unwilling yet to expose themselves to that "civilization," presumably because they see the peacefulness as well as the other benefits of their own society clearly to be related to the absence of men.

Moreover, Bradley's men on Isis are accorded many of the characteristics at present attributed to women—sentimentality, self-pity, timorousness, sexual insatiability—but they are allowed to express their maleness in regulated hunting. Further, both pro-matriarchs state that men are held in check because they too easily indulge the urge to dominance and war.

As we observed earlier, the two remaining novels (*Woman on the Edge of Time* and *Kin of Ata*) indict the male of our species in much less outspoken ways. Piercy simply shifts to men the so-called fundamental female characteristic, nurturance, the contrary of violence. Bryant affirms in her idealized characters the full spectrum of the non-masculine psychological paradigm. Nine of the eleven novels, then, make a case for the male's association with violence and the other two imply the connection.

THE USES OF TECHNOLOGY AND THE RELATIONSHIP TO NATURE

At a recent conference on technology and women[3] two distinct groups emerged out of the discussion of women's relationship to technology. One group saw technology as the instrument of women's liberation and the inevitable wave of the future. The second group saw technology as a process of alienation and either espoused an extreme "back-to-nature" position or recommended a use of limited (appropriate) technology accompanied by a high awareness of what tools and machines do to nature and to human beings.

On the whole, the feminist utopias stand with the second group. Most of them are suspicious of technology and all hold a "same" rather than an "other" relationship to nature. The principle of empathy is played out not only in human relationships but in each individual's interactions with the earth, the sea, the air, the forests, and other animals. None of the societies is highly technological, in some cases because the opportunity for such advancement has not arisen and in other cases because the culture has deliberately chosen against the kind of alienation that high technology invariably entails in Western culture.

A selective technology is a part of the culture in *Woman on the Edge of Time* (where test-tube babies release women from pregnancy and where the jobs no one wants to do—like dishwashing or stuffing pillows—are mechanized); *The Female Man* (where "induction helmets"—Russ's version of the computer—make easy some of the large and essential jobs on Whileaway); and *Retreat* (where the society has the capacity to communicate with other planets and to engage in interstellar war). All three cultures, however, seem to deny the precept of Western science that "if it's possible then it must be done." Instead, the author either makes a point of explaining the vast sensibleness of limiting technology or else lets her story itself make obvious the reasons for that choice.

Isis wants more technological aid from the rest of the galaxy, primarily to control its devastating earthquakes and tidal waves, but we're given to understand that there is never to be any imbalance between the material (technology) and the spiritual (nature) needs of the people—the implication being that though the planet is opening up to foreign relations it will not be as "progressive" as other worlds. Both Demeter and the Wanderground argue eloquently as societies for the use of limited technology and in the case of the Hill Women psychic power will soon substitute entirely for more cumbersome electronic or mechanical devices. The Kin of Ata live so simply that they do not use eating utensils.

We may like to think that, if given the opportunity, all feminist societies would choose nature above technology. But that conclusion is not obvious. The Free Amazons (*The Shattered Chain*) remain silent on this matter as do Charnas' Riding Women and Wittig's Guerillas. Each of these societies is a subculture struggling for its existence on a hostile planet. And in each society there is little reflection about the sanctity of nature. The Amazons must protect themselves, the Guerillas already use bazookas, and the Riding Women are becoming aware of some threat from the Holdfast. If offered the technological advancements that accompany "progressive" warfare, any one of those societies might choose it in the service of their cause.

Another symptom of a renewed or ongoing empathic relationship with the environment shows up in the attitude that these cultures have toward animals. In traditional utopias, meat-eating, the use of animals for entertainment and education, and even forms of factory farming are common. And, in some of the feminist utopias, there is only a conventional consciousness about animals—Whileawayans care about cows and the Free Amazons are kind to beasts of burden. But in at least half the feminist novels a keen sensitivity toward animals crops up. Most extreme in this sensitivity are the Kin and the Hill Women whose reverence for animals equals or exceeds their regard for human life: everyone on Bryant's island is in relationship with a particular animal and, in *The Wanderground*, the Hill Women communicate with trees and animals as easily as, sometimes more easily than, with other humans. The Riding Women have a special relationship to their horses, even beyond their respect and care of them for their own reproduction. The Demeter women will kill only when necessary and are outraged at the visiting man's attitude toward a goat. And in Herland, cats hold a special place even though the women have for practical reasons had to let most other animals die out. In Mattapoisett, a chimpanzee has become a national hero and cats can be addressed ritualistically. The point is made that we cannot assume any human superiority over animals.

One final element of the ecological awareness: several of these utopias deal with the issue of overpopulation, one of the concerns beginning now to be understood as a feminist issue. Most of the authors have created cultures which must struggle still to produce rather than to limit their offspring, but, in three of the novels, there is a high consciousness about the human responsibility in the overall ecology: *Woman on the Edge of Time, Herland,* and *The Kin of Ata.* Luciente, the future character of Piercy's novel, explains the delicate balance of the biosystems and the necessity for maintaining a steady population figure; "the inhabitants of this next century attempt to live as partners with water, air, birds, fish, and trees" (p. 125). Everyone knows exactly the number of children in a village and, when there is a death, the brooder is notified to start another baby. The women of Herland regret the time in history when they were not yet in control of their population and had to sacrifice a number of animal and plant species for their own survival. The task for these fecund and happy Mothers was to stop the conceptions, to limit them ultimately to one per woman so that their numbers could be maintained at three million. The Kin of Ata see themselves so much a part of nature that disturbing that balance is nearly impossible for them. Knowing what pregnancy and birth are, both to themselves and to the community, Atan women do not ordinarily have more than one child. They know when they are fertile and when they are not and the experienced ones can mentally hold in check even that fertility. The coming of outsiders (like the hero) provides for varied physical types among them. Both death and the occasional departure of highly developed Kin into the world account for population loss.

There are thus several ways in which the societies affirm their commitment to good ecological principles: in the use of a selective technology, the attitudes in many of them toward animals, and a consciousness of species responsibility or population control.

RACISM

Most of the novels fail to be anti-racist and in this failure end up supporting a stereotype of the dominant culture. In his *Ecotopia*,[4] Ernest Callenbach implies that all the intercourse and strong female characters in his book demonstrate a vision of sexual liberation. He tries hard, but what comes across has nothing to do with sexual liberation. It's a nice view of what a man wants and what he hopes women want. Callenbach can talk about "sexual freedom" on every page—and our feminist utopian writers consistently point to the dark skin and non-Caucasian features of their characters—but Callenbach's images are male-made and those of our feminists are of pale construction. Callenbach does women no favor with his vision. By telling only a male truth he perpetuates in an insidious way his own privileged reality and the oppression of women. The analogy holds to the racism in feminist utopias.

Bradley (in both books), Gearhart, Gilman, Russ, Singer, Young, and Wittig make no successful attempt to paint ethnic differences among women or to identify conflicts that might arise because of such differences. Gilman might be excused because she wrote sixty years before the second wave of feminism. And there are token moves among these writers: Singer's Calliope is about to bring forth "another black baby" (p. 3); Wittig uses a litany of names throughout her book which suggests specific women of globally varied backgrounds; Gearhart describes dark-skinned women. But the action and the critical question for these writers clearly lie in the strife between women and men. That is their concern, that is what their novels reflect, and other political/social issues get interpreted in that light or entirely lost in the shuffle.

Charnas and Bryant make more respectable efforts. Charnas deliberately and carefully distinguishes between the Motherlines, delineating particularly Nenisi and the (Black) Conors. Her painting of a whole nomadic culture that barely forces out survival from a bleak landscape sets a tone of hardship, and the resulting behavior among the women is far from the familiar patterns of middle-class life. But even Charnas's Riding Women and her commitment to toughness and diversity do not convince the reader of any awareness on her part of the injuries committed on the basis of race. Bryant's society, apparently a melting pot of all the world's peoples, openly emulates the dream culture of the Senoi Indians. Among the Atans the value system, the eating practices, the shelter and clothing, the communication, the rituals and tales all stand in contrast to the protagonist's white male standards and behavior—precisely Bryant's point. But whether Bryant intended it or not, the Atan culture comes off as a contrast to maleness, not to whiteness. There are no racial issues here; no points are made that suggest any deep consciousness on the author's part of Western civilization's stigma of race.

When Piercy's *Woman on the Edge of Time* is measured against other feminist utopias, it emerges as the most wholehearted effort to engage the issues of race and class and relate them to larger social scenes. Piercy achieves this, I think, partly because she creates a dialectic between Connie's present (the hospital) and the possible future that she imagines (Mattapoisett). No other feminist utopian protagonist is as much a victim of the present system as is Consuelo: poor, Mexican-American, imprisoned, child-batterer, certified insane, and abused alike by pimp, lover, family, bosses, government, and the psychiatric profession. Her here-and-now influences her envisioning of the future, *e.g.*, the food, the dress, the physical interactions, the nursing, and the play of children, remind her of her childhood, and she even calculates the number of generations between her own daughter, Angelina, and the Mattapoisett child who reminds her of the lost Angelina. Thus, while Mattapoisett is in contrast to Connie's drugged and depersonalized self, it is as well a continuation of it. Further, Connie deliberately initiates a discussion of racism, giving Luciente and others the chance to explain how that evil has been dealt with. Granted the device is forced, none of the other writers even mentions the subject. The conscious effort is made globally in this future world to retain the heritage of specific and varied cultures. (Luciente's village re-creates the world of the Wamponang Indians, no matter how Irish or German or Black its citizens are.) The whole rationale for that policy is a part of every child's understanding.

Piercy gives us in Connie a full-blown hero of considerable stature whose progress through future good and present evil culminates in a righteous rebellion against her doctors—an inspiration to many readers in their own revolutionary or rebellious action. Piercy's book is not white. Her characters are not tokens. She alters and deepens the reader's perspective on the present world. Her book is a revolutionary tool precisely because it bends the utopian genre to good political purpose.

For me moving myself out of a non-racist stance and into an anti-racist one is like trying to push an idle steam roller: I can't get moving, it seems hopeless, and it's easier to do something else that I have more passion about, more success in doing. That word "passion" turns out to be the key for me. Obviously, it's easier to feel deep rage and pain when I'm the victim rather than when I'm the oppressor. And, truth to tell, in comparison to the rage and fervor that I instantly muster over other issues (*e.g.*, homophobia, sexism) I hardly have any passion at all to confront racism. Being an oppressor means in fact cutting off my feelings, and so the whole enterprise for me at once becomes an effort to feel, a search for passion. The thing that has worked best is going back to my childhood and early teens when I had intense experiences with Black people that I reacted to at the time with sheer outrage, fear, hurt, or embarrassment. When I can touch those feelings again, I am genuinely "moved" to action, *i.e.*, there's some passion to my politics.

A generalized summary of the novels suggests that there is a movement towards collective approaches to action, a strong statement of lesbian separatism, an indictment of men as the source of violence, a pervasive skepticism of high technology and, except for Piercy, an almost nonexistent awareness of the issues of race and class. Thus do feminist utopias make their political statements. We do well to explore them for they mold our ideas, our struggles and our strategies in the present.

NOTES

1. All but one of these novels were written since 1973. The exception is Charlotte Perkins Gilman's *Herland*, 1915, whose resurrection and reprinting in the 1970's further testifies to the recent surge of interest in feminist utopian fiction.

2. I include *The Ruins of Isis* in spite of the fact that I'm not *always* convinced that Bradley feels the matriarchate she has created on Isis is better than societies presently in existence.

3. "Technology and the Future of Women," sponsored by the Department of Women's Studies, San Diego State University, March 5–7, 1981.

4. Ernest Callenbach, *Ecotopia* (New York: Bantam Books, 1975).

Fantasia

EVE MERRIAM

I dream
of giving birth
to
a child
who will ask
"Mother,
what was war?"

Contributors

Martha Ackelsberg teaches government at Smith College, where she is also a principal investigator with the Project on Women and Social Change.

Mischa B. Adams holds a Ph.D. in Anthropology from the University of California, Santa Cruz. She works as a secretary by day, and teaches night courses in Anthropology at a community college. Her other interests include writing, feminist science fiction, and playing guitar in an all-woman rock and roll band.

Harriette Andreadis holds a Ph.D. in English Renaissance Drama from the University of Wisconsin, Madison. She has published a critical edition of John Lyly's play *Mother Bombie* and writes on feminist pedagogy, women writers, and women in film. This study of the Belton community is an offshoot of her work for a book on the private writings of women in nineteenth-century Texas. Since 1975, she has been teaching literature, film, and women writers at Texas A & M University.

Eleanor Arnason has had stories published in *New Women of Wonder, Amazons II,* and the science fiction issue of *Room of One's Own.* Her second novel, *To the Resurrection Station,* will be coming out in 1984.

Elaine Hoffman Baruch holds a Ph.D. in English and Comparative Literature from Columbia University. She is Associate Professor of English at York College, City University of New York and faculty associate at The Center for the Study of Women and Society, The Graduate Center of the City University of New York. Her articles have appeared in *Comparative Literature, Etudes Anglaises, Commentary, The New Republic, Partisan Review, Dissent, Alternative Futures, The Massachusetts Review, The Yale Review,* and *1984 Revisited,* edited by Irving Howe. She is the General Editor of the "Women's Studies Series" of the Everett/Edwards *Cassette Curriculum.* She is currently working on projects in reproductive engineering and psychoanalytic approaches to literature.

Marilyn Bensman is an Assistant Professor in the Department of Sociology of Lehman College, City University of New York. She has written on the family and the nineteenth-century women's movement. More recently she has been working in the area of death, dying, and bereavement.

France Burke is a poet, novelist, and playwright. Her work has been published in *The Paris Review, The Agni Review,* and *Confrontation,* among other journals, and presented at The American Place Theater. She has received a Ford Foundation grant for work in theater.

Blance Wiesen Cook, historian and journalist, is the author of *Crystal Eastman on Women and Revolution, The Declassified Eisenhower: A Divided Legacy of Peace and Political Warfare,* and senior editor of the Garland Library of War and Peace. Currently Professor of History at John Jay College, City University of New York, she is writing a biography of Eleanor Roosevelt.

Tucker Farley teaches Women's Studies and English at Brooklyn College, City University of New York. She has been active as a radical, lesbian feminist for many years. Her work has been published in a variety of journals and anthologies, including *The Future of Difference, Power, Oppression* and *The Politics of Culture.*

Sally M. Gearhart is Chair of the Department of Speech and Communication Studies at San Francisco State University where she also works with the Women's Studies Program. She appeared in the gay documentary *Word Is Out,* authored *The Wanderground* and *A Feminist Tarot,* and is involved in issues of animal rights.

H. Lee Gershuny is Professor of English at Manhattan Community College, City University of New York, and received a Kenyon Award from the International Society for General Semantics for her doctoral dissertation: *Sexist Semantics in the Dictionary* (1973). She has published and presented numerous papers on gender in language and literature and co-authored *Sexism and Language* with Alleen Pace Nilsen, Haig Bosmajian, and Julia P. Stanley. She has also published poetry and fiction, and won the 1982–83 Jacksonville University Playwriting Contest for her one-act play, "Play With Voices."

Ann Sutherland Harris holds a Ph.D. from the University of London and has taught Art History in the United States since 1965. She has also been Chair for Academic Affairs at the Metropolitan Museum of Art. With Linda Nochlin, she put together the exhibition *Women Artists, 1550–1950,* for the Los Angeles County Museum in 1976, which later travelled to Austin, Pittsburgh, and Brooklyn. She is currently on the advisory board of the National Museum of Women's Art in Washington, D.C., which is now in an advanced planning stage. As of Spring 1984, she is the Mellon Professor of Art History at the University of Pittsburgh.

Jill Harsin holds a Ph.D. from the University of Iowa and is now Assistant Professor of History at Colgate University. Her major field of research is nineteenth-century French history, with a particular interest in women and the law.

Nancy M. Henley is Professor of Psychology and Director of Women's Studies at the University of California at Los Angeles. She is editor of the *Psychology of Women Quarterly,* author of *Body Politics: Power,*

Sex and Nonverbal Communication, and co-editor of *Gender and Nonverbal Behavior,* and of *Language, Gender and Society.*

June Jordan is Professor of English at Stony Brook, State University of New York, and a winner of many awards, among them, the NEA and the Prix de Rome. She is the author, most recently, of *Civil Wars* and *Passion.*

Lee Cullen Khanna holds a Ph.D. in English and Comparative Literature from Columbia University and is Associate Professor of English and Director of English Graduate Studies at Montclair State College. She has published articles on Thomas More's *Utopia,* renaissance images of women, feminist utopian fiction, and Doris Lessing's speculative fiction. At present she is completing a book on feminist utopias.

Cheris Kramarae is Associate Professor of Speech Communication at the University of Illinois, Urbana-Champaign where she teaches courses in language and gender, and in issues of language and power. She is author of *Women and Men Speaking,* editor of *The Voices and Words of Women and Men,* and co-editor of *Language, Gender and Society.*

Diane LeBow has taught Women's Studies and English in California, New York City, and the Netherlands during the past twenty years. She developed and directed the Women's Center, Women's Studies, and Women's Re-entry Program at Cañada College in northern California, where she teaches in the Humanities Division. She writes poems and fiction, and is currently working on a book entitled *Feminist Consciousness in Twentieth-Century Fiction: Novels by Black and White American Women.*

Susan H. Lees is Professor of Anthropology at Hunter College and the Graduate Center of the City University of New York where she teaches in the Anthropology and the Women's Studies Programs. She has published extensively in her field of specialization, third world rural development, and has done research in Latin America and the Middle East. She is also editor of *Human Ecology, an Interdisciplinary Journal.*

Audre Lorde teaches English at Hunter College, City University of New York. She has published seven volumes of poetry as well as a work of non-fiction, *The Cancer Journals.* Her latest work is *Chosen Poems—Old and New.*

Geraldine Day McNelly holds a Ph.D. in Anthropology for Women's Studies from the New School for Social Research. She teaches at the College of Staten Island, City University of New York, originated a course in Irish Women at the Irish Arts Center in New York City, and has published "Child Socialization & Education: Innovative Open Education," in *Resources in Education,* February 1980, ERIC, Boulder, Colorado.

Eve Merriam is the author of over forty books, among them, *After Nora Slammed the Door, Growing Up Female in America, The Club,* a feminist play that received rave reviews as far away as Japan, and *The Inner City*

Mother Goose. In 1981, she was the winner of the National Council of Teachers of English Award for Excellence in Poetry for Children.

Carol S. Pearson, an Associate Professor of Women's Studies and American Studies at the University of Maryland, College Park, is the co-author with Katherine Pope of *Who Am I This Time: Female Portraits in American and British Literature,* and the author of *The Female Hero in American and British Literature.* She has also written many articles on women and literature.

Marge Piercy, poet and novelist, is the author of several books, among them, *Dance the Eagle to Sleep, Small Changes, Vida,* and the feminist utopia *Woman on the Edge of Time.* Her most recent book of poetry is *Circles on the Water.*

Dinnah Pladott holds a B.A., M.A. and Ph.D. on William Faulkner from Columbia University and Tel Aviv University. She teaches American Literature at Tel Aviv University, and has just completed a year of post-doctoral research into experimental American drama ca. 1900– 1950, as a Fulbright Fellow at Columbia University.

Ruby Rohrlich is Professor Emeritus of Anthropology, Manhattan Community College, City University of New York, and Research Associate, University of California, Berkeley. She is the author of *The Puerto Ricans: Culture Change and Language Deviance,* and *Peaceable Primates and Gentle People,* as well as editor of *Women Cross Culturally, Change and Challenge.* Her earlier works were written under the names of Leavitt and Rohrlich-Leavitt. Her articles appeared in the anthologies *Women in Sexist Society, Toward an Anthropology of Women, Politics of Anthropology Humanness: An Exploration into the Mythologies about Women and Men, Women's Studies: The Social Realities, Becoming Visible: Women in European History* and in various journals including *American Anthropologist, Signs, Feminist Studies, Heresies, Critique of Anthropology,* and *l'Homme.* She is now doing research with Eleanor Leacock on Samoan sexuality following Derek Freeman's attack on Margaret Mead.

Ntozake Shange, novelist and playwright, is the author of several works, among them, the widely acclaimed *For Colored Girls Who Have Considered Suicide When the Rainbow is Enuf, Sassafras, Cypress, and Indigo,* and *Daughter's Geography.*

Mary Anne Shea is Humanities Research Scholar at New York University where she edits *VNIVERSITY,* a review of academic life at NYU. She co-edited *Around the Square: Life, Letters, and Architecture in Greenwich Village, 1830–1890* and has written and edited a number of books for children.

Arlene Sheer is a writer and artist. She lives in New York City, works as a motion picture projectionist and has been involved in the women's movement for fourteen years and a spiritual discipline for the last nine years.

Barrie Thorne is Associate Professor of Sociology at Michigan State University, where she also teaches in the Women's Studies Program. She is co-editor of *Language, Gender and Society,* and editor of *Rethinking the Family: Some Feminist Questions.*

Ruth Wangerin holds a Ph.D. in Anthropology from the City University of New York. She has taught at the City College of New York, and is currently underemployed. Originally a Midwesterner, she has a long-standing research interest in agriculture, as well as in political economy, kinship, and male dominance.

Batya Weinbaum is author of *The Curious Courtship of Women's Liberation and Socialism* and *Pictures of Patriarchy,* and fiction and poetry from *Radical in the Woods.* She works as a coordinator of healing at Michigan Women's Music Festival and is developing alternative spaces for women in Vermont.

Frances Whyatt is a poet who divides her time between New York City and Islamorada in the Florida Keys where she grew up. She is the author of a recent book of poems, *American Gypsy,* and a novel, *American Made.*

Jan Zimmerman directed the Conference on Future, Technology and Woman in 1981 at San Diego State University, where she is an adjunct faculty member of the Women's Studies Department. A writer and consultant in the fields of telecommunications, computers and technology, she has written numerous articles on those subjects and is the editor of *The Technological Woman: Interfacing with Tomorrow.* In January 1980 she was named by *Ms.* magazine as one of the "80 Women to Watch in the '80s."

Index